Torn

Torn

Casey Hill

W F HOWES LTD

This large print edition published in 2014 by
W F Howes Ltd
Unit 4, Rearsby Business Park, Gaddesby Lane,
Rearsby, Leicester LE7 4YH

1 3 5 7 9 10 8 6 4 2

First published in the United Kingdom in 2012
by Simon & Schuster UK Ltd

A CIP catalogue record for this book is available
from the British Library

ISBN 978 1 47125 417 8

Typeset by Palimpsest Book Production Limited,
Falkirk, Stirlingshire
Printed and bound by
www.printondemand-worldwide.com of Peterborough, England

This book is made entirely of chain-of-custody materials

To Andy and Kay –
the best parents /in-laws we could wish for

CHAPTER 1

Sandra Coffey was desperately struggling to breathe.

The smell, an over-ripe suffocating stench, completely overwhelmed her, making her nauseous and dizzy. She shook her head in panic, suppressing an urge to gag, thinking she wouldn't be able to hold out for much longer.

Suddenly she heard the crunch of tires on the gravel outside, and through the window she saw drawing to a halt a white van with familiar blue writing on its side.

At last, help had arrived.

Thank God, thank God . . .

Sandra stood up, smoothed down her trousers, and, trying to regain her poise, headed quickly for the front door.

'Morning, Mrs Coffey,' Paddy Murphy, the local plumber, greeted her amiably. He had a round, red face, long, white muttonchop sideburns, and his bulky frame filled every inch of his extra-large, navy-blue boiler suit. He looked up at her, a frown of concern on his face. 'Toilet backing up, you said?'

'Not just one, Paddy. All of them. The smell . . . it's unbearable.'

His frown deepened. 'Probably your septic tank then.' The plumber removed his cap to reveal his shiny bald head and scratched at it thoughtfully. 'Sounds unusual. Maybe a rat or something found its way in there. Only way we'll know for sure is to go and have a look.'

Paddy set his toolbox down, loosened the cap of the inspection pipe, then stood back and averted his face. He didn't want to be hammered by the acrid funk he knew would rush his nostrils when the system was opened.

He rummaged in his toolbox and came up with a large industrial torch. Tapping it on the heel of his hand, he flicked it on, aimed it down the tank and peered into the murky depths.

The inspection pipe was narrow – maybe sixty centimeters across – and didn't show much of the tank itself. He moved the torch around and peered in as far as he could to see if he could identify a blockage, but all he saw was the layer of scum that floated on top of the mottled and putrid grays and browns. Instinctively he held his breath. Helluva way to make a living . . .

'Can you see anything?'

Paddy jumped, startled.

Unheard, Mrs Coffey had come up behind him, her feet in a pair of patterned wellington boots, a Barbour jacket draped across her shoulders.

He grunted as he stood up, trying to regain his composure. The woman was standing very close and her proximity was unaccountably disconcerting.

'You can never really see much down these. Reckon I'll just have to open up the manhole cover.' He sighed as he recapped the pipe.

What a pain in the arse – digging around in a heap of shite was not what Paddy had in mind just before lunchtime on a Friday morning, especially with yer woman over his shoulder watching his every move.

He grabbed his toolbox and trudged across the sloping lawn and around a line of low-growing shrubs, Mrs Coffey hard on his heels. Then he stopped so suddenly that she almost stumbled into the back of him.

'What is it?'

He turned and looked at her, puzzled. 'Have you had someone else in to check the system lately?'

'No. Why do you ask?'

'Someone seems to have been digging for the manhole cover, but from the looks of that mess, they didn't know exactly where to find it.'

They both observed the turned-over soil, dark and rich from the recent rain.

'Maybe Tony noticed it was backing up before he left and tried to fix it, though he didn't mention anything . . .'

The plumber approached the metal manhole cover. 'Someone's been at this for sure.'

He kneeled down, slipped a small crowbar from

his toolbox, and placed it under one edge of the cover. He glanced over his shoulder at Mrs Coffey. 'You might want to stand back a bit – these things reek to high heaven when opened.'

She duly took a couple of steps back and pulled her jacket tightly around her. Paddy flipped the cover off, and once again averted his nose to evade the malodorous stink racing up to greet him.

Waiting for the air to clear a little, he was reaching for his torch when a horrified cry from behind stopped him short. He shook his head. Serves her right for standing over him – this was no place for a—

But Paddy quickly realized that it wasn't merely the stench that had affected Mrs Coffey.

Once, twice, three times her high-pitched screams split the cold, damp air, before she finally clamped her hand across her mouth, her eyes wide with horror.

What the . . .? Paddy stared at her, puzzled, before slowly turning back to the tank to see what had so affected her.

Floating up to greet him was the bloated, distorted face of a man, his eyes protruding, skin purple with putrefaction, sewage spilling from his open mouth as he bobbed in the effluent pool.

Frozen with shock, the plumber just stared, unable to take his eyes away. The dead man's deeply veined, bloodshot eyes seemed to be staring back at him in mute accusation.

Behind him, Mrs Coffey was whimpering little sobs of pure animal fear and horror.

Finally Paddy Murphy gagged and fell backwards onto the damp grass.

'Jesus Christ Almighty . . .'

CHAPTER 2

'Can you please state your name and occupation for the benefit of the Court?' the lawyer asked.

The oak-paneled courtroom was still, all eyes on the woman sitting in the witness stand.

She sat upright, her piercing blue eyes fixed on the man who was questioning her. Patrick Masterton was a picture-perfect lawyer in his immaculate dark suit, crisp white shirt, and just enough gray in his hair to make him appear distinguished.

As Masterton referred to his notes, a court artist worked quickly to capture the scene. He had already finished drawing Masterton – he looked elegant, determined, powerful, even – and was now working on the witness.

With quick strokes he portrayed the shape of her head, the sheet of blond hair falling onto her shoulders, her high cheekbones and strong jaw line. Her eyes were an unusual shade of deep blue and her strongest feature. In just a few strokes he managed to capture the fierce light of intelligence – defiance almost – that shone through. She wore an

6

elegant charcoal skirt and jacket, her shirt a complementary pale pink. The only adornment was a small brooch in her lapel, shaped like a dragon.

'Reilly Steel, GFU investigator,' she replied, in a strong American accent.

'GFU?'

'Garda Forensic Unit,' she clarified. 'We collect and analyze evidence from crime scenes.'

'And how long have you been in this profession, Ms Steel?'

'I've been employed by the GFU for approximately thirteen months. Before that, I led an ERT – Evidence Response Team – out of the FBI San Francisco field office for almost seven years. Throughout this time, my Office carried out extensive crime scene investigative work with contacts in local, state, federal and international law enforcement agencies.'

Her answers were clear. Absolutely no hesitation – just statements of fact.

'And your qualifications?'

'In 2003 I graduated in Crime Scene Investigation from the FBI National Academy in Quantico, Virginia.'

'Impressive credentials, I'm sure the Court will agree,' Masterton said.

He smoothed his tie, and looked from the jury back to Reilly. 'Ms Steel, can you tell us about the evidence you found at Elizabeth Walker's house on the night of the 15th of August last?' the lawyer asked, pointing to a nearby projector

7

screen, upon which two photographs were displayed side by side. The first photo showed the head of a bed, a heavy bloodstain on a pillow against the wooden slatted headboard. The second was a close-up of the same image, displaying a dark, frizzy hair wedged between the pillow and the headboard.

Reilly's voice was even. 'The hair was collected from the victim's bed.'

Masterton moved a step closer, once again focusing the jury's attention on her. 'What can you tell us about it, based on your forensic analysis?'

'It's male, Caucasian.'

'You were able to extract DNA from it?' Masterton had his notes behind his back, but he had no need to refer to them.

'Yes. The follicle was attached, so we were able to extract primary DNA from the sample.'

'And you compared this with a saliva sample obtained from the accused?' He nodded toward a young man with dark curly hair, who sat slouched between two guards, his ill-fitting suit making him appear uncomfortable, out of place in these formal surroundings.

'Correct.'

'The hair was a match?'

'It was.'

Masterton moved toward the jury, making sure he had their full attention before asking the key question. 'Ms Steel, what would you estimate as the likelihood that the hair you found on the pillow belongs to the accused?'

Reilly sat up even straighter. This was her world – forensic evidence, scientific certainties. She could answer with complete confidence. 'The likelihood that the hair we found on that pillow belongs to the accused is 99.97 percent.'

A small murmur went through the courtroom. One or two members of the jury gave slight involuntary nods. This type of evidence – precise, cold, scientific – always hit home hard, and helped sway wavering minds.

Masterton resumed his questions. 'Ms Steel, could you now please tell the Court what you found beneath the victim's fingernails?'

'Samples of blood and skin tissue.'

'These are typically evidence of a struggle?'

'That's correct,' Reilly replied.

A photo of the female victim's upturned hand appeared on the projector, the woman's elegant fingernails darkened by the blood beneath them. The jury's gaze turned toward the image – there was something brutal about those cold, lifeless hands, the blood-flecked nails mute testimony to just how hard Elizabeth Walker had fought for her life.

The artist glanced quickly at the jury – faces were hardening, decisions were being made, and cold glances flashed across the room at the accused, Danny Doyle.

Masterton continued, relentless now that he was

closing in on his prey. 'Ms Steel, you were able to extract DNA from these samples also?'

'We were.'

'And the DNA matched that of the accused, Daniel Doyle? Matched that of the hair sample, as well as the saliva sample you obtained from the accused?'

'Correct.'

The word hung heavily in the air, and rolled around the courtroom with a resounding air of finality. Whatever else the defense might say, whatever tricks or stratagems they might come up with, the science had spoken – clearly and incontrovertibly. Danny Doyle had been in Elizabeth Walker's bed the night she died; his hair was on her pillow, his skin and blood beneath her battered, broken fingernails.

Masterton allowed himself a smile. 'Thank you, Ms Steel.' He turned to the defense. 'Your witness.'

The defense lawyer wore a tired, defeated look. In his late fifties, with a thousand tough cases behind him, Michael Liston knew when to attack, or when to regroup and look for a weak point elsewhere.

Reilly Steel, GFU investigator, had revealed no chinks in her armor. She had a rock-solid chain of evidence, unimpeachable scientific credibility, unshakeable conclusions, and a manner that spoke of unquestionable competence. Experience told him there was no value in pursuing her – what he needed was to get her off the witness stand as

10

quickly as possible. Liston shook his head. 'No further questions, Your Honor.'

The judge nodded to Reilly. 'Thank you, Ms Steel, that will be all.'

As the GFU investigator stood and walked quickly back to her seat, the artist noticed that all eyes were on her. She had delivered her evidence with such certainty, such an air of confidence, that it was hard not to feel admiration for her.

Even as the next witness was called to the stand, he began a second sketch of her, his quick strokes filling in the details that had been hidden while Steel sat in the witness stand – her slim figure, long legs, elegant way of walking . . .

It was on days like this that he loved his job.

As she exited the courthouse, Reilly exhaled, finally able to release some of the tension, the strain of being the key witness. The entire trial hinged upon her evidence, and she had come through.

With Doyle's denial of guilt blown out of the water, the case should proceed smoothly toward a conviction.

Did the system always convict the right person? Of course not – Reilly wasn't naïve enough to believe that – but she did believe that most of the time, if there was sufficient incontrovertible evidence, the correct decision would be reached.

In this instance it had all come together. Doyle had pleaded not guilty, and had denied even knowing Elizabeth Walker, but Reilly's evidence – the evidence so carefully collected and analyzed by her team at the GFU – had placed him at the scene of the murder, in Elizabeth Walker's bed.

Justice was about to be served.

Making a mental note to thank her team for their Trojan work in preparing for the case, Reilly pulled out her iPhone to type a reminder to herself, and also to check her messages. There were a few, but one in particular caught her attention: a text message from Detective Chris Delaney. He rarely texted unless it was important. Reilly opened the message.

'Hope the trial's going well and you nail Doyle to the wall. Call when you're finished? We've got a weird one.'

Reilly arched an eyebrow. A weird one?

Exactly how she liked them.

CHAPTER 3

Detective Chris Delaney climbed from his car and looked up at the Coffey house. His partner, Pete Kennedy, hauled himself out of the other side and followed Chris's gaze. 'Didn't realize tabloid journalists made that much money.'

Chris slammed the door of the Ford closed. 'They don't. According to the file, Tony Coffey married well.'

Kennedy glanced around and straightened up, trying to hitch his trousers up over his beer belly. It was a hopeless task, but one he nonetheless repeated constantly. 'Who's the missus, then?'

Chris ran his dark eyes over the house. A former Franciscan friary, the imposing sandstone building was three stories tall and solidly built, mostly large assemblies of intricately cut masonry, and decorated with delicate filigree woodwork.

'Webb. Big local family, construction money. They're part of the horsy set.'

Kennedy vainly hitched up his trousers again. 'I don't get it. Wasn't Coffey a bit of a radical?'

Chris bent down to look in the wing mirror,

straightened his tie and ran a hand through his dark hair. He nodded. 'Yep – every Sunday he wrote a column in the *Herald* supporting this or, more often than not, denouncing that. But he's probably best known for his attacks on animal cruelty and foxhunting, that type of thing.'

Kennedy raised an eyebrow. 'I'll bet that went down a treat at family get-togethers.'

They headed across the gravel toward the rear of the house. Chris glanced around the graveled parking area. There were several garda cars, a couple of white vans, and a battered black Volvo estate.

The autumn leaves blew round his feet in hurried swirls, as though they were looking for a way to escape from the garden. It was mid-afternoon, but the gray bruise of rain-clouds covering the sky from horizon to horizon made it feel later.

'I see the doc is here already – have you managed to get hold of Blondie yet?' Kennedy asked.

Chris shook his head. 'She's in court today, remember? The Walker murder. And she'd have your balls for breakfast if she heard you call her that.'

No better woman than Reilly Steel to put Kennedy in his place, Chris thought wryly, and it was something she did repeatedly. He was glad for more reasons than one that it was she, and not grouchy old Jack Gorman, that was the GFU investigator handling this particular crime scene. She and Chris had become close since teaming up on an investigation earlier in the year that had

14

involved Reilly's family, during which he had almost been killed.

He was pretty certain that, unlike the older investigator, Reilly Steel wouldn't bat an eyelid at the rather 'difficult' circumstances they were facing today. Fearless and unflappable, he knew that some members of the force thought her standoffish. 'Steel by name, steel by nature,' he'd heard said about her.

Chris knew, however, that behind the cool façade was a woman who'd spent much of her life trying to overcome major demons in her past.

During their first investigation together, he'd discovered a side to her that others rarely saw: fun-loving, warm and sometimes vulnerable. She was a demon on a surfboard (and with a gun, it was rumored), and her driving scared the life out of him. She ate like a horse, yet could barely cook.

And she had a devilishly croaky laugh that made his skin prickle.

Chris and Kennedy pushed through a gate set in a high sandstone wall into a large back garden. A group of uniforms stood nearby, two forensic techs in their protective suits and booties were checking the ground around it, while Karen Thompson, the medical examiner, could be seen kneeling in the grass. Chris's gaze ran over the area. The house was beautifully kept – double French doors opened onto a tiled terrace, and another door led out onto the garden from what he guessed was the kitchen.

The inspection pipe stood in the grass, half hidden behind shrubbery on the left-hand side of the house; nobody wanted to be looking at the mechanics of human waste removal while they sat on the terrace with their gin and tonic, so the tank must have been strategically placed to be almost invisible from the house. Easily achieved here, as the grounds were extensive.

The detectives nodded briefly toward the uniforms and the lab techs, then approached the doctor. Karen was bent over an exposed manhole cover, a breathing mask covering the lower half of her face, but still barely protecting her protruding nose.

In his four years working city homicide, Chris had experienced some acutely nasty odors, but the location of this particular corpse exacerbated the pungent stench of death with the ripe aroma of human excrement.

Suppressing his urge to gag, he automatically stepped back from the septic tank hatch. The manhole cover still lay a few feet away, where it had evidently rolled after the poor bastard who'd discovered the body had dropped it in shock.

The corpse was vertical, submerged up to the neck in sewage, and bore a horrible, twisted expression, a grimace of deep, soul-crushing despair.

Chris heard Kennedy emit a low curse. 'Christ, that's rank!' he said, putting a hand over his nose and mouth.

Having seen enough, they both retreated hastily from the opening. Quick as a flash, Kennedy reached into his pocket and brought out a packet of JP Blue.

Chris looked at him speculatively. 'Thought we'd finally agreed that that stuff will kill you,' he said.

Lighting up, Kennedy glanced back at the tank and shuddered visibly. 'Looks like there are worse ways to go.'

A couple of minutes later, the medical examiner stood up. Peeling off her slime-covered latex gloves, she slipped the mask away and moved over to where the detectives stood. She coughed, and wiped her nose on the back of her hand. 'This one's a real mess.'

'Bit of an understatement . . .' Kennedy muttered.

'Anything to go on?' Chris asked, trying his utmost to keep his nostrils closed.

There was no question that foul play had been involved here; the manhole cover had been replaced and closed over, which wouldn't have been the case if Tony Coffey had fallen into the tank by accident. He was already trying to picture the scenario of someone dragging a heavy body across the grounds to dump it into the manhole. The only access to the garden was via the gate they had come through; the wall, seven foot high, blocked any other access from the front of the house, and it was unlikely that anyone had come over that with a body.

Chris turned toward the rear. The back garden was

huge – about half an acre, he guessed – and was either walled or fenced on all sides. To the north was a small patch of orchard, to the east a wooded area, and to the west the road, separated from the garden by a tall hedge. Whoever brought Tony Coffey here had most likely come via the house, or through the gate from the gravel driveway. 'How long's the body been down there?'

Karen shrugged. 'I won't know for sure till I get him cleaned up and take a proper look, but I'd guess he's been dead for two or three days at least.'

'Someone certainly worked really hard to put him down there,' Kennedy said.

She turned her huge saucer-like eyes on him. 'You don't know the half of it.'

'How's that?' Chris asked.

The ME grimaced. 'Well, I'm almost positive that the poor man was submerged alive.'

Reilly shifted down through the gears, revved hard, and moved the GFU van out into the opposite lane and past two slow-moving cars. The spray from their tires temporarily blinded her, but she knew she had time to make the maneuver.

She kept her foot to the floor, and enjoyed the muted roar of the engine, the low rumble as the acceleration kicked in. Despite a rocky beginning, driving on the left – the opposite of back home in California – was now becoming second nature to her.

She zoomed past another car, cut back into her

18

lane, then slowed just a little for a sweeping left-hand bend. She felt the van's grip transmit through the firm leather seat as she took the curve at speed, the g-force keeping her pressed firmly against the seat.

Part of her knew that driving like this was childish, but it put a smile on her face, and reminded her that there was more to life than peering down a microscope and speculating on the motives and methods of criminals.

Given the nature of the job, it was essential that she found some down time when she could live for the moment, forget the job, and allow her brain simply to relax. Surfing was how she used to get her kicks, but there wasn't much opportunity for that around Dublin, so fast driving had naturally become a substitute adrenaline rush. For Reilly, California was now figuratively, if not literally, a thousand miles away, and Dublin was gradually becoming home.

She glanced at the sat nav – the house was just ahead – and wished guiltily that the journey could take just a little longer, and include a couple more tight bends.

The police at the gate of the house waved Reilly in, and she pulled up beside the detectives' silver Ford. She glanced round and nodded in satisfaction. Everyone was already there – she had called ahead, and her team from the GFU was expecting her.

She slipped a contamination suit over her clothes – she was by now an expert at getting changed in the narrow confines of the van and could do it in thirty seconds flat – and having traded her heels for trainers, she grabbed her forensic kit and climbed out.

A uniform waved her over to the walled back garden, and immediately Reilly began assessing the environment; asking questions, narrowing options, and beginning the process of analysis.

Kennedy and Chris looked up as she appeared.

'Hey, Miss Baywatch is here!' the older detective joked.

From anyone else it might have come across as sexist and derogatory, but Reilly knew Kennedy well enough by now to understand that the teasing was good-natured, and he'd say anything to wind her up.

She didn't mind in the slightest and, in truth, was just glad that the detectives she worked with were supportive of her. It had taken a while, particularly with the older guys on the force including Kennedy, but Reilly figured she'd done enough to prove her worth in her first year at the helm of the GFU.

Besides, she flat-out refused to waste energy on a battle of the sexes, having seen many of her female Quantico buddies back home crash and burn trying to overcome the inevitable prejudice that existed in such a male-dominated field.

They were guys, she was a woman – deal with it.

She always enjoyed working side by side with Chris; to her he was the best kind of investigator:

logical, open-minded and willing to approach a case from any angle, however unlikely it might seem. Unusually for a detective, he had little ego, and possessed a calm, quiet strength that always managed to put those around him – particularly witnesses – instantly at ease. She guessed his dark good looks probably played a part in that, too. In short, Chris Delaney was the kind of guy you could trust with your life, and Reilly hadn't met too many of those.

Kennedy glanced at her contamination suit. 'I thought you were giving evidence this morning – tell me you didn't wear that to court?'

Reilly winked at him. 'Haven't you learned yet? I always wear this – even to bed.'

Chris guffawed and Kennedy hitched up his trousers. 'Helluva image,' he muttered to himself, but at least it had the desired effect of shutting him up.

Reilly looked around, her eyes taking in the scene. 'So what do we know?' she asked. 'Anything helpful?'

'Dead guy is a journalist, Tony Coffey, well known on the tabloid scene,' Chris told her. 'Plumber came to check on a blocked toilet this morning, opened up the septic tank and . . .' He grimaced.

Reilly's eyes were wide. 'The body was found in the septic tank?'

He nodded. 'I know. Nice, isn't it? And a forensic nightmare for you, no doubt.'

'I'll say.' Her mind was already racing with the inherent difficulties of processing a scene like that. Every piece of potential evidence soaked in filth . . . 'Well, seeing as we're all here, I'm guessing the guy didn't fall in there by accident.'

'Right.' Kennedy pinched the stub of his cigarette out between his fingers, and dropped the residue into his pocket – he knew better than to contaminate Reilly's crime scene. He rubbed at his eyes. 'Manhole cover was on and, according to the doc, the poor fucker was alive when he was put in there; may have been stewing in it for two or three days.'

Reilly winced. 'What a way to make a guy suffer.'

'I know,' Chris agreed. 'The question is, why?'

The answer was something that would have to wait for the moment, Reilly thought, looking again toward the golgothic pit that was the septic tank. She gulped. For possibly the first time in her career she wasn't champing at the bit to start processing a scene.

Chris followed her gaze as if sensing her reluctance.

'Body's still in the tank. Karen reckons it's going to take a bit of work to get him out.'

'Well, good luck to whomever gets that task,' Reilly muttered. 'Have you talked to anyone yet?'

He shook his head. 'We arrived only about ten minutes before you. We're heading to the house now to talk to the wife, see what she knows. We're thinking he was most likely brought in through the gate or from the house, but we need to cover all the options.'

Reilly nodded. 'I'll have my guys sweep the perimeter, let you know what we come up with.'

'Thanks.'

'The plumber's still around too; I think I saw a van on the way in?'

'Don't miss a trick, do you?' Kennedy grumbled good-naturedly. 'All right, Steel, work your magic. We're off to do the dirty work.'

Reilly looked again at the tank and shuddered. A gentle geyser of putrid mist spewed from the opening.

Nope, this time the dirty work was unquestionably all hers.

CHAPTER 4

Reilly hefted up her kitbag and headed back toward the opening of the tank. The November sky was darkening, and heavy rainclouds drifted menacingly across the fields from the east.

She approached the tank and nodded a brief greeting to the ME before getting down to business. The stink from the opening was so strong that, for once, Reilly didn't get a whiff of Karen Thompson's favored perfume, Red Door by Elizabeth Arden.

Smells were Reilly's thing. She'd discovered a long time ago that her sensitive nose had some sort of weird talent for cataloging scents, particularly perfume. And while it often came in handy for the job, today she was cursing that particular ability.

'How soon before you get the body out?' she asked.

Despite the circumstances, Karen Thompson looked typically calm and unruffled, and Reilly marveled at the woman's strong stomach.

'Shouldn't be too much longer – I've got a team

24

on their way now,' the doctor replied, fixing her big, almost oversized eyes on Reilly. 'I pretty much have to sit on my hands till then so if you want to get in there before they arrive, be my guest.'

Reilly nodded, grateful for the opportunity to inspect the area around the manhole before it got trampled even further. Between the uniforms, the wife and the plumber, there was already a lot of disturbance, to say nothing of what it would be like after they'd hauled the corpse out. But such contamination was nothing new and Reilly did love a challenge . . .

She bent down and peered closely at the ground. As expected, the area around the manhole opening showed signs of heavy traffic. Blades of grass were bent and crushed into the damp earth by several sets of footsteps going back and forth from the gate to the tank. There had been some heavy rain recently, and the various footprints had left deep indentations in the soft ground. Reilly would have her GFU colleagues collect everyone's shoeprints later for elimination, but for now she wanted to see if there was anything of immediate interest.

She cast her gaze around, trying to understand what had been done, get a feel for it. It seemed to her that there were several ways into the garden: from the house or the gate behind her; over the hedge from the road to her left; through the woods to her right; or across the orchard straight ahead.

She tried to put herself in the perpetrator's shoes, tried to imagine what the murderer had been thinking. Someone had gone to a lot of trouble to kidnap the journalist, never mind the effort of dropping him into a septic tank. If the guy had been alive at the time, like Karen suggested, choosing to murder him in this way was making a point, a very visible one. The killer would have planned it all out, have known where the septic tank was, have had every detail figured. Reilly was prepared to put money on his coming in the normal way, through the gate.

She scooted round to the side of the lawn, took a new path out toward the septic tank, walking lightly, and checking the grass in front of her as she moved. As she had expected, there were no signs of footprints from the direction she was traveling. She stopped about two meters from the limestone opening.

Trying to muster courage and steel herself for the inevitable, she paused for a moment and gazed up at the gray sky. She needed to be calm and composed when she looked at the body, her mind neutral, assessing everything . . . unaffected.

She stepped closer to the opening and peered inside it.

Tony Coffey's face floated gently on the scummy surface, framed by a thick, viscous soup of gray foam. His eyes were open, staring upwards, the moment of his death captured forever in his ghastly grimace.

What had the poor guy been thinking? Reilly wondered. What goes through your mind as you slowly drown in sewage or choke on lethal fumes, all alone in the dark confines of a tiny space surrounded by human filth? Did he know his murderer? Did he have any idea why he was being subjected to such punishment?

She bent down to take a better look at the area below. The tank itself looked old – ancient, actually – and she figured it must have been there for decades, perhaps part of the original friary. The original waste system was just as old, as was often the way with these period houses, and the entire lower portion of the tank was hewn directly into living rock, with heavy limestone blocks stacked above it, creating large walls over which giant crosspieces were laid.

Between the layers of limestone were delicate frets of a soot-like substance, as if the whole thing had been constructed with burned or burning wood between the stones: plenty of dark little corners in which Reilly hoped trace evidence might lurk.

They'd be draining the tank once the body was removed, but until then . . .

Catching a whiff of methane that almost made her dizzy, yet again Reilly bemoaned her delicate nose. Normally when working a scene all her senses were hyperaware, but this time she was definitely going to have to do without her trusty nose.

Taking one last gasp of fresh air, she slipped on a gas mask to shield her from the toxic fumes, and

27

kneeled down properly on the damp grass. If she felt the cold wet ground through the knees of her contamination suit as she tried to look past the purple-splotched face of the body, she barely registered it. Her focus was now entirely on collecting evidence, finding clues as to how this had happened, and who might be responsible.

Not for the first time, Reilly wondered how in the world she had ended up here – on this occasion hovering over an open sewer with only a putrefying corpse for company – instead of spending her days sitting at a desk and exchanging pleasantries and coffee with colleagues, like most normal people.

Faced with a situation like this – with such a disgusting horrific mess – wouldn't most sane people throw up and run away screaming? The fact that she could face it all with such equanimity made her wonder what kind of person that made her. As bad as the killer if this was just another part of the day job? Or as bad as . . .? A thought surfaced unbidden and, attempting to banish the notion from her mind, she flicked on her torch, and began carefully examining the rim of the manhole opening. It was wet, rusting and crusted with a thick layer of dried scum.

She knew that chemically, 99.9 percent of the dank gray soup in the tank consisted merely of water, yet it was amazing how that other tiny percentage of offensive fecal bacteria was responsible for the assailing reek, and the main reason Reilly was restricting the majority of her person to outside the tank.

She choked back a gag, and began searching along the rim. After a few minutes, a short hair clinging to the damp metal on the inside caught her attention. It looked to be human, with the follicle still attached, and while she knew it could be anyone's (and being coarse and curly was likely to be a pubic hair that had passed through the Coffeys' toilet) at least it was something. She gently lifted it with her tweezers and dropped it into an evidence bag.

She continued to scan the area, following the beam of the torch as it illuminated the dark interior, then leaned further inside the opening, her face just inches from the dead man's. The putrid foam moved gently as the victim bobbed on the surface, the gases in his stomach keeping him there, but by now any last traces of disgust had left her – she was completely and utterly absorbed in her work.

Reilly felt a little *frisson* of excitement tickle her spine.

Despite the circumstances, she had to admit that these cases – the difficult ones – were what made the job for her. Intrigue, puzzlement, frustration . . . these were all in a day's work for a crime scene investigator.

Afterwards, Reilly checked on her fellow GFU techs.

'We've covered the perimeter,' Lucy reported. She was in her mid-twenties, with curly fair hair cut into a stylish bob, and dark-framed glasses. Energetic and enthusiastic, she often provided the impetus the team needed when energy levels flagged. 'I went from the wall, Gary from the house, and we met up in the middle.' She pointed to the fence line behind the septic tank, where the property ended and the woods began.

'Anything?' Reilly asked, although she suspected she already knew the answer.

'No one has entered the property from those directions anytime recently,' confirmed Lucy.

'The ground is soft from all this rain,' Gary said. He was older, late twenties with an open, appealing face, and a scruffy beard. He was more detail-oriented than Lucy, but lacked her intuitive skills, the ability to take disparate facts and make connections. 'Anyone climbing over the fence would leave deep prints where they landed.'

Especially if they were hauling a body, Reilly thought. 'Dr Thompson believes Coffey was still alive when he was put in the tank,' she reminded them.

'I know,' Gary nodded. 'But I can't imagine he went in voluntarily, so I'm thinking he would need to have been bound or sedated.'

'True. I don't think anyone would be dumped in there without a fight.'

Lucy shuddered. 'That's got to be a horrible way to die – in the dark, flailing around in sewage, choking on all those fumes . . .'

30

Reilly could see the discomfort in her face. She really was young to be doing this kind of work. But then again, there was no way of being fully prepared to deal with the things the GFU investigated.

'That's why we're here,' Reilly reminded her. 'To act on behalf of those who can no longer defend themselves.' Even as she said it, it sounded trite, but it seemed to have the desired effect. Lucy's face lost its emotion, and she turned her focus back to the case, to the evidence.

She looked at Reilly, her bright-eyed enthusiasm returning. 'Did you find anything in the tank?' she asked. 'I'll bet that was fun.'

'Nothing obvious. The whole area outside it is a mess of footprints – the plumber, Mrs Coffey, the uniforms . . .'

'Just once,' Gary said frustratedly, 'just once could we get an uncontaminated crime scene?'

'And what would be the fun in that?' Reilly said drily. She gazed out over the trampled sod. 'No, this is what we get, and it's down to us to make some sense of it.' She paused. 'But I did have an idea.' She looked at Gary. 'Can you do me a favor?'

'Of course, what do you need?'

'My iPhone's back in the van, and because I can't get down and dirty in the tank—'

'I've got the camera here if you need to take some shots,' Lucy interjected.

'No, that's not what I had in mind.'

Gary's eyes widened. 'iSPI? You're going to use

31

it?' he asked, his enthusiasm almost palpable, as Reilly anticipated it would be.

'iSPI' – Investigative Scene Processing Integration – was a portable app Reilly had promised to beta-test for one of her old Quantico classmates, Jet Miller, a former master hacker, now working in the FBI's forensic science division. The Academy had tasked Jet with researching the application of mobile computing technology to forensic field investigation, and he'd recently developed a suite of software designed to simplify and improve scene-processing by forensic technicians. Currently in development stage, the app was able to render a 3D image of a location using key photographic and video information, enabling investigators to 'run the scene' repeatedly after they'd finished doing so physically.

It was aimed at particularly challenging or potentially dangerous locations, such as the aftermath of a nuclear explosion, or a chemical fire. The Academy administration hoped the software could eventually be sold to investigative agencies throughout the world, and were making plans to begin negotiations for its commercial release once it was ready.

To this aim, Jet had recruited a number of guinea pig beta-testers from law enforcement friends in varying locations. And while Reilly had been hovering over the reeking septic tank and trying her best not to fall in, she figured this might be as good a time as any to give iSPI a try.

Gary was back with the phone almost as fast as was humanly possible.

The three returned to the septic tank and, slipping on her mask, Reilly once again took position over the opening. Launching the iSPI app, she aimed the phone low in the tank well below the rim, moving it slowly around in a 360-degree angle, and hoping to goodness she didn't drop it into the malodorous soup.

'Did you get everything?' Gary asked, when a few minutes later she stood up, hoping that she'd done all she needed to construct a usable map based on Jet's standard protocol.

'I think so. I also took some photo footage from the inside looking out. For a scene like this, where a victim has been confined in a tank or perhaps a well,' Reilly continued, automatically slipping into instructive mode, 'it's always a good idea to have an image from inside, so we can try and imagine what our victim was looking at, what he might have been thinking before he died. It could well be part of the motivation for the murder.'

'I'd imagine he was thinking that he really wished he had a ladder.'

'Gary!' Lucy poked him in the side.

'What? Wouldn't you?'

Reilly shook her head. 'OK, guys, show's over. Now it's back to good old-fashioned crime scene work.' She pointed to two young uniformed policemen standing by the gate. 'Those two were first on the scene. Gary, why don't you get their shoeprints for elimination purposes?'

He nodded and went to do as he was bid.

'Why does he get the cute uniforms?' Lucy complained.

'You think? I'd have thought this would be the last place you'd want to look for a date.'

The younger girl shrugged. 'Needs must. I'd try my chances with hunky Detective Delaney if I thought I had a chance,' she added, and despite herself, Reilly felt a little irritated.

'I'm sure your dad would just love to see you stepping out with a cop,' she said, referring to Jack Gorman, a fellow GFU investigator who also happened to be Lucy's father – something Reilly had only discovered after taking up work at the unit. To her horror, she'd been unashamedly vocal to her protégée about Gorman's old-fashioned, chauvinist attitude, completely unaware that the two were related.

Lucy winked. 'Like I've said before, what Dad doesn't know won't hurt him.'

Reilly had been lucky that Lucy and her father weren't especially close, and that Reilly's complaints hadn't affected the younger girl's impression of her – in fact, it was obvious that father and daughter had a complicated relationship and, if anything, Lucy shared Reilly's opinion of the senior Gorman.

'Well, now I need you to deal with Mrs Coffey and the plumber. Check their shoes for elimination purposes. They'll both be shaken, and you have the gentler touch.'

Reilly watched as Lucy, too, went off to carry

out her orders. The team were good kids – heck, Gary was only five years younger than she – but they seemed so young. Too young to be dealing with something as gruesome as this.

So what made her any different? How come she was able to deal with these things with such ease? Was it because she'd had no choice but to grow up fast, after her mother abandoned the family when Reilly was barely into her teens? She'd had to step in and help her dad raise her little sister, try to become a kind of mother figure to Jess.

And look how that had worked out.

Reilly swallowed hard. The root of her equanimity around violent death was something she often wondered about. Her only explanation was that once she was in the middle of an investigation, she'd taught herself over the years to let the more horrific circumstances go over her head. It was the only way she could remain unmoved. Or if not completely unmoved, then unscathed.

And Lord knew she'd had lots of practice.

Often, the messier the murder, the more focused and determined she in turn seemed to become, the more driven to read the clues, decode the science, and reveal the murderer. This case would certainly provide her with plenty of grist for the mill.

She remembered Chris's words earlier. *A forensic nightmare* . . .

Heaven help them.

CHAPTER 5

'I hate this.'

The detectives stood outside the front door, waiting for Mrs Coffey to answer.

Chris looked at his partner 'Hate what?'

'You know, interviewing the wife.' Kennedy hitched up his trousers and looked up at Chris, who was easily a foot taller. 'For feck's sake, her husband's just been stuffed in a septic tank – and here we come asking questions and making her feel like a suspect.'

'You're long enough in the tooth to know it's not like that,' Chris protested.

Kennedy gave him a look of incredulity. 'Yeah, and how would you feel if two flatfoots came knocking at your—'

He never finished his question. The door slowly opened, revealing a shaken-looking woman. In her mid-fifties, Sandra Coffey was trim and tidy in a navy trouser suit, her styled hair lightly colored to hide any encroaching gray.

Her face was ash-colored, her eyes red-rimmed. She looked dazed, as though, like Alice in Wonderland, she had stepped into a strange world where nothing made sense, and everything was turned upside down. She stared blankly at the detectives, clearly unaware of who they were or what they wanted.

'Mrs Coffey?' Chris smiled, immediately employing his natural propensity for putting people at ease. 'So sorry to bother you – I'm Detective Delaney, and this is Detective Kennedy.'

Her face maintained its blank expression, and she said nothing, just looked back and forth between the two of them as though their presence made no sense; was just another strange event in a bizarre and surreal day.

Chris continued, 'We're so sorry for your loss and know this is an exceptionally difficult time for you, but we wondered if we might ask you a few questions. Just to help us all try and understand what might have happened to your husband.'

Finally Sandra Coffey's face registered comprehension. Visibly composing herself, she took a deep breath and tried to force a polite smile through the grief and shock etched deeply into her face. 'Of course. Please come in.'

She held the door open for the detectives and they stepped inside. As the door closed behind the three of them, there was a moment of awkward silence as Mrs Coffey stared at their feet. Chris looked down and saw that their shoes were muddy from the garden.

'Should we . . .?'

She nodded. 'I'm sorry, but the housekeeper

was here just yesterday . . .' She pointed to a place by the door where two pairs of wellington boots stood neatly side by side. His and hers, a sight seen in thousands of houses up and down the country – except now there was no 'him' anymore. Then her gaze rested upon the boots for a moment, as though she was starting to understand that this reality was her future, and would be repeated again and again, over and over in the coming days. She suddenly caught herself and looked up, as if finally realizing how insignificant a muddy carpet was, considering . . . Her eyes welled up. 'Forgive me, of course it doesn't matter.'

'No, the last thing you need is to have to clean up after us,' Chris said gently, already using one foot against the heel of the other to slide his shoes off. Kennedy's were sturdier, black brogues tightly laced. He huffed and puffed as he bent over to untie them and struggled for a moment before straightening up, red-faced.

'Why don't we sit in the drawing room?' She led the way down the hall and the detectives padded along behind her.

Chris took in the details of the house. There was money here all right. The place was decorated in a restrained way, but all the furnishings were solid, antique pieces – no Ikea flatpack here – and the artworks were originals: oil paintings of rural scenes. Tradition ruled. He wondered how her supposedly 'down with the people' journalist husband had felt in a house that represented many of the values he purported to hate.

Mrs Coffey led them into the drawing room and pointed to a floral couch. 'Please, take a seat.'

Chris lowered himself into the sofa, Kennedy beside him. The cool light of late afternoon flowed through the tall wood-framed windows, and half-lit the room.

Mrs Coffey stood over them, her hands working, rubbing each other over and over as though trying to remove an invisible stain. 'Can I get you some tea? I could certainly do with a cup.' She framed it in such a way that refusal was not an option.

Chris again offered his most comforting smile. 'That would be great thanks – we'd both love one.'

Her face registered relief, and she turned and hurried from the room, her footsteps tap-tapping on the wooden floor as she disappeared down the hallway.

Chris watched her as she left. 'She seems composed, but she's having to work really hard to hold it together.'

Kennedy nodded, his eyes taking everything in too. 'I think we surprised her just for a second, but she pulled it together really fast.' He ran his gaze over the piano, a cluster of family photos arranged on top. 'Have you ever seen a more . . . . I don't know . . . old-fashioned house?'

Chris smiled as his partner struggled to find the right word to describe the décor, but he knew what Kennedy meant. Someone from the 1950s would feel completely at home here. Apart from the digital radio standing unobtrusively on a small side table, there was nothing that would have been out of place in a post-war house – the comfortable floral-print couch and chairs, the real fireplace with a grate, the piano, a wall of bookshelves, and a couple of antique side tables.

'No point looking *her* up on Facebook,' Kennedy commented, right before Sandra Coffey reappeared with a small tray, three elegant china teacups and a plate of biscuits.

She set the tray on the side table by the couch, took her own tea and stood gazing out the window. 'Help yourselves – there's milk and sugar.'

Kennedy passed a cup to Chris, then spooned three mounds of sugar into his own cup, and grabbed a chocolate digestive as if he'd never see one again in his lifetime. He dipped his biscuit into the tea, and maneuvered it into his mouth in one bite, then slurped his tea.

Chris had just picked up his teacup when out of nowhere, his hands began to tremble.

Dammit . . .

He'd been aware of a slight tingling in his fingers earlier in the car on the way here, but hadn't thought too much about it, just putting it down to the cold weather.

Suddenly he felt nauseous. He sincerely hoped it wasn't a recurrence of his former mysterious affliction. Even having some idea of what it might be would make it less frightening . . .

'Once again, we're sorry to bother you so soon,' Kennedy was saying, 'but the quicker we begin our investigation, the greater the chance of finding your husband's killer.'

'What do you need to know?' The window at which Mrs Coffey stood looked out onto the fields beyond the garden and orchard at the back of the house. She answered without turning round, her gaze seemingly captured by the wide sweep of a newly plowed field, the soil lying in rich, deep lines, churned and opened, marching off up a gentle slope toward the gray horizon.

Kennedy slurped again at his tea, and looked at Chris, as if urging him to continue the questioning.

Chris and Kennedy had been partnered together in the Serious Crime unit shortly after the death of Chris's father almost four years ago. At that time, Kennedy had automatically taken over much of the heavy lifting in the workplace, no questions asked, and Chris was forever grateful. As a result, they had very quickly become good mates as well as partners and by now the two had worked out a well-worn, almost instinctive interrogation routine. Chris laid the groundwork, asked all the right questions and set the witness at ease, while Kennedy listened carefully, allowed the information to wash over him and waited for anything that sounded unusual or out of place.

Trying to concentrate and refocus on the task at hand, Chris set his teacup down and

41

surreptitiously opened a small notebook so as not to break the thus-far cozy façade, all the while trying his utmost to conceal his shaking hands. 'When did you last see your husband?'

Mrs Coffey lifted her cup, and sipped from it again, before finally turning round. He could see the tension in her shoulders. 'The weekend. He was going to a conference down south somewhere earlier this week – Limerick, I think.' She paused. 'His secretary should have the details. Or assistant, as they like to be called these days. He has an office here at the house, and works mostly from home rather than at the *Herald* building.'

Chris and Kennedy exchanged glances, both noticing how there was a brief change in her voice when she mentioned the secretary. Gripping the pen tightly so as to steady his hand, Chris scribbled a quick note. 'And had you spoken to him since then?'

Sandra Coffey shook her head. 'That's not unusual, though. When Tony's away he works unsociable hours. As you can imagine, part of his game as a journalist is to hang around in bars to get what he calls "the lowdown" on a situation. We often don't talk when he's away – after twenty years of marriage the need to speak to one another every day seems to fade.' A look of sadness flitted across her face. 'We usually just catch up when he gets home – often find we have more to say that way.' She paused for a moment, as if again suddenly remembering her new-found situation. Her voice caught. 'Or I should say, we did . . .'

Chris glanced at Kennedy, who gave a barely perceptible shrug.

'Did your husband have any enemies, Mrs Coffey?' Kennedy asked, but something in his tone seemed to catch her attention, and she turned to look at him directly.

'I can see why you would think that, of course.' She suddenly shivered, as though a cold draft had hit her, and her voice broke a little. 'It must have been such a horrible way to die.'

They said nothing, just let her continue.

'For someone to do that to him . . .' For a brief moment it seemed as though she was going to let her emotions show, then just as quickly the shutters came down again and she strengthened her resolve. 'I'm sure my husband had lots of enemies, Detective. He was an investigative journalist, after all. He wrote hundreds – if not thousands – of highly opinionated pieces over the years. People tended to either love him or hate him.'

Chris nodded. 'I believe he was a big supporter of bringing in a ban on hunting with dogs, similar to the one in the UK?'

Sandra gave a dry laugh. 'Yes, you can just imagine how well that went down around here.'

'Ever any trouble over it?'

She nodded. 'A few months ago, when it was all very heated. It was what I would call silly, anonymous stuff – a dead fox left on the front step, slashed tires

43

on the Range Rover. I insisted that it was all reported to the police, of course – you should have it on record somewhere – but nothing ever came of it.'

Mrs Coffey walked to the middle of the room, and stood looking down at the detectives, sitting side by side on the low couch, Kennedy with his teacup still on his knee.

'Searching for my husband's enemies based on his writing would be a lifetime's work, Detectives. There's hardly a sector or group in Irish society that he hasn't attacked or upset at some point.'

She glanced toward the family portraits on the piano.

'He was very good at what he did. Almost too good.'

'Meaning?'

Sandra gave a brief smile. 'Uncovering dirt, being controversial, winding people up.' She sighed. 'Tony could wind anyone up if he had a mind to. Give him five minutes and he'd find your weakness, and exploit it mercilessly.'

'He must have pissed off a lot of people in his time then,' Kennedy commented, with a frustrated glance toward Chris.

Sandra looked reflective. 'The thing about Tony – something that when I first met him was very attractive – was that he would always find a way to get what he wanted, whatever it took. He was no respecter of anything – position, power, privacy – they were just trivial obstacles sent to challenge him. And he loved a challenge.'

44

Chris looked at her. 'Mrs Coffey, are you suggesting your husband operated on the margins of the law?'

She shrugged. 'I'm not sure Tony would describe it that way. As far as he was concerned, he just did whatever it took.'

Wonderful, Chris thought darkly. He tapped his pen against his notebook. 'Didn't he have any principles, any causes that he believed in?' Even as he said it, he regretted the question, realizing it sounded too harsh, too judgemental.

Mrs Coffey gave a bitter laugh. 'Principles – Tony? Except for a vague belief in the freedom of the press, he was completely without beliefs, morals or scruples. If you wanted some dirt on someone, wanted a hatchet job, an assassination, he was your man. Believe me, he wrote for the highest bidder.'

She stared out the window once again. 'Detectives, the reality is – was – that my husband was an arm twister, a digger of dirt, a discoverer of secrets. And it's no surprise that many people hated him for it.'

CHAPTER 6

Reilly woke suddenly, instantly awake even though it was the middle of the night. Her eyes flicked quickly to the alarm clock. The red digits glared back at her: 3.27. Three and a half hours until the alarm blared into life, starting another day. So what had woken her? A noise of some kind? She listened carefully. Was there something happening next door . . . or outside?

Lying completely still, she strained her ears to hear the faintest sound, but she could make out nothing but the steady beat of her own pulse. She lifted her head off the pillow – still nothing. The street was quiet, peaceful – the reason she had moved to Ranelagh in the first place. That and the fact that it was the nicest area in the city she'd been able to afford the rent. Though only a couple of miles from the center, it had a villagey feel to it that really appealed to her, with a multitude of restaurants, cafés and cute little shops that weren't yet suffering the effects of the ongoing economic recession.

Now, she focused her attention on the rooms around her – not a sound from the living room, no creaking floor-boards, not even a radiator ticking quietly as it cooled.

She settled her head back on her pillow, sighed deeply, and tried to relax, tried to let herself unwind and go back to sleep, but the harder she tried, the more sleep eluded her. Something was lurking there, hiding in a quiet corner of her mind, waiting to ambush her as soon as she started to drift off.

She turned over again, seeking that perfect position that would help her to relax. What was playing on her mind? Was it the Coffey case? She would have the ME's report in the morning, and the lab were analyzing the samples they had collected. Sure, it was a weird situation, but at this early stage, and with so little evidence uncovered, it wasn't at the point where it preyed on her mind.

That would happen soon enough, Reilly knew, but not until later, not until she had enough pieces of the jigsaw to see if there was a pattern. Then her brain would go into overdrive, trying to fit the pieces into coherent order, and striving for that elusive part, the keystone, the one that would make sense of everything. Then she would work days, nights – and barely sleep while she drove herself crazy trying to make sense of it.

Reilly rolled over, and pulled the covers tightly around her. She had been in Ireland for over a year now, but she still hadn't got used to the biting cold. While she'd thought that winter back home in San Francisco could be chilly, really she'd had

47

no idea. Two blankets and a duvet covered her, but still her toes felt like blocks of ice. She curled her legs up to bring them into the warmer part of the bed and slowly began to relax.

The climate was something she hadn't really considered when, the previous year, she'd got an invitation from the Irish Police Commissioner offering her the job of bringing the new Garda Forensic Unit up to date.

With her Quantico qualifications and her law enforcement experience, Reilly knew there was a lot she could bring to the job, but another reason she'd accepted the position was to keep tabs on her father, who in the hope of starting afresh after family life had been shattered, had moved from San Francisco back to Ireland, the land of his birth. At the time of Reilly's arrival in Dublin, Mike Steel was living in a scummy city center flat, drinking himself into oblivion.

Recently, though, he'd cleaned himself up, was staying off the bottle, and had even found himself a lady friend in one of his neighbors. Reilly was glad; after all the shit that had gone down in their family, he deserved to be happy.

But it also meant that there were fewer opportunities to spend time with him now, and Reilly missed checking in on him, missed taking care of him. Mike had moved on and it was almost as if he didn't need her anymore. She shook her head, annoyed with herself. Her dad was a grown man – of course he didn't need her. Still, his new relationship was a sure sign that his relocation from the US had been a success, whereas Reilly still wasn't certain if the same could be said for her own move . . .

Finally her breathing began to even out, and she felt a ripple of calm wash over her. Her eyes gradually felt heavier as sleep began to creep in.

She was almost gone, right at that delicious point where you know you are about to sleep and you can luxuriate in it when – *bam*– it hit her again.

Like an icy grip the dream grabbed her mind, started to play itself out, started to move toward its inexorable conclusion. It had visited her many times before, always when she was at her most vulnerable, when she had something else on her mind. There it was, coming out of the mist of her subconscious, a reminder of past defeats, a reminder that if you don't figure things out in time, you have failed.

Reilly was running – running as fast as she could – but getting nowhere.

Ghostly images floated around her, trees like sticks appearing in the mist . . . tiny snippets of conversation with Chris and Kennedy . . . Reilly's feet moved as though she were struggling through thick treacle, each step taking an agonizing minute, each minute bringing death one step closer.

She tried to run faster, strained, cursed the air, ripped at it with her hands as though it were a physical thing that she could tear aside by sheer willpower, but at the same time she already knew that she was doomed to fail.

Just as she had failed with her sister.

Hours later, an exhausted Reilly was at the lab to begin analysis of the samples they'd taken from the Coffey scene. There would be no weekend breaks while this investigation was going on.

The first sample was from one of the footprint indentations around the opening of the tank, and it was of interest because she'd noticed a slight glistening in the soil at the bottom of one of the soleprints around the heel area.

Something the killer may have walked in on the base of his shoe? She couldn't be sure but it was worth a look.

Reilly approached the mass spectrometer, placed the swab of soil into a sample cup, and fed it into the input slot at the base of the machine. After a brief irradiation and some molecular weight calculations, the machine spat out an answer.

Water, caramelized sugar, vinegar, sodium chloride and capsicum.

Reilly frowned. A soft drink perhaps? Strike that; no soft drink would use vinegar as one of its ingredients. So it had to be savory, maybe some kind of cooking sauce?

She racked her brains for a cooking sauce that might consist of such ingredients, and immediately came up with several: chili, taco, sweet and sour, Tabasco . . . She'd get Julius to track it down, crosscheck all the major brands available commercially to see if he could pinpoint it to something specific. The older lab tech was like a dog with a bone when it came to things like that.

Still, the type of sauce was perhaps less important than where it had come from. Had the killer walked it in from his own kitchen? Perhaps he'd made himself a bite to eat before taking poor Tony Coffey off to stew in his own filth.

Or perhaps it had been on the bottom of Coffey's shoes, and had slipped off onto the mud as he was being dragged to the opening? She made a mental note to get Chris and Kennedy to ask Mrs Coffey what her husband's eating habits and preferences had been, although the ME's analysis of Coffey's stomach contents during autopsy should determine if he'd eaten anything savory beforehand.

Water, sugar, vinegar, salt and capsicum . . .

As with all unidentified trace, Reilly found that this simple piece of evidence threw up more questions than answers.

'Hey.' Later that morning, Chris stood in the doorway of Reilly's office. It was a fair reflection of herself: small, meticulously organized, with minimal personal touches.

She was reading a file and was so engrossed she hadn't even heard him approach.

'Hey there. Thanks for coming by. I've got the ME's report, and I'm going over it for the second time to see if there's anything I missed on the first reading.'

He came in, and slumped down into a chair in front of her desk, his dark hair flopping over one side of his forehead. 'You look a bit gray today,' he said. 'Did you sleep?'

She pushed the file aside, and looked at him properly. 'Gee, thanks, you sure know how to make a girl feel good,' she joked. She leaned back in her chair. 'I slept some. How about you?'

Chris shook his head. 'Not great, to be honest.'

'Oh?' She gave him a questioning look. But before she could say anything more, Kennedy barged in, holding three paper coffee cups.

'Ah, quit your whingeing, lightweights,' he said. 'Has the bogyman been haunting ye with nasty nighttime visions?' He handed out the coffees, hitched up his trousers and flopped down into a vacant chair beside Chris. It creaked a little under the strain.

Reilly grabbed the cup, lifted the lid and blew at the steam. 'Let me guess, you slept like a baby?'

He nodded. 'Just like every night.'

'The joys of a happy marriage,' Chris said with a wry smile, winking at Reilly.

'Yeah, yeah, laugh it up. But I *am* happily married, something at least one of you might consider trying before you're too old and cynical.' He looked back and forth between their amused faces. 'Laugh all you want. You might think it's sad, but every day when I get home from work,

52

Josie's there waiting for me with a kind word and some good grub. Can't argue with that – or a sound night's sleep.' He stirred his coffee with a slim plastic stirrer, and flipped it into the nearby rubbish bin.

'So anyway, Reilly, much as we love you, we didn't drive all the way over here to chat about my home life. Do we have anything?'

'Well, here's Karen Thompson's report, for starters.' Reilly duly slid the document across her desk toward the two detectives.

Kennedy waved dismissively at the paperwork, and sipped his coffee. 'Save us the time – just give us the edited highlights. And no fancy medical talk either – you know I'm a meat-and-spuds man.'

She suppressed a smile. Kennedy liked to wind her up about her use of technical jargon, but she'd come to know that underneath all the bluster, the guy was a lot smarter than he let on. After all, she had him to thank for pinpointing her location and coming to her rescue on a previous case when things went bad. Nope, there were no flies on Pete Kennedy.

'All right, seeing as you asked . . . Autopsy for Dummies, page one.' She flipped open the report. 'First of all, the doc confirms Coffey had been in the tank for at least forty-eight hours.'

'That would make it Wednesday when he was put in there?' Kennedy clarified.

'Yeah.'

'When Mrs Coffey would have been at her

weekly bridge club meeting,' Chris put in, looking at his own notes. 'Sounds like the killer had some idea of their schedule.'

'Right. And like you said yesterday, he was indeed alive when he was put in the tank.'

'Ugh, the thoughts of that . . .' Kennedy grimaced.

Chris looked pensive. 'So what was the actual cause of death? Drowning . . . sewage poisoning?'

'Those fumes would have asphyxiated him pretty quickly,' Reilly agreed, 'but yes, actual cause of death was drowning.'

'Oh Christ . . .' Kennedy said wincing. 'You're saying the guy drowned in his own shit? The press are going to have a field day with that one.' As it was, media interest was already heightened in the case, given that the victim was a fellow journalist.

Reilly cocked her head to one side. 'Actually, I would never say anything that inelegant, Detective Kennedy, and neither would Dr Thompson. As the report says, Mr Coffey drowned in human excrement – you're the one saying he drowned in his own shit.'

Kennedy waved a hand. 'OK, I get it – but stop saying it. It's making my breakfast rise up in rebellion.'

Chris smiled at their banter, but remained focused on the details. 'All of this suggests a high degree of planning and premeditation. This was very definitely no accident. We're interviewing Coffey's secretary this morning to see if she can shed any light on why the poor guy ended up like that. Anything else to go on before we talk to her?' He looked hopefully at Reilly. 'Did your guys turn up much since?'

'Well, we've really only just gotten started but . . .' She went on to tell them about that morning's sauce discovery. 'Going by his stomach contents at autopsy, apparently Coffey was like Kennedy, a meat-and-potatoes man, so it's unlikely the sample came from him.'

'What about the plumber?' Chris asked.

'He was wearing boots, and this was definitely a shoeprint. Size ten, which suggests our killer would be of average height and build.'

'Aren't they always?' Kennedy grumbled. 'What I wouldn't give for a shoeprint that, for once, gives us a guy that's eight foot tall and twenty stone. Would be easy to pick him out in a crowd.'

'Like I said, we've just gotten started, and there's quite a bit of isolation to do first. I may have picked up some potentially interesting trace from the limestone inside the tank opening – lab's working on that as we speak – but the sewage would have obliterated any trace around the body.'

Chris nodded as if expecting as much.

'So all we know for the moment is that someone average, who may or may not enjoy a spot of Chinese food, wanted Coffey dead,' Kennedy said, sighing.

'I never said anything about Chinese—'

'Yeah, yeah, I know, *some* kind of sticky sauce. Doesn't much matter either way, does it?'

'Actually—'

'OK, I get it, it's a start. But until you can tell us what this stuff is, it's no good in helping us catch our killer.'

'It may be no good anyway, but we still have to check it out.' Despite the huge strides in forensic science and its application to police work, Kennedy was dubious, and much more of a fan of the old-fashioned methods.

'I've sent the manhole cover to the specialized tool marks lab in Edinburgh,' Reilly continued. 'Results will take some time, but this might help us identify how the culprit got it off, and that in turn may yield something helpful in itself.' She picked up a sheaf of papers from her desk. 'I was also interested in the construction history of the tank – you saw yourselves how old it looks – so I called the plumber and asked him about it.'

Paddy Murphy had still been pretty shaken up by his unexpected discovery, but when Reilly asked him about the specifics of the tank, he'd quickly perked up.

'It's a completely natural system,' he'd told her. 'And when I say it's old, I mean ancient. I always figured it operated so well because it was fed from an underground spring of some sort. Maybe it was a kind of sacred cave before the monks claimed it for the friary sewer. Regardless, it doesn't need any chemical assistance and is by any standard a remarkable feat of septic engineering,' he'd added with an enthusiasm that only a specialist in waste

56

management could muster. 'It quickly digests any organic material it's fed, and distributes the resulting nutrients out under the orchard and into the garden.'

'So what's a history lesson on the tank going to tell you?' Kennedy sounded skeptical.

'Well, I wondered if there was anything significant in the tank itself as the manner of death.'

'Ah, I was thinking you'd start soon on that . . . erm . . . shite,' he muttered irritably. Reilly's tendency to look at not only the physical elements of a murder scene, but also any potentially meta-phorical significance in how it was executed got on his nerves. It was difficult not to, when one of their previous investigations had been determinedly metaphorical in tone. It also stemmed from Reilly's behavioral psychology training at the FBI Academy.

'Well, I suppose a lot of journalists are considered to be full of shit,' Chris said, nodding in agreement. 'And someone certainly wanted to deliver a strong message, killing Coffey the way they did. Maybe that's what he's hoping to get across.'

'That's pretty much what I was thinking,' Reilly said. 'Might be worth going through Coffey's most recent articles, see if he's annoyed anyone badly enough to do something like this. No harm in cross-referencing the cause of death with other cases either.'

Kennedy stood up, headed for the door. 'Cheers, we'll be sure to let you know when we graduate from homicide high school too,' he said sardonic-ally, but Reilly knew him well enough by now to realize it was merely banter. 'God knows what we'd do without the FBI's finest to show us how to run a case, eh? Speaking of which, how's our old buddy Agent Forrest?'

'Retiring, actually,' Reilly replied, referring to her friend and former mentor Daniel Forrest, with whom the detectives had consulted on a previous case involving Reilly's sister.

It had been a surprise to her to hear that he was hanging up his boots. Reilly had expected the man to be buried clutching a half-completed profile in his hands, so dedicated was he to unraveling the most twisted of human minds.

'He's continuing his lectures at Quantico but staying out of the field, apparently.'

'I reckon he has the right idea,' Kennedy said, and both Reilly and Chris looked at him in surprise. If anything Reilly had expected the older cop to greet the news with derision.

'Workload getting you down, Detective?' she queried, arching an eyebrow.

Kennedy shook his head, looking uncharacteristically defeated. 'Last week, one of our boys is turned into a human Popsicle,' he said, referring to the murder of a former colleague. 'This week, guy drowns in his own shite, and in both cases we've got no clues, suspects, or motive – not to mention having the press all over it.' He shrugged. 'What's not to love?'

CHAPTER 7

There were secretaries and there were secretaries, Chris thought, and he'd make an educated guess that shorthand wasn't among Kirsty Malone's key skills.

Tony Coffey's assistant was the type of woman the most trusting of wives would worry about spending time with her husband. Chris guessed she was in her mid- to late thirties, but today she was dressed far younger, in a short denim skirt and tight-fitting red sweater, with highlighted blond hair and too much make-up. Not his type, but nice to look at, all the same.

Kirsty had agreed to meet them at the journalist's office, where she had some corrections to make to Coffey's final piece before sending it through for tomorrow's edition. The decision to run the column on the week of the journalist's untimely death was bound to be controversial, but from what Chris had already learned about Coffey he figured that the man wouldn't have wanted it any other way.

The office was situated in an extension of the main Coffey residence, and was a large airy room, the walls lined with books, files, and stacks of magazines. There was an oak desk on the far side, in front of a bay window, a couch, and two comfortable chairs arranged beside the fireplace. A fire crackled in the grate, flooding the room with a faint orange glow.

Kirsty was perched on a chair, displaying entirely too much perma-tanned thigh. She dabbed at her eyes, which were red-rimmed apparently from crying. When the detectives entered the room she stood up and offered them a gentle handshake.

'Miss Malone,' Chris asked, 'we need to ask you a few questions about Mr Coffey. Do you think you're up to it?'

Kennedy always let him take the lead in interviewing women. Chris had a way about him, particularly with attractive ones, seeming at first to be besotted, taken in by their charms, while in reality he was very much in control, using flattery to disarm.

Kirsty nodded. 'Of course.'

He waved her back into her chair, and she obligingly sat down once more, crossed her legs, and gripped her notepad like a security blanket. He gazed out of a nearby window to avoid staring at her.

'Where was Mr Coffey supposed to be this week?'

Kirsty sniffed. 'At a conference in Limerick. He left on Monday . . . Monday morning, early.'

'And you hadn't spoken to him since?'

She shook her head.

'Was that unusual?'

Kirsty looked up at Kennedy – he was standing much closer to her than Chris was – invading her space almost, forcing her to look upwards. 'A little, but he'd just got a new mobile – one of those iPhones – and he was really struggling to figure it out. Technology wasn't his thing.'

Chris smiled sympathetically. 'I know what you mean. Sometimes it's hard to learn how to make a simple phone call on these newfangled machines. So did you try to get in touch with him while he was away?'

'Several times – and I sent him a couple of texts. But he didn't reply.'

'Weren't you concerned? I'd imagine you two were quite close.'

Kirsty gave him a sideways glance, unsure what he was implying, but Chris's open face was the picture of innocence.

'I was a bit bothered,' she admitted. 'We usually talked most days when he was away, but you know what a journalist's life is like. I just thought he was busy, had a few late nights boozing, or he'd let the phone run out of battery or something. He never kept up with things like that.'

Chris continued to nod sympathetically. 'Did you talk to Mrs Coffey about your concerns?'

Kirsty shot him another look, peering up through her thick black eyelashes. 'Me and Mrs Coffey, we don't exactly . . . see eye to eye on everything.'

61

'Like her husband?' As usual, there was no treading softly where Kennedy was concerned.

Kirsty averted her gaze and fiddled nervously with the notepad in her lap, rolling the corners of the pages up and down, up and down. Suddenly she looked up. 'Mind if I smoke?'

Chris nodded. 'Go ahead.'

She stood quickly, and picked up a small gold purse from the desk, before taking out a packet of Malboro and a lighter. Her hands shook as she lit the cigarette, and it took her three attempts to get it alight.

'Got one to spare?'

She looked up and met Chris's smile. 'You too, huh?' She strode across the thick carpet and offered him the packet, while Chris prepared to use a well-worn feint, employed to put witnesses like her at ease.

That Kennedy was a smoker was obvious from the broken veins on his face and the giveaway persistent cough, but most people found it unexpected in the clean-shaven picture of health that was Chris Delaney, and he figured it was a decent leveler of sorts.

Kirsty stood and inhaled deeply from the cigarette, visibly unwinding. 'Tony loved to smoke too, but had to keep it from the missus. Old witch doesn't like smoking in the house,' she continued.

Chris immediately picked up on the reference to Sandra Coffey. Definitely no love lost between those two.

He lit up, and nodded sympathetically, his eyes never leaving hers, but he said nothing.

Kennedy was on the far side of the room checking out a wall of photos. Tony Coffey featured in most of them, along with a selection of local celebrities and politicians. He had obviously enjoyed mixing with the rich and infamous, and had an oily smile on his face whenever he was up close with a well-known personality. Chris looked at the pictures then back at Kirsty, wondering what on earth someone like her saw in the squat and decidedly unattractive man.

'What was he like?' Kennedy asked suddenly. He was still gazing at the photos, and had picked up one of Tony pictured at some bash with a woman who was neither Sandra Coffey nor Kirsty Malone. His companion was in a glamorous black dress that barely contained her ample cleavage, and Tony had his arm around her waist as he beamed at the camera.

Kirsty turned to look at him. 'Tony?' A little smile played across her face. 'He was funny. Could always make me laugh.'

Chris's tone was level. 'Mrs Coffey doesn't look like she laughs much.'

Kirsty gave a snort of derision. 'You got that right – oul wagon's face might crack if she smiled.' She inhaled deeply, and breathed the smoke out hard; it formed a shroud around her face. 'Don't miss much, do you?' she added, meeting his gaze square on.

He shrugged. 'It's my job.'

Kirsty walked over to Kennedy, and looked at the photo he was holding. 'Journalists' Association dinner last year,' she informed him. 'That's Tony and our features editor. Bit of a drunken bash, but we had a laugh.'

'Tony didn't take his wife to events like that?'

Kirsty raised her eyebrows. 'Given the choice, would you? No, Sandra prefers not to get down and dirty with the gutter press,' she said. 'Too high and mighty for us, although that didn't stop her from marrying Tony. Could never quite understand what he saw in her.'

Chris looked around the large room and outside to the neat little country estate, and reckoned he could figure out exactly what.

'Doesn't seem like the happiest of marriages,' Kennedy commented.

Kirsty looked at another photo of Tony and gazed at it wistfully. She shrugged. 'I guess she learned not to ask too many questions. For the most part Tony kept this life . . .' she paused slightly, as if talking about something other than his work, '. . . completely separate from his home life with her and the country crowd.'

'I'm guessing they didn't mix all that well?' Chris ventured.

Kirsty gave a bitter laugh. 'Tony was an out-and-out socialist. He was forever banging on about how his dad had worked on the railways for forty years, salt of the earth, real working man, all that stuff.' She followed Chris's gaze, and settled on a portrait of Tony and his wife behind his desk. 'The whole country set thing? He hated it, hated the dinner parties, the crusty formality of it all. Bunch of old fakes in tweed and twinsets, he called them.'

Kennedy had been listening carefully, waiting for his opportunity. Having worked so long together both he and Chris knew instinctively when to press, when to pull back, when each had set the other up with an opening. Now was the time.

'So what was the attraction, Kirsty?' he said, deciding not to tiptoe around the obvious reality. 'You're an intelligent, attractive woman. He was married and must have been, what, twenty years older than you?'

Kirsty carefully set the photo down, and turned to face Kennedy. She took a drag on her cigarette, and sent a cloud of smoke up toward the high ceiling.

'I don't know, hard to put a finger on it really. I suppose he had a way of making me feel needed.' She paused, teary-eyed once again. 'We all want to be needed, don't we?'

Chris looked briefly at Kennedy – their eyes met, a faint nod. The door had opened, now was the time to push through.

'You weren't the first, were you, Kirsty?' Chris probed softly.

She gave a bitter smile. 'His first assistant or first affair?'

'You tell me. Were they one and the same thing?'

Kirsty gave him a sharp look, but said nothing. She walked slowly across the room, and sat down on the sofa.

An uncomfortable silence filled the room. Chris let it sit. It was easy to talk too much, to fire one question after another at people. The trick was not to say anything, to let the pauses and the silences do their work. Let Kirsty think about what she'd said, wonder if she'd said too much, worry what they might be thinking of her . . .

Kennedy was now standing by the desk, checking it over as if he was no longer interested in what was being said. Chris looked slowly back and forth between the photo collection and Kirsty. She was obviously uncomfortable, flicking nervously at her cigarette while repeatedly glancing toward the detectives waiting for one or other of them to say something. The only sound in the room was the hum from Tony Coffey's computer screen.

'Any idea who would want Tony dead?' Chris asked finally. 'Want him to suffer by stuffing him alive in a septic tank, buried in his own filth and left to die?'

Kirsty shot Chris a look of utter horror. 'What? He was alive when they . . .' She hugged her arms close to her chest. 'Oh my God, that's disgusting . . . it's sick!'

'It is,' Chris agreed quietly, going to stand in front of her. 'That's why we want to catch the bastard who did it.'

Kirsty fiddled again with her cigarette and looked down at her brightly painted nails, studiously avoiding Chris's piercing gaze. 'Look, I'm not suggesting in a million years that something like that was justified, but Tony was a hard man to like. He was harsh in his opinions, said exactly what he thought, even though a lot of people thought he was full of . . . Oh God!' she said, putting a hand to her face. 'Is that what this was all about? Someone trying to imply he was full of shit? But why? Who?'

'You're saying he had a lot of enemies?' Kennedy asked quickly, unwilling to let her become distracted.

She took a last hard drag on her cigarette, before stubbing it out roughly in a cut-glass ashtray nearby. 'You name it, he'd pissed someone off over it. You only have to read last week's column to know what he's all about.'

Chris had; it was a nasty, sneering piece about same-sex marriage and what he called 'the gay abomination'.

He glanced again at Kennedy, then turned his focus back on Kirsty. 'So from what you've said, we should be looking at anyone from an angry husband to an irate fox hunter to a pissed-off homosexual?'

'That's Tony.' Kirsty gave a sad laugh. 'To know him was to hate him.'

And Chris thought, frustrated, it seemed there were many who did just that.

CHAPTER 8

Reilly was running. She liked to do so when her brain was overloaded by work, and nothing was making sense. Sometimes the change in brain chemicals seemed to help her think more clearly, and rearranged her pattern of thoughts in a way that made what had previously seemed to be random bits and pieces suddenly click into place.

The cool evening breeze on her face felt good. It had rained earlier in the day, but now the air was fresh, clean, and the late autumn leaves were thick on the grass as she ran past Herbert Park. She was tempted to cut through it and savor the feel of soft grass under her feet, but even in this leafy suburb it was too risky for a woman to go alone there after dark.

She contented herself with the quiet streets, almost deserted now that the rush hour was over. She glanced at the brightly lit houses, each one a small oasis of light and warmth and safety, televisions casting ghostly blue light on the ceilings and curtains. No doubt filled with happy loving families, the way hers used to be back home in California before . . . everything.

Her footsteps tapped out a steady rhythm, her blond ponytail bobbing in time against her neck, muscles moving fluidly, comfortably, on autopilot, allowing her brain to run free. She had spent that afternoon researching old case files, trying to find another incident of the mode of killing – drowned in a septic tank – without success. Though there were hundreds of such incidents as a result of accidental drownings, as far as she could tell there was none suggesting murder.

She turned a corner, and startled a cat lurking in the shadows beneath a parked car. It scooted out and across her path, almost causing her to stumble, then across the road. It paused on the far side and shot her a fearful glance before finally disappearing into a dark patch of shrubs on the far side of the road.

Reilly quickly found her rhythm again, willing her mind to relax as her feet beat out a hypnotic beat.

Later, back home, she showered and toweled her hair dry as she stepped into her living room. She had brought a couple of lab reports home from the office to read, but wasn't in the mood to start on them just yet.

She sat down on the couch, idly turned on the TV, and tried to concentrate on what was showing, but nothing could capture her attention. She surfed through the channels for a few minutes more before finally switching off.

Reilly sat for a moment in the silence of her

small one-bed apartment. Kennedy was right – loneliness could be a bitch sometimes. It was fine when she wanted to be alone, but there were also times when she longed for company, for a hug when she walked through the door, for someone to be there, waiting for her. They would talk about something inconsequential, cook dinner together, maybe exchange foot massages . . .

Of course she wasn't completely alone in Dublin. Her father lived a few miles away in the inner city, but that wasn't the same, and anyway, by all accounts Mike Steel had a hectic social life these days, whereas Reilly was feeling increasingly lonely in this strange, and sometimes inhospitable city. While people were for the most part friendly, she could sense an undercurrent of frustration about the collapse of what had once been a vibrant, thriving economy.

She and Chris had spent a lot of time together last summer, during her temporary suspension from the GFU following an issue surrounding their first investigation, and while he was recovering from shooting injuries related to the same case. She'd tried (without success) to teach him how to surf, and he'd shown her around the city, and made her dinner once or twice in his apartment. But since her reinstatement, and the increase in their respective workloads, the opportunities for these occasions had been few and far between. It was a pity, as she'd enjoyed chilling out with someone who understood the pressures of the job, but ironically it was those very pressures that had been keeping them apart lately.

The thought of those lazy dinners at Chris's place and the rumbling of her stomach reminded Reilly that she hadn't eaten anything since lunchtime, and the run had only made her more hungry.

Pulling open the door of her fridge, she looked dejectedly at the miserly contents for a few moments, before a flash of inspiration hit.

Taking down a large cast-iron skillet from the hook beside the stove, Reilly sparked up one of the gas burners and melted a little butter in the pan.

She grabbed three corn tortillas that remained from a pack of eight in the fridge, and tossed them into the now bubbling butter. Selecting two brown eggs from their box and a small jar of tomato salsa, she shut the fridge door and deposited all three items on the counter top. With a wooden spatula, she slid the sizzling tortillas into a stack at one side of the pan and then, cracking open the eggs on the skillet's edge, she added them to the butter.

Placing a lid atop the pan, she turned to her fruit basket and selected a large avocado that was slightly overripe but it would have to do. As the eggs basted, she halved and stoned the fruit, slicing the flesh then arranging the thin wedges on a plate.

By now the egg yolks had developed an opaque white film so she dished the crispy tortillas on the plate next to the avocado wedges and carefully topped them with the eggs. This short stack

71

was topped with a dollop of the tomato salsa and – ta-dah – Reilly had, in the heart of Dublin, recreated heuvos rancheros, an old student favorite from her Quantico days. It was actually a Mexican dish, and technically breakfast, but it had always been a major comfort food for her, and tonight she figured that was exactly what she needed.

Returning to the fridge once more, she poured herself a healthy serving of orange juice, and was just about to settle down to eating when her cellphone rang.

Checking the screen, her face fell. This was not a call she wanted to take, but it wasn't one she could really refuse either. 'Reilly Steel speaking,' she announced quietly into the mouthpiece.

A booming voice with a strong Midlands accent filled her ear. 'Steel, Inspector O'Brien here. I trust this is a good time?'

Reilly looked dejectedly at her heuvos rancheros. 'It's fine, sir,' she lied. 'What can I do for you?'

'Good, good,' he rumbled. 'Just watching TV or something, were you?'

'About to have dinner, actually but it's OK.'

'Dinner, yes . . .' He paused as if the very concept was alien to him. 'Steel, I'll get straight to the point. I was wondering if you have any news on Crowe, preferably good news? I couldn't contact Jack this evening, and as his number two . . .'

Reilly bristled. Technically, she and Jack Gorman, the older GFU investigator, were equal in rank,

72

but as he was an incumbent of the previous forensic unit, old habits died hard.

She could hazard a guess that Gorman was uncontactable because he was currently on location or, unlike Reilly, he merely had the good sense to switch his phone off at dinnertime.

The investigation O'Brien was referring to was another the GFU lab were immersed in at the moment, the death of a former cop John Crowe. The thinking was that the man had been murdered by an ex-collar. Crowe had come up through the ranks alongside the chief, so O'Brien had a personal interest in securing a speedy outcome.

Reilly took a deep breath. What to tell him? The case was one of Gorman's and she'd had little involvement in it thus far.

'Nothing substantial, as far as I know, sir. I'm sure Gorman's got the lab working on any trace he found. Of course, we've had to move some resources to the Coffey murder lately.'

'That journalist? Of course, I understand that, yes.' O'Brien paused. 'And I completely understand that resources are stretched. I don't want us to lose focus on Crowe, though. He was one of ours, and it sends a bad message if people think they can get away with killing members of the force. It's the beginning of a slippery slope, if you get my meaning . . .'

'Of course, sir. I'll chase it up.' Reilly understood completely; understood that for the next few days, sleep was likely to be something of a luxury. She walked into the kitchen and slid the now-cold remainder of her meal into the bin.

Sleep was already a luxury for Chris. For the third night in succession, he was awoken in the early hours by crucifying pain. His body racked with tremors, his threadbare sheets were a tangled mess of cotton and wool soaked through with cold sweat.

He'd experienced something similar about a year ago, something that had worried him enough at the time to confide in Reilly about it, and ask her to investigate further. He didn't want to risk anything popping up in his force medical. But the blood tests she'd run had turned up nothing untoward, and when in the meantime the symptoms had stopped, Chris had put it down to exhaustion or probably closer to the truth the onset of middle age.

But now the tremors and discomfort were back with a vengeance. He lay motionless for a while, letting the worst of the pain wash over him, trying to figure out just what the hell was going on.

Eventually, when the sun was finally up, he rolled gingerly out of bed and stood up, half expecting his legs to crumple under him. But no, for the moment at least he was still able to stand on his own two feet.

Striding determinedly into the bathroom, before his traitorous limbs changed their mind, he retrieved a small bottle of extra-strength ibuprofen from the cabinet and took two, crushing the pills between his molars and enjoying the brief, acrid taste before swilling them down with a gulp of water from the tap.

He stoppered the sink and drew a basinful of scalding hot water. Then folding a small cotton washcloth in half to produce a strip of fabric, he dropped it into the water, poking it with a comb to submerge it.

Once it was well and truly saturated, he gingerly grabbed it by the corner, pulled it from the basin's watery embrace, and plastered it across the bottom of his jaw. A red-hot ripple of pain flushed through his face, momentarily distracting his embattled nervous system. He held the boiling-hot rag tight against his skin and slowly counted to sixty, allowing it to soften his facial stubble from the texture of dry pasta to that of *al dente*.

Next, lifting a small ivory-handled badger-hair shaving brush from the brass stand next to the sink, he dipped it into the hot water, using it to whip up a nice head of foamy lather from the bar of shaving soap he kept nearby. Applying the soothing balm to his engorged skin, he gave it a moment to set and cure. Then, with a few deft strokes he brought the razor to a fine edge and, turning to observe himself in the mirror, began slowly and methodically to scrape it across the planes of his jaw.

'Damn!' Chris cursed out loud as, out of nowhere, another rod of pain shot through his arm. He

75

cursed a second time when he noticed the streak of dark crimson running down his jaw. Tearing off a strip of toilet paper, he laid a thin piece on the cut, and waited for the bleeding to subside.

It took him about five minutes to complete the rest of the shave, and when he was finished he spritzed a little aftershave lotion into the palms of his hands and clapped both tight to his cheeks, reveling in the short, sharp sensation of the astringent tightening his pores.

If he didn't feel like a dynamic detective at the peak of his health, the least he could do was try and look the part.

Pleased with his efforts, he shuffled out of the damp, clinging pyjamas and flung them into the wicker clothes hamper next to the shower. Feeling too dizzy to risk a shower, instead he managed a brisk, thorough wash.

Ready to face the day, Chris walked back to the bedroom, where in the wardrobe a freshly laundered uniform awaited. He pulled off the plastic bag, trying to remember the last time he'd worn full blues – usually when working he got away with jeans and a succession of practically identical cotton shirts and a leather jacket. This morning was different, though: he was part of a guard of honor for Johnny Crowe's final send-off, hence the formal threads.

With the uniform smartly enshrouding his tall frame, he went into the galley kitchen, which abutted his living room area. The linoleum floor hadn't seen a mop in some time, and the counter tops were crowded with boxes, cartons and other remnants of too many takeaways.

He shook his head. He'd better be careful or he'd turn into one of those clichéd detectives that appeared in TV shows – the alcoholic workaholic, who spent his evenings alone surrounded by takeaway boxes and whiskey bottles. He laughed. Not likely. For one thing, he rarely drank other than socially, and for another he was actually quite a decent cook when he could find the time.

Chris sighed. As for the workaholic part, well, in the murder business that was non-negotiable.

CHAPTER 9

The GFU building was almost deserted when at seven thirty Reilly arrived. She liked to get in early, and have some time to think in peace and quiet before the interdepartmental phone calls and questions started.

She settled in behind her desk with her coffee – black, no sugar. Today she'd decided to see if the iSPI software could reveal anything about the Coffey scene that the investigative team had missed.

Grabbing a cable with a mini-USB connector on the end, she plugged it into the recessed slot on the side of the iPhone, and the other into her PC.

The computer immediately sprang into life and displayed a password confirmation screen. Reilly keyed in 'Cassandra', her late mother's first name, and the terminal hummed, a status bar indicating its progress as it downloaded the data from the iSPI app.

When that was complete, it displayed a second progress bar, under the words 'aggregating image data', and she waited patiently to see what would happen next.

Eventually the rendering engine displayed a 'complete' icon, and prompted her to enter a file name. Reilly saved it using the Coffey case file number and date, and then as directed, keyed in the command to begin a further render.

As the progress indicator began another maddeningly slow advance across the screen, Reilly went to the comfortable chair that sat next to a small table supporting two data gloves and a head-mounted display: the second piece of Jet Miller's toy, and the stuff that really sent Gary into spasms of excitement. She'd let him try it out later, but first she wanted to see for herself how the software performed.

Relaxing back into the chair, she laced the display onto her brow like some sort of intricate hat. Two small viewing panels folded down over her eyes and reflected, through a series of prisms and mirrors, the visual output of two small high-resolution color LCD displays. Sliding the data gloves onto her arms, she made an 'OK' gesture with her right hand – as Jet's instructions directed – and the terminal flared to life.

The goggles displayed a boot menu, and using subtle movements of her right hand, she reached across the screen through the network, and grasped the freshly rendered scene from the storage attached to the rendering engine. Turning her palm face up, she clenched a tight fist and then splayed her hand out open. As if by some miracle, the machine responded by unfurling a finely stitched virtual reality mosaic of the Coffey septic tank.

Whoah . . . Reilly felt goosebumps.

Poking around at the edges of the illusion, she was amazed to find that for a first attempt she had actually followed the instructional protocol fairly well, and all the vital data needed to reconstruct the scene seemed to have been properly captured.

In fact, it was so close to the real thing it was scary. OK, so there was no way a machine could replicate the sounds . . . smells . . . *feel* of a crime scene for real, but in this situation that was a good thing. This time there was no stink, no toxic stew.

Nice work, Jet.

Reilly smiled, ran her hands over the gloves and prepared to walk the Coffey scene for the second time, iSPI-style.

As she worked, the GFU building gradually came to life around her – footsteps in the corridor, voices and greetings, phones ringing, the buzz and the pace gradually picking up as people settled into their daily routine.

Reilly ignored it all. She had her door closed this morning, both to shut out sound and also discourage casual visitors.

'Reilly?' There was a brief knock before the door opened and she looked up to see Lucy leaning inside. Reilly glanced at the clock: it was after ten a.m. and she had been working on the scene for over two hours. Lucy stared at her headgear. 'Wow, that looks so . . . futuristic.'

'I guess that's exactly what it is.' Removing the headset, Reilly rocked back in her chair and stretched. Her neck and shoulders were tense from sitting still for so long. She picked up the remains of her coffee, now stone cold.

'Is that the Coffey scene from the other day?' Lucy moved closer to the computer screen, immediately interested. Reilly had placed a virtual placemarker inside the rendering of the tank, similar to the ones they used to mark something of potential interest at a real-life crime scene. Lucy screwed up her eyes. 'What's this?'

'I'm not sure yet,' Reilly replied truthfully, 'but I think it might be some form of blockage, and the real reason the tank backed up.'

She was slightly reluctant to conjure a theory until the 'real' tank had been fully drained, and she was able to examine it physically, but iSPI – through its molecular analysis of the tank – had identified an irregularity on one side of the pit about half a meter beneath the surface.

Had Coffey's murderer purposely blocked up the offshoot pipe so that the tank would become backed up, and the journalist's body would be found? The plumber had mentioned that the system automatically redistributed the effluent out beneath the orchard. If this had happened as it was supposed to, Tony Coffey's body could have been stewing in the tank for weeks, even months

81

before it was found. As it was, the corpse had been discovered within a couple of days.

Granted, it might be nothing, but Reilly was impressed at the software's ability to pick up on potentially interesting evidence that might other-wise have taken considerable time to reveal itself, if at all.

'Crikey, the software showed you that – deep down in the tank? That's so cool.' Now it was Lucy's turn to be awed, making Reilly feel vaguely uncomfortable. If iSPI was that reliable, they could all be out of their jobs soon.

'Like I said, I'm not sure what it is – it could be nothing. And it's definitely nothing until we find physical evidence to support it. Anyway,' she turned her chair to Lucy, 'what's up?'

'Well . . .' The younger woman couldn't keep the enthusiasm out of her voice, '. . . we think we might have something from one of the soil samples from this very scene.'

'Great. And you obviously think it's of interest.'

Reilly felt relieved; she wasn't pessimistic by nature, but given what little trace evidence they'd collected, it was a pleasant surprise to think that her team might have been able to isolate something potentially helpful from the sewage-soaked sludge.

'Come take a look and see what you think,' Lucy said, and Reilly followed her down the hallway to the lab.

The GFU laboratory was a brightly lit open space. Two long benches of equipment ran the length of the room, and in the corner at the far end was a pair of small desks with computers and printers for the lab techs to share.

Lucy led Reilly over to where she had an electron microscope set up. She was talking quickly, almost tripping over her words to get them out. 'We've gone through everything we brought back. Firstly, you were right: that hair sample was Mr Coffey's. It matched one of the pubic hairs we took from his corpse for comparison.'

Reilly nodded, expecting as much.

'Most of the soil samples we collected were consistent with the type found in Coffey's garden,' Lucy continued. 'But there was something different about one batch in particular.'

'Go on.'

'Not only is it a much more alkaline soil, but it also had traces of something rather interesting.' She slid the microscope toward Reilly. 'Take a look.'

Reilly swept her hair back off her forehead and leaned into the microscope, adjusted the setting so that the specimen was in focus. 'So what am I looking at?' she asked.

'Traces of chloride, sodium, potassium, creatinine . . .'

'. . . and urea?' Reilly straightened up.

Lucy nodded.

'So it's urine. Not much of a find, considering,' Reilly said, decidedly unimpressed. 'This sample was taken from the region surrounding a septic tank, Lucy; what did you expect to find?'

She quickly assuaged her misgivings. 'Of course. I was inclined to dismiss it at first too, but then I looked more closely at the composition. It's not human.'

'Oh. You caught me there,' Reilly said quickly. 'Well, if you know what it isn't, I take it you also know what it is?'

Lucy smiled. 'Would I drag you in here if I didn't?' She slid a printout toward Reilly. 'This is what gave me the strongest clue. It's the chemical composition of another substance we took from the very same sample.'

Reilly ran her gaze over the elements. Barley, wheat, bran, soybean, canola meal, molasses, vegetable oil, limestone, salt, dicalcium phosphate. She racked her brains, trying to figure how such a seemingly random group of ingredients could relate to the urine sample.

'OK, I give up, what's this then?' she asked.

'The ingredients commonly found in horse feed. Horse pellets, to be precise. What we got was most likely fine dust residue from the pellets. So I'm thinking that the urine has to be from a horse.'

'I see.' Something clicked in Reilly's brain, and her mind raced to work out why this should be significant. Then she recalled something Chris had said about Coffey's wife being part of the horsy set.

Which meant it may not be so significant after all.

When she mentioned this to Lucy, the younger woman frowned. 'Yes, but that garden is pristine, not somewhere you'd ordinarily let horses loose to feed and pee. And the Coffeys don't keep horses themselves, do they?'

'No. That's true.'

'So while there's a chance that Mrs Coffey or one of her horsy friends walked it in, there's just as much of a chance that whoever put Mr Coffey in the tank might have done so,' Lucy persisted.

'OK, let's go with that for the moment, until we discover otherwise. What about the samples from Mrs Coffey's boots that you took for elimination? Any traces of it on those?'

Lucy shook her head. 'Not a sausage,' she said, and Reilly smiled. It had taken her a while to get to grips with some of the team's idiom, but she figured she could translate most of it by now.

'Then we can probably count her out as the source for the moment. I'll ask the detectives to find out if any of her friends were in the garden area recently; see if we can maybe isolate it to one of those. If not, then we may well have something.'

Lucy grinned but Reilly wasn't convinced the new find gave them anything more to go on with the investigation.

Cooking sauce, horse feed, and one hell of a load of shit.

How on earth was any of it going to help them find Tony Coffey's killer?

CHAPTER 10

Kennedy set two pints of Guinness on the table and groaned as he lowered himself into a chair. 'I hate days like today . . .'

He and Chris were in a small city-center pub, and in a mood to blow off some steam after John Crowe's funeral earlier.

Music blasted out way too loud from the jukebox in the corner. A gaggle of girls in micro-miniskirts stood in a cluster drinking alcopops, exchanging flirtatious glances with a bunch of young guys who were cranking loose change into the machine. Ninety percent of the people in there were under twenty.

Kennedy looked thoughtfully at his drink. 'Ah, my friend in need . . .' He buried his face in stout, then looked around the pub as if seeing it for the first time. 'Jesus, I'm getting old. Look at this place. Remember when it had ratty old stags' heads on the walls, and you got change back from a fiver when you bought a pint?'

Chris grinned. 'No, Granddad, I don't.'

'Ah, feck off.' Kennedy slumped back in his seat. 'I *am* getting old, though. Days like today sort of bring that home to you.' He stuck his head in the glass again.

Chris wrapped his hands around his own pint, and took a long sip.

Although the funeral of a fellow cop always got you in the gut, he hadn't known John Crowe personally, unlike Kennedy, who'd graduated from training college at the same time as him. And there was no doubt that funerals forced you to think about your own mortality. Especially when you weren't feeling a hundred percent.

Chris swallowed hard, then raised his voice a little so as to be heard above the noise. 'It's never easy, is it? I always feel so sorry for the family in these situations. Sometimes I wonder if the whole guard of honor thing makes it even harder for them.'

When Kennedy finally came up for air he looked a little happier. 'I know it would break my Josie's heart, definitely.'

'Well, luckily you're not planning on going anywhere anytime soon. Are you?' Chris added jokingly, trying not to think about the irony of that with regard to himself.

'Not if I can help it. But sometimes you wonder, with all the shit that's going down these days.'

'Speaking of, erm, shit . . . where are we on the Coffey murder?'

The smile quickly left his partner's face. 'Buggered if I know. Like I said, no clues, no suspects, no motive.'

Chris nodded in agreement. It was four days since the discovery of Tony Coffey's body, and they needed something to move the investigation forward soon, an opening, something to give them direction. He gazed at his half-empty pint glass. The stout wasn't bad, and it was definitely relaxing him a little, relieving some of the tension and worry he'd been experiencing these last few days about the tremors. Maybe the odd Guinness was the answer?

'With regard to motive, did the editor have much to say yesterday?' Kennedy asked.

Coffey's editor at the *Sunday Herald* had shed little light on anything, other than to insist to Chris yet again that Tony was 'a total arsehole, but he had a way with words. If you wanted someone to be provocative, to stir up a storm of controversy, then he was your man.'

Chris shook his head. 'Sounds like everyone hated Coffey – the left, the right, old people, young people. The guy lived to wind people up.'

Kennedy sipped thoughtfully. 'Did you ask the editor about death threats, irate calls or letters in response to his articles, anything like that? Stalkers, even?'

'He said there have been some inflammatory responses down the years, but no stalkers, no one who swore they'd kill him or whatever. What about the wife?' he asked, referring to Kennedy's second interview with Sandra Coffey in light of Kirsty Malone's revelations.

The detective looked grim. 'I tried beating about the bush, but she knew where I was coming from.'

Chris nodded sympathetically. There was no easy way to ask a woman about her dead husband's affairs.

The music seemed to grow even louder, battling the chirping of the crowd. Kennedy leaned toward Chris to make himself heard. 'She admitted knowing that Coffey had had several "secretaries" throughout the years. She gave me a couple of names – I'll follow up on them tomorrow, see if there was anything unseemly, unpleasant, whatever.' He sighed. 'We're pissing in the dark, Chris, and I'm not sure we're hitting anything except our own shoes. Think about it, a provocative middle-aged journalist with a string of affairs, and by all accounts an arsehole too. The question isn't who would want him dead – it's more like who *wouldn't*?'

Chris nodded tiredly. This was making him feel drained yet again. 'My guess is it's more than that,' he said. 'I reckon we can forget the girlfriends, or any wounded husbands, to be honest. It's the whole setup of the killing. This isn't a crime of passion – it's a carefully planned, meticulous job, and it's intended to make a point.' He picked up his glass again. 'Think about it – you're a killer, you've got it in for a guy for whatever reason. Fair enough, we know that happens.'

'All too often, unfortunately,' Kennedy grunted.

Chris was warming to his theme. 'But why do something so elaborate – sensational, even?' he asked. 'Stuffing a guy in a septic tank to drown in his own shit . . . that's pretty imaginative even by the standards of the low-lifes we come across.'

Kennedy picked up his own pint and knocked it back. 'Ah, what the hell. We aren't going to solve anything on this one without a lot of work and a little bit of luck. Right,' he licked froth off his lips, 'I'd better go home to the wife.'

'Do – while your dinner is still warm and you can still walk.'

The older cop gave him a look. 'Sneer all you like, but what do you go home to, eh? An empty flat and the Playboy channel?'

Chris grinned. 'Admit it, you miss the bachelor's life sometimes.' As he spoke, two attractive women passed their table – one of them looked over and gave Chris an appraising glance.

Kennedy caught the look. 'Some parts of it, yeah.' His eyes followed the girls across the bar. 'Trouble is, Romeo, I never got the kind of looks you just did.' He stood up and shook his head. 'Guess some women just have no taste.'

At the GFU lab, Reilly spread Tony Coffey's clothes out for examination, the dried sewage-encrusted garments looking incongruous against the gleaming white counter top.

Lucy and Rory, another lab tech, stood either side of her, face masks in place, although these weren't much help in protecting them from the stink. Even a big strong rubgy player like Rory,

90

who was well used to getting down and dirty, was having trouble.

Reilly wore a mask too, not for protection from the smell – she'd become accustomed to that by now – but because they were going to get up close and personal with the victim's clothes in the hope of finding some crucial piece of evidence on them that might have been trapped beneath the layer of sewage.

At the time of his death, the journalist had been wearing a dark blue shirt, a small-check-patterned tweed jacket, and gray woolen trousers. She slid the trousers toward Lucy and the jacket toward Rory.

'So what are we looking for?' Rory wore his usual slightly anxious look; he was aware of the increasing media coverage of the crime because of Coffey's profession, and it was clearly weighing on him.

Reilly smiled and tried to look reassuring. The last thing she wanted was uptight lab techs who had trouble focusing on the job. She needed the team sharp, paying attention to every detail.

'The usual,' she told them. 'Anything goes – lint, fluff, skin flecks. Basically anything that's out of place, we want it.'

Rory nodded. 'So we're focusing around the collar and cuffs to start with?'

'Yes.'

For a few moments the three of them worked in silence, each going over the clothes meticulously using a hand-held magnifying glass.

This was one part of the job that Reilly loved. There was something soothing about focusing the mind on the most minute details, poring over a tiny area, searching in the nooks and crannies like a hunter creeping stealthily over a wooded hillside in search of prey.

At times like these she was able to clear her mind, let her worries and problems go, allow the creative side of her brain to roam free while her conscious mind was completely absorbed in a task. All she could hear on either side was Lucy and Rory's steady breathing as they too concentrated on the job at hand.

Coffey's jacket was a wool and synthetic blend. Under Rory's magnifying glass – which increased the image forty-fold – it looked like a rolling hillside, a nightmare tangle of crossed threads running at ninety degrees to each other. There were literally thousands of little ridges and valleys, places where a microscopic piece of material could hide.

Every so often one of them would find a tiny particle of trace on the clothes. They would remove the particle with their tweezers, bag it, label it, then resume. They all knew from experience that there was no point getting excited at such times. Unless they found something large or very obviously out of place, there was virtually no way of knowing what it was until it was analyzed. For every vital piece of evidence that they recovered in this way, they analyzed a hundred bits of household dirt and toast crumbs.

Reilly relaxed and enjoyed the hunt, hoping that somewhere out there she would find her elusive prey. And while she worked, she let her mind wander, speculating on what a sad lonely death Coffey's must have been. Whoever had it in for him had conjured up one hell of a punishment.

Not that freezing to death in a bathtub of ice would have been a bed of roses either, she mused, thinking about John Crowe's equally strange manner of death. The former policeman's funeral had taken place early that day, and she knew that some of the older members of the GFU who'd worked alongside Crowe in the past, including Jack Gorman, had been in attendance.

The thinking was that Crowe's death was all to do with punishment – revenge from one of his former collars, or payback from someone who'd borne him a grudge.

Reilly shivered. Criminals were getting more and more inventive these days, coming up with ways of sending out strong, defiant messages to their opponents.

What kind of message they were trying to send out by immersing a guy in ice was anyone's guess. She shrugged, thinking that they'd probably picked the idea up from one of those TV cop shows; you got a lot of that these days – criminals styling themselves on hotshot mafia types.

'Take a look at this.' Rory's voice broke into her thoughts. She turned and saw that he was delicately tweezing open a folded piece of paper. 'From the inside pocket of his jacket,' he told her. 'Looks like a note.'

'Seems to be in pretty good shape too,' Reilly commented, pleased that whatever it was, it had escaped the sludge. The outside of the jacket would have got the worst of it, and while the paper still looked wet, Rory was slowly but expertly teasing the folds apart.

'Generic lined notepaper – nothing distinctive,' he continued, answering Reilly's unspoken question. 'There's something written on it all right . . . just on a single line, from what I can see. Ink looks like blue ballpoint, but the words are blurry from the moisture.'

Reilly handed him the magnifying glass. 'This might help.'

'No, I think I can make it out actually.' He seemed reluctant to accept assistance, and was being almost protective of his prize find.

Reilly knew that feeling well. For the most part forensic work was tedious and mostly fruitless, so finding anything out of the ordinary was akin to uncovering buried treasure.

'Oh. It's not words, it's numbers,' he said.

'Just numbers?'

'Yes, a sequence, almost like . . . yeah, that's exactly what it is – ten digits. It's a phone number,' Rory confirmed, triumph in his face. 'It starts with 086 so it's a mobile number.'

'Nice work.' Reilly smiled. It might ultimately

get them nowhere but for now it was at least something. 'Is the rest of it legible?'

'I think so . . . just not sure if this one is a three or an eight.' Now he accepted the magnifiying glass and peered closely at the sequence of numbers.

'Want me to take a look and then we can compare?'

He nodded. 'Go ahead.'

Reilly bent down and examined the blurred ink. Actually, the digits on the note were surprisingly legible, considering what the jacket had been through. But yes, it was difficult to tell whether the edges of the three had blurred into the shape of an eight, or if it had been an eight to begin with.

Reilly continued studying each digit and when she was finished, she wrote down the number sequence as she'd identified it.

When she compared it with what Rory had written, they realized they had the same mobile phone number. It was obviously relevant to Tony Coffey in some way, but the question was, was it relevant to his murder?

Leaving the others to continue the examination, Reilly removed her gloves and headed for her office.

From there she called the station but both Chris and Kennedy's direct lines went to voicemail, so next she tried Chris's mobile.

When he answered she could hear crowd noises in the background.

'Hey there,' he said, and Reilly thought his greeting sounded unusually chirpy.

'Where are you?' she asked, and was faintly surprised when he told her he and Kennedy were in a pub. Then she remembered Crowe's funeral and recalled that drinking after a burial was an Irish tradition. A wake, wasn't it? Another quirky local custom Reilly couldn't quite get her head round, despite being the daughter of an Irishman, not to mention one who'd never needed a funeral for an excuse to hit the bottle.

Unsure of the protocol surrounding a wake, especially a cop's, she felt slightly wrong-footed. 'Well, maybe this can wait till—'

'No, whatever it is, fire ahead,' Chris assured her. 'We're just about to head off now anyway.'

'OK . . .' Reilly went on to tell them about the find in Coffey's clothes.

Chris was impressed. 'Nice one. Could you make out the number?'

'Would I be calling if I didn't?' she replied, faintly teasing. 'Got a pen handy?'

'Hold on a sec, it's a bit noisy in here, and we're just going outside.'

There was a brief rustling and Reilly heard a creaking noise, which she guessed was the pub door opening. After that, the background din disappeared.

'OK, shoot,' Chris said. 'Kennedy has the notebook out.' Reilly read out the number sequence and heard Chris recite it to Kennedy in turn.

'It's a cellphone number so should be easy enough to identify – unless of course it's prepaid,' she went on. 'Whether it's any good or not is anyone's guess.' When there was a brief silence at the other end she said, 'Chris? Are you still there? I don't know if the signal's—'

'I'm still here,' he said in a strange voice. 'That's definitely the number you found in Tony Coffey's pocket?'

'No question. Why – does the sequence sound off to you or something?'

'The sequence is fine.' Chris's voice was grim. 'And seems we'll have no trouble identifying it.'

'What? How?'

'Well, according to Kennedy, that's Johnny Crowe's number.'

CHAPTER 11

C hris sat in the back of a taxi, his thoughts filled with Reilly's latest discovery and its significance or otherwise.

Why would Tony Coffey have had John Crowe's mobile number?

There could be any number of reasons: the most obvious being that Crowe was Coffey's source on a story he was researching for the *Herald*. Yet, Coffey wasn't a crime reporter and, as a rule, didn't write about drug dealers, organized criminals or the other unsavory types Crowe had been typically involved with.

More importantly, was there anything significant in the fact that the two men were now dead, both murdered in bizarre circumstances?

Kennedy, with his personal links to Crowe, was going to follow up on it tomorrow, talk to Crowe's former colleagues and partner to see if any connection between him and the journalist was immediately apparent. If not, then it was simply another loose end in this increasingly frustrating case.

After Kennedy had left for home, on a whim Chris decided to head for his best mate Matt

Sheridan's house for a long-overdue visit. He'd called ahead; Matt and his wife were home and delighted at the prospect of seeing him. The couple were parents to Chris's goddaughter, a gorgeous 18-month-old called Rachel, and he rarely got the opportunity to spend time with her.

'I'll just pop in for a few minutes to see Rach before she goes to bed – then I'll be out of your hair, I promise,' he'd told Emma on the phone.

'Not at all, you're staying for dinner and that's the end of it,' she'd insisted. As there was nothing in his own fridge but out-of-date milk and a few moldy vegetables, Chris didn't need too much persuading. After such a somber day it seemed fitting to spend time with people he really cared about.

'Kiss!' Rachel demanded when he was barely in the door of the Sheridan household – her own special way of pronouncing his name, and demanding a cuddle at the same time. Faced with such a bundle of cuteness – Rachel was all blond curls, bright blue eyes, and a big baby-toothed smile – Chris was happy to comply, although it troubled him how much the toddler had grown in the few weeks since he'd last seen her.

He and Matt played happily with Rachel until her bedtime at seven, and while his mate got the little girl ready for bed, Chris chatted with Emma in the kitchen as she prepared dinner.

'So how's work these days?' she asked him, before adding pointedly, 'And your lovely American colleague, what was her name again?'

Chris rolled his eyes. Emma was a notorious matchmaker, and he rued the day he'd introduced her to Reilly. A few months back, when he'd had a stint in hospital following the work-related shooting injury, a visit from Reilly and his friends had overlapped.

Like the majority of the force, Chris certainly wasn't immune to Reilly's charms. There was no denying she was a knockout: great legs, silky hair, huge, appealing eyes . . . and more than once he had surreptitiously observed the slim, muscular lines of her body when she was working at a crime scene.

But despite getting to know her better recently, he still felt like he'd barely scratched the surface. To say that Reilly Steel was a complex woman was a huge understatement.

And complex women scared Chris.

'Work's fine, and yes, we're all busy – Reilly too,' he answered briskly, refusing to be drawn. 'Can I help with anything?' he asked, changing the subject as Emma went about setting the table.

'Same old Chris, all work and no play,' Emma scolded, shaking her head. 'But seeing as you asked . . . can you organize the glasses?'

'Sure.' As he went to the cupboard, his gaze rested on a cream-colored card propped up against the wall on the worktop.

'I see you guys have a wedding coming up,' he remarked casually, as Matt returned to the room. He nodded toward the invite; the elaborate gold-colored script on mother-of-pearl card a dead giveaway. 'Need a babysitter?'

Emma stared at her husband, and was it Chris's imagination or did a strange look pass between them?

'Um, my mum is taking Rachel – but thanks,' Emma replied quickly.

'Grand. I'm sure you're looking forward to a night off – not to mention a lie-in,' he joked, aware that since Rachel's arrival, time away for the couple was as rare as hen's teeth. 'Anyone I know?' he went on, wondering why the mood seemed to have altered all of a sudden.

'Well, now that you say it . . .' Matt murmured, and all at once Chris figured out the reason for this silent exchange, and the uncomfortable vibe that had suddenly descended upon the conversation.

'It's Mel's wedding, Chris,' Emma said gently, confirming his suspicions. 'We weren't sure if you would have been—'

'No, I wasn't invited,' he said, keeping his tone even. 'She told me a while back she was getting married all right, but I wasn't sure when . . .' He placed a wine glass in front of each table setting. 'I'm sure it'll be a great day. Give her my best, won't you?'

Emma looked at him worriedly. 'Of course.'

The conversation about the wedding had ended at that, but for Chris the incident lingered in his mind much longer thereafter.

Later that night, as he lay wide awake in the darkness, he was still thinking about Melanie, and trying to remember what she had been like back when they were together – happy together.

But all he could focus on was Melanie afterwards, when everything had fallen to pieces.

Five years earlier

Chris walked slowly up the path to the small semi-detached house, a bag of groceries tucked under one arm. His dark jacket was slightly crumpled, overdue a visit to the dry cleaner.

His eyes took in the peeling paint around the windows, the tightly drawn curtains, the overgrown garden. The house didn't quite look abandoned, but there was no question it wasin an advanced state of neglect. The person living within had long ago given up caring what other people thought.

With a deep sigh, Chris reached up and rang the bell, making sure to position himself directly in front of the sun-bleached front door.

'Who is it?' The woman's voice was nervous, crackly as it came out of a small intercom on the wall to the left.

He pushed the button to speak. 'It's Chris.'

'Chris who?'

He sighed. 'Chris Delaney.'

'Show me your ID.'

He was already reaching into his pocket, by now familiar with the routine. He held his detective's badge up to the glass panel.

The shadow moved against the peephole again. Chains and locks rattled back one by one, until finally the door opened just enough for him to step in. It was slammed shut the moment he was inside.

'Hi, Mel.' He stood inside the narrow hallway, and held out the bag. 'They were out of pears so I got you some apples instead.'

She took the bag, scuttled down the hall. 'Gala? You know I only like Gala apples.'

Chris bent to pick up the pile of junk mail that lay on the doormat, before following her down the narrow gloomy hall and into the kitchen. 'Of course.'

Melanie set the bag on the table, and began unpacking, her movements quick, full of nervous energy. 'Cup of tea?'

'Please.'

It was a small kitchen with pale blue 1970s cupboards, a square Formica table in the middle of the floor, two cheap plastic chairs tucked neatly in to the table. A blue and white checked tablecloth covered the table, a small glass vase with a large faded plastic sunflower the only attempt to brighten the cold room.

He watched as Melanie scuttled around the kitchen – she was thirty-two years old, but could have passed for anything from twenty to forty. She wore a gray woolen skirt, pale blouse, baby-blue cardigan. Her shoulder-length brown hair was scraped back in a tight ponytail, her thin face free of make-up.

The kettle rattled as it boiled, and Melanie

pulled two matching mugs from the cupboard, dropped the teabags in and poured the hot water, the steam rising up briefly to wreathe her face. 'I've been thinking . . .'

Chris looked at her carefully, knowing by her tone exactly what was coming. He folded his hands in front of him on the table. 'You promised.'

She reached for a tea towel, and began wringing the end of it fiercely between her hands, wrapping it tighter and tighter until her knuckles were white and stretched.

Chris leaned forward, tried to make eye contact with her. 'Mel, it's been almost a year. The psychologist said —'

' I know!' she snapped. She kept her back to him, ignoring his imploring looks. 'And I will, I will . . .'

'But not just yet,' he finished softly.

'Not just yet,' Melanie repeated. She set the two mugs of tea on the table and finally turned to look at Chris. Then, in a flash, her face changed and her eyes brightened. 'Oh, you bought me a packet of digestives!' she beamed. 'You're so good to me, Chris. I don't know what I'd do without you.'

Chris smiled, his heart automatically softening at the sight of the rare, but achingly familiar smile.

Be patient, he told himself. Give it time. Just a little more time . . .

CHAPTER 12

Father Byrne never felt closer to God than at this time of day, and in this place. Just before dawn, when the cold gray of the early morning fog shrouded the area, he turned the key in the wrought-iron lock. The hinges on the heavy wooden door groaned as he opened it to enter the beautiful old country church.

Such a shame to see it falling into decline, the priest thought, but with so few parishioners in the area and St Joseph's only two miles away in Blessington, the parish couldn't keep the building permanently open. The best they could do was morning communion once a week. There was no lighting, the electrics being decades old and in complete disrepair. And sadly, these days the numbers were dwindling, the faith of the flock sorely tested by revelation after revelation about dark moments in the Church's past.

Father Byrne liked to get in early and make sure everything was in order before nine o'clock Mass. In truth, he enjoyed spending time in this wonderful old building. There were so few like it in Ireland these days, and he admired its traditional features:

rough stonework, mahogany carvings, and of course the awe-inspiring stained-glass windows above the altar.

It was a calm, peaceful location; the opposite of the functional, purpose-built church in the town. The interior was small, the gray stone walls wearing a tired look. Ten rows of wooden pews ran up each side of the central aisle, cloaked in shadows.

He walked down the aisle, marveling how, at this time of day, the colored glass caught the light and redistributed it throughout the interior in myriad rainbows – as though God Himself was sprinkling the room with His light and love.

Heading into the vestry, Father Byrne hung up his robes. A movement outside caught his eye, and he moved toward the tiny window that looked out over the church's expansive rear grounds.

Magpies, circling the hawthorn tree.

The birds were always plentiful around here, and he'd spied many of them on his way in. Yet this morning they seemed oddly . . . agitated. And there were *so* many; considerably more than was typical.

For reasons he couldn't quite fathom, Father Byrne felt compelled to investigate what was making the magpies so excitable. He had plenty of time; it was just before eight, and worshippers wouldn't begin to arrive for another half-hour or so. A walk through the grounds would be enjoyable, actually.

Using the vestry's rear door, the priest went outside. He rubbed his hands together to try to ward off the biting chill, and took a deep lungful of the fresh morning air.

But, he realized, suddenly growing tense, there was something else present in the air that morning – a heavy odor that almost certainly wasn't fresh. He frowned and looked again toward the hawthorn tree.

Was that it? he mused. Had the magpies come across a dead animal – a badger or squirrel perhaps – and were feasting on the remains? In these parts, squirrels were almost as plentiful as magpies so that wasn't unusual. Well, whatever had the birds' attention, he noted, it was in the vicinity of the tree.

Shuddering, but this time not from the morning air, Father Byrne strode in the direction of the tree, all the while watching the magpies and their delighted swooping dance.

But when the object of the birds' attention suddenly came into view, the priest immediately revised his earlier belief. Reeling back in horror, he fell to his knees and invoked all the angels and saints in heaven to protect him.

Far from feeling close to God, right then Father Byrne was certain he had come face to face with Satan himself.

Reilly was taken aback by the size of the hulking stone church.

Located in a small town just outside Blessington, an area famous for its beautiful mountain lakes, the church had been shrouded in the cold gray of the early morning fog on Reilly's arrival.

Although the Wicklow countryside was only a short drive out of the city, Reilly was unfamiliar with the area and she had forgotten to bring the GFU van's sat nav. After she'd taken a few wrong turns, Chris had sent a patrol car to meet her and guide her to the location of what he'd described on the phone as 'yet another brain-fry murder'.

As the sun rose, the church appeared huge, but an almost menacing darkness still clung to it, as though the mist had not moved on, but rather simply condensed back down into the masonry.

As the clouds parted further, the church grounds sparkled with droplets of moisture, each diffracting so that everything seemed rainbow light, except the church, which brooded with a heavy gothic gravity of mass. It sat upon a raised mound, and a macabre cast-iron spiked fence encircled it protectively.

Entering the sanctified space, Reilly noticed that the building felt cold and forbidding, far removed from the vibrant and resplendent churches she had come across elsewhere.

It was decorated in an austere manner that suggested respectful worship a great distance removed from an unsympathetic deity.

'Who found the body?' she asked Kennedy.

'The priest, Father Byrne. Chris is interviewing him now.'

As Reilly followed Kennedy through the doorway,

a woman popped up from the long wooden pew upon which she had been praying.

'Hello,' she gushed. 'You must be the crime scene people. Father Byrne asked me to assist you – he's with that nice-looking detective at the moment.' She turned and shook their hands with a perfunctory grace obviously acquired by glad-handing her way through many church socials. 'My name is Henrietta. I'm the chairperson of the lay committee. I help Father Byrne with the admin, and also make sure that nobody walks off with the donation box. This is just terrible,' she babbled. 'I really can't believe such a thing could happen, especially around here. It's such a quiet little place; nobody bothers anyone else and you'd never think . . .'

The woman's words went right over Reilly's head when she looked down the aisle toward the altar.

'Wow,' she gasped.

A larger-than-life-size Technicolor statue of Jesus suffering horribly on the cross towered above the altar, backed by large stained-glass illustrations of the stations of the Cross.

'Erm, very nice,' Kennedy said, obviously confused as to what the interior of the church had to do with anything, when the dead body had been found in the grounds.

'Look up a little,' Reilly told him.

Above the statue and the stations, dwarfing them both, was an immense carving depicting a huge gnarled hawthorn tree, its twisting limbs running around the corners, and back out of sight into the recess.

The screen that separated the nave from the chancel bore a hawthorn leaf motif, and was topped with a hawthorn branch curled into a shepherd's crook instead of a more traditional crucifix. Reilly had the botanical knowledge to pick up on how deeply the image of the hawthorn tree had permeated this place of worship.

Kennedy let out a long, low whistle. 'Now I get you. That's a big tree.'

'Yes it is,' Henrietta continued giddily. 'Almost as big as the real one. Come on, I'll take you to it.'

She started down the aisle, continuing a steady stream of chatter, Reilly and Kennedy in step behind her. 'Marcus, our groundsman, is out there keeping an eye on the poor soul since Father Byrne found him earlier this morning.'

Reaching the transept, Henrietta turned right, and then left again, pulling back a gray curtain with 'Private' embroidered across it. She then led them through the vestry, which was spartan and smelled of bleach and disinfectant. Jeyes Fluid, to be precise, Reilly's trusty nose informed her.

From there, Henrietta opened a side door and took them out into the church's rear grounds. Reilly immediately spotted the tree the funny little woman had been referring to.

The church property backed onto deep woodland, the plot long and deep, and cleared back to well over a hundred yards.

110

About two-thirds of the way down, the gentle rolling lawn was interrupted by a large, circular earthwork, in the center of which grew a huge hawthorn tree. The gnarled and twisted branches of the tree seemed innumerable, and it wasn't until she had appreciated the sheer majesty of it that Reilly could comprehend how a body could be hidden there in plain sight.

'See him just there?' said a man nearby, whom Reilly deduced was Marcus, pointing to an incongruous patch of bright orange nestled on the side of the tree facing them. It was a quarter of the way up, located in the twisted confines of the thorny labyrinth. 'We managed to get a tarpaulin over him before the rain really set in,' the groundsman continued, 'but it's pretty obvious he's been up there for a while, so it's definitely not the first shower he's had to endure.'

'Come on. Let's get a better look,' Kennedy said, and they tramped cautiously down through the grass toward the foot of the tree.

The detective reached up and pulled away the tarpaulin, and even Reilly felt her stomach turn over.

Thanks to the elements, the body – that of a man – was in execrable condition. But the first thing she noticed was the teeth. They were clean and white, a pearly parade. The dentalwork stood out as the focal point because it glowed with a bright white light compared to the rest of the corpse, which was naked, gutted and somewhat weathered.

Reilly had seen enough corpses in her life no longer to be affected or nauseated by them, but what she was seeing now was definitely making her woozy.

The stomach, colon, intestines and other lower abdominal organs of the victim appeared to have been torn out of his body, and suspended from the thorny branches that curled overhead. The trauma of this seemed directly reflected in the searing, suffering aspect of his face.

Even while Reilly gaped aghast at the horrific spectacle, a large crow dropped down from higher up in the canopy and, blithely ignoring the small group standing only a few feet away, began scavenging amongst the dangling innards.

Reaching into his pocket, the groundsman quickly withdrew a palmful of sand and aimed it up at the bird.

'No!' Reilly cried out, aghast. 'It's a crime scene, you can't—' But it was too late; the damage was done, and there was sand scattered everywhere beneath the tree. Her stomach sank.

Aggravated, the bird leaped into flight and landed on a branch not far from where the group still stood, obviously intent on keeping them under its watchful and unblinking gaze.

The groundsman reddened, horrified. 'I'm sorry, I didn't think—'

'Of course you didn't,' Reilly snapped irritably.

Another forensic nightmare. She'd need to take a sample of the sand he had left so as to dissociate

112

it from any evidence they might now be lucky enough to find.

Soon afterwards, the ME arrived and began to make arrangements as to how best to extricate the body from its thorny throne. While she waited for the all clear to run the scene from Karen Thompson, Reilly surveyed the site from afar.

As she did, she was reminded of one of Daniel Forrest's lectures at Quantico. Her former mentor was a stickler for analysis, and, adopting his attitude, Reilly couldn't help but notice the almost theatrical way the victim had been displayed: suspended from a branch in a tree – but with his head facing toward the hulking form of the church.

She couldn't be sure, but it was almost as if the killer had intended for the dying man's tortured gaze to fall directly onto the imposing church tower.

Significant or just coincidence?

She looked at Kennedy. 'Somebody show me how to get up into that tower.'

CHAPTER 13

C hris followed the beam of light into the darkness. He could hear Kennedy's breathing behind him. They stepped up and past the altar, heading for the door in the back corner of the church.

The door was dark, and the ancient wood creaked as Chris gently nudged it open. His torch intruded into the gloom beyond.

'What is this place?' Kennedy asked. 'I came through here earlier with Reilly.'

'The vestry.' Chris followed the beam of light into the small room.

It had a dry, musty smell, the scent of old air, scurrying mice and thick layers of dust overlaid with disinfectant. The white painted walls were bare except for a heavy wooden crucifix on the far end. There was a small table in one corner with a sturdy wooden chair, and a recess half covered by a faded velvet curtain.

'This is where the priest gets changed before the service,' explained Chris, 'like his little office at church.' He looked sideways at Kennedy. 'Clearly you were never an altar boy.'

Kennedy chuckled. 'Do I look like the altar boy type to you?'

'Well, I was.' Chris gave a little grin to himself in the darkness, imagining his partner's expression

He got the expected snort in reply. 'Hard to imagine that. I'd assumed you were a right little terror when you were young.'

'Oh, I was,' admitted Chris. 'That doesn't stop you from being an altar boy, though – it's a good grounding in divilment, actually,' he added, thinking of all the hijinks he and his mates used to get up to, during and after Mass.

His torch highlighted the lock on the back door. 'Here we go . . .'

It was not quite closed, and there were clear signs of damage around the lock. 'That must be how he got in.' He shone the torch on the floor. There were several sets of footprints in the thick dust. Someone had gone back and forth recently.

'So did the priest have anything useful to say for himself?' Kennedy asked as they looked around the small area.

'Not a lot, to be honest. He was pretty shaken up, obviously.'

Poor Father Byrne, Chris thought, what must it have been like for him, coming into the church by himself, calm, and at peace with the world, as he got ready for morning Mass, and finding that horror? And what lasting effect would the intrusion of such profanity and evil in a place he would normally have regarded as safe have on him?

Would it shake his faith? Or would it strengthen it – reinforce his conviction that the devil was at large, and that he needed to tend his flock in order to help them stay vigilant and safe?

'Apparently they just do daylight services here,' he told Kennedy, 'but the Mass calendar is posted on the boards both here and at the church in town.'

Kennedy cursed. 'So anyone would be able to see the schedule, know when someone was here, or wasn't?'

'Exactly. Plenty of opportunities for someone to sneak a body onto the grounds unseen.'

'So what do you reckon?' Kennedy asked. 'Think it could be some satanic cult, or weird shit like that?'

Chris wondered the same thing. Was there some religious significance to this particular murder? Or was it another in a recent succession of murders bizarrely similar in their ghoulishness?

'Too early to say anything at the moment,' he replied noncommittally.

Soon, the GFU crew arrived, and the detectives headed out of the vestry and back into the main church.

By the altar, Kennedy paused for a moment, his head down.

Chris stopped beside him, curious. 'What's up?

116

Have you got some kind of thing against churches?' he asked, amused. 'Some deep fear of religious iconography, or something?'

Kennedy turned and gave him a scathing look. 'Me? Nah.' He grimaced. 'But it's Sunday and from the looks of things, it's going to be a long oul day.' He headed back down the aisle, Chris at his heels.

'Yes, it's Sunday, but why should that matter? You and I both know this gig's a million miles from nine to five.'

His partner sighed heavily. 'It's just Josie always does a lovely roast beef with Yorkshire puddings, the whole works,' he added, his tone mournful. 'And I bloody hate missing Josie's Sunday roast.'

Reilly went inside the church and made her way down the aisle to the transept.

Next to the pulpit was a tightly twisted spiral staircase that would be completely unacceptable under modern building codes. It led up the tower.

She studied it for a few moments, trying to ascertain if it had been used recently.

Henrietta had advised that the tower was rarely used, so by rights there should be a thick coating of dust, which would easily show up any footprints. Then again Reilly imagined that the older woman would be the type to make a mission of keeping the interior of the lovely little church spick and span.

Unfortunately.

Unable to find any sign of recent use, she took the steps and slowly ascended to the level of the thin, ornate wrought-iron gate that accessed the room at the top of the tower.

Sliding the heavy deadbolt back out of the frame, she stepped inside the tiny room. Immediately, the first thing that struck her was the smell, a heavy alkaline scent that was almost like cat pee or . . . human, even?

She inhaled the air, letting the scent flow through her delicate nostrils, trying to catalogue it. Perfume she was good at; foul scents, not so much.

It was very heavy in ammonia, though, and did indeed smell like very strong urine. Actually . . . Reilly paused and inhaled again, realizing that the smell put her in the mind of skunk spray. Skunk? Were there skunk in Ireland?

Taking out an evidence bag, she tried to pinpoint the area it seemed strongest, but it was impossible to tell. In any case, she swabbed a small area from the wall and then the ground, bagged them, and in addition picked up a sample of grit from the same area on the floor.

The tower, with its two battered old wooden slat windows, was completely empty, save for some pigeon droppings. As birds didn't urinate, Reilly already knew the foul smell definitely wasn't coming from them.

Moving tighter into the wall, she began stepping in concentric circles inwards, her gaze scanning the ground area. Then, her keen eye noticed some tiny bluish dots that were slightly incongruous amongst the grit and the droppings.

She pulled out her tweezers and, bending low, carefully lifted one up for inspection. With some idea of what it was, she held it to her nose, sniffed, and removed all doubt.

Rubber.

Reilly's mind raced, wondering if this was of any significance. Had the killer dropped it? Probably not. Whoever had hoisted that poor man up into the tree and slashed open his torso surely wouldn't have then gone to the trouble of coming all the way up here to watch him die.

Or would he?

She craned her neck, looking upwards into the gloom, then made her way to the window. As she did, she let out a breath.

There, framed perfectly in the opening as if it were a painting, was the hawthorn tree, the unfortunate victim dramatically hanging front and center.

Leaving little doubt in Reilly's mind that such positioning was completely intentional.

It took a while, but eventually the local police managed to arrange for a mobile elevating platform to be sent to the site from the nearest town.

The ME, having repositioned the man's innards as best she could, wrapped the mutilated body in the tarpaulin and, with the platform operator's assistance, accompanied it down to the ground, where she could examine it more closely.

Reilly took a lint roller from her bag and rolled the victim's clothes and hands. Then she concentrated her efforts around the perimeter of the tree, walking in concentric circles around the base amongst the humongous roots poking through the soil. Granted the victim was not a heavy man, but even so, it would have been no easy task to hoist a body, dead or alive, up onto the branches of a tree.

Reilly was looking for imprints from a ladder, or anything that might have been used for such a job. While the ground itself was wet, the immediate area beneath the tree was largely dry, mostly because the canopy of branches was so thick and spanned so widely.

She was unable to spot anything that remotely resembled ladder markings, but something irregular in the grass approaching the tree caught her eye. At first it looked like a track of some kind, perhaps a path worn through by a dog, or some wild animal. But no, there were actually two matching indentations, consistent in width, about as narrow as the wheels of a bicycle. Bicycle tracks?

Taking out her camera, she shot the tracks from various angles. Then, finding little else of interest beneath the tree, she picked up her kitbag and headed toward the platform, ready to take a closer look amongst the branches.

Kennedy was watching her. 'No way you'd get

me up on that rickety contraption in the midst of all them poison thorns.'

'You do know the tree's not poisonous, right?' Reilly replied.

'Yeah, but I know evil when I see it.'

Looking back up at the tree, Reilly shivered slightly as she realized that perhaps he was right.

She was also somewhat dubious about the platform operator's ability to bring her up into the branches intact, so thick was the enveloping canopy. She needn't have worried, though, as he seemed to have taken great pains to position the apparatus in the precise location necessary to extend unobstructed to within a foot and a half of the crooked branch where the body had been hung.

While Reilly waited, he fiddled with the lift's control panel, which was mounted atop a sturdy steel box affixed to the rail enclosing the machine's operating deck. Raising the panel's protective Plexiglas rain cover with one hand, he stuck the other in his pocket and retrieved the keys.

Reilly was impressed by how his fingers instinctively found the right one without his so much as glancing at the fob; her wide range of responsibilities at the GFU required her carrying multiple keys of all types, which, try as she might, she could never identify instantly. Inserting the key into the ignition slot, the operator gave it a quick clockwise turn, and the gas motor that powered the lift's hydraulic articulation sputtered to life.

Then, opening a hatch on the front of the box below the control panel, he retrieved two bright red safety harnesses made of a heavy polyester webbing and secured to heavy lanyards by spliced loops ending in large carabiners.

'You'd better put this on before you go near those branches,' he said, handing her one of the harnesses and proceeding to illustrate how to put it on. 'Safety first, that's the company motto. It goes over your head and around the back, fastening in front, like this.' Reilly copied his movements, securing her frame in the loose but reassuring embrace of the safety equipment. 'OK, now pass the end of your lanyard back to me.'

Using the carabiners, he secured both their lanyards to the bottom rail of the safety railing. 'Ready to go then?'

'Yes, let's do this.'

The guy kept up a steady stream of chatter as they ascended. 'I suppose you've seen a lot of horrible things, doing what you do, but I thought I was pretty tough, and well, when I saw that poor divil, I was rightly shocked. I mean, I've seen dead bodies before, at funerals and that, but I didn't realize that they could be so . . . well, so sad, I suppose. The guy looks so sad that it made me feel sick.'

Reilly nodded, thinking that it was largely a good thing that most people never got to experience first-hand how horrible and ignoble death could be.

Using his palm, the operator depressed the large green button with an arrow pointing upwards, and the interlaced steel members accordioned up out of the mechanism's base, shuddering under their combined weight. Doing Archimedes proud, they cleverly levered the earth away from them while providing a place to stand.

As the lift platform drew level with where the body had been positioned, the operator released the button, bringing them to a stop. Up close, the tree appeared many times more menacing, covered as it was in inch-long pin-sharp splinters.

Reilly duly handed the man the lengthy cord now securely fastened to her form, and, opening her forensic kitbag, set about her examination of the victim's final resting place.

From below, she'd spotted some markings on one of the branches that looked out of place – it was as if part of the bark had been worn away. Now she realized that she was right.

She took out her camera and snapped a couple of shots of the marks close up, and from various angles. It looked like the killer had used an industrial hoist or pulley of some kind. He'd definitely used something to get the body up here, that was for sure, in order to bear not only the victim's, but his own weight, once they were both amidst the branches.

If they could track down the type of hoist, and perhaps narrow it down to make and model, it might be helpful in finding out who had taken upon themselves to crucify the poor as-yet unnamed man, and leave him to the mercy of the elements and the scavengers.

Back on the ground, she quickly flicked through the digital shots of the body in the tree she'd taken from the tower.

Since her descent she'd been grappling with the thought that there was something familiar about this entire scenario, something oddly reminiscent.

It was almost like a real-life version of a Renaissance painting, a medieval torture scene. Was that what was going on – a re-enactment of some kind?

Jack Gorman would go bananas if he could hear her thoughts. He was forever accusing her of making wild leaps, and forging connections where there appeared to be none. But it was how Reilly had always worked, and indeed, such odd disparate thoughts often helped her make her breakthroughs, so she couldn't ignore them.

There was without doubt something familiar, something recognizable about the setup.

She looked again at the image of the victim in the tree. But what? And what kind of person could orchestrate something so grotesque, so evil?

A magpie squawked loudly in the distance and Reilly felt a fresh chill run up her spine.

CHAPTER 14

The following morning, Reilly, Chris and Kennedy assembled in the incident room at Harcourt Street Station, where they were scheduled to meet with Inspector O'Brien.

The disemboweled man in the tree had made front-page news, and the garda chief superintendent had ordered an immediate autopsy and more manpower for the investigation.

'Last Rites – Police Baffled by Church Killing' one of the more restrained headlines screamed, and outside the station Reilly had to battle through a media scrum demanding answers, their cameras and microphones recording everything.

As it was, the team were only beginning to try to put things together.

Through a dental match, Karen Thompson had by now identified that the dead man was 58-year-old Dr George Jennings, a well-respected Dublin GP who had been reported missing a week ago.

The ME had suggested that, based on the severe deterioration of his biological tissue due to prolonged weather exposure, he had most likely been up in the tree for most of that time. More disconcertingly, she ascertained that when strung up there, Dr Jennings had been very much alive, and was vivisected as a feast for the scavenging birds.

Upon Reilly's instructions, Julius was currently seeking out various makes and models of mechanical hoists, and their suppliers or hirers, trying to ascertain how easily the killer might have got hold of one. Such a task was always difficult, though. The killer may have been in possession of such an item for years, and a supplier search would likely be fruitless. But with someone as dogged as Julius on the case, you just never knew . . .

'Three men dead, and all in the weirdest circumstances I've ever come across in my time!' O'Brien thundered.

The team (as well as the media) had little choice but to contemplate that the recent murders, all so macabre in nature, should no longer be viewed in isolation. The elaborate manner of all three deaths was just too coincidental.

Reilly guessed that O'Brien was rattled, not only by the murders, but by the intensifying media demands. To try to keep them at bay, at least temporarily, he'd scheduled a press conference, and she guessed he was hoping this meeting would give him something to help calm the situation and reassure the public that the authorities were in control.

'One drowned in his own shite, another frozen in a block of ice, and now some poor creature strung up with his guts hanging out! What the hell is going on in this country? Is it gangs, huh? Is that what it's all about? Are they trying to outdo each other by seeing which one can come up with the freakiest?'

'We don't think it's gangs,' Chris put in quietly. 'With the exception of Crowe, the victims had no connection to gangland crime that we know of.'

Tony Coffey had rarely tackled national crime issues in his newspaper column, and Jennings, who had lived in leafy Killiney, was as far away from the city's seedy underbelly as you could get.

'Well I'm delighted you *are* thinking, Detective Delaney,' O'Brien snapped. 'But thinking alone won't get this thing stopped.'

'The victims are all middle-class professionals from the same social spectrum,' Kennedy put in. 'We're working on a possible link, we suspect they knew each other . . . met up socially, members of the same golf club, that kind of thing.'

'God bless us and save us,' O'Brien muttered. 'You think they might have been knocked off over a game of golf – from a sore loser or something?' His eyes bulged. 'Jesus, Kennedy, I've been in this job a long time and I've never, *ever* seen anything like this. It's a spectacle of the most horrific order! And to think there are sick fuckers out there with minds like that. I mean, where the hell do they get these ideas? Is it from the television, the internet—'

'Actually, I think it might be deeper than that,'

Reilly said, speaking for the first time since the meeting began.

They all turned to look at her.

'This isn't some guy stealing ideas from a TV program,' she continued. 'There's a real medieval brutality to the stagings and tortures employed. Old Testament, almost wrath-of-God-type stuff, with overtones of Christianity. The man in the tree . . . well, it could be considered a crucifixion of sorts, couldn't it?'

She'd been thinking about it all night, suspicious now, like the others, that the horrific and theatrical manner of the recent murders was just too similar to be coincidental. With the discovery of the third victim, it seemed that there was some form of symbolism attached to the manner of each death. Given that their most recent victim was found in a church, she wondered if there was a biblical element.

'My guess is that we're dealing not with some low-life gang lord,' she continued, 'but someone with a classical education, who is being very definite about the message he wants to get across.'

'What kind of message?' Chris asked.

'I'm not sure. Clearly there's a personal element to the killings, with all the trouble he goes to. But perhaps with the ice, the sewer and now the tree, I wonder if we might be dealing with somebody environmentally sensitive?'

'A tree-hugger? For the love of God, Steel, what kind of sick bastard loves trees enough that they'd hang some poor bugger alive on one and leave him for the birds to feed on?'

She sat back. 'I don't know, sir. It's just a theory.'

'Jesus, I hate this job sometimes. Right, enough talk, there's no time for hanging around. You two,' O'Brien stabbed a finger at the two detectives, 'talk to Johnny Crowe's wife, and see if she knows anything about golf buddies, or if he knew either of the other two victims. Steel, I take it you've got plenty to occupy yourself with from that tree yesterday?'

'Yes, sir, but taking into account the harsh elements—'

'I don't want to hear it. Just work your mumbo-jumbo magic and find me something amongst it all that'll help us find this madman, or at least figure out what he's up to before he does it again. And seeing as Johnny Crowe's killing looks to be connected to the other two under your remit, it makes sense for you to oversee that one too.'

Reilly winced. Her older colleague, Gorman, would no doubt go ballistic at the idea of her taking over one of his open files. But it was nothing personal, and in reality another file was no great bonus to Reilly, who now was likely slap-bang in the middle of a serial killer investigation.

'Jesus Christ, I can't keep up with criminals in this godforsaken country anymore,' O'Brien was muttering. 'And what am I going to say at the press conference later, huh? That a bunch of crusty hippies are responsible? They'll eat me alive!'

'Sir, the environmental angle was merely a theory. I wasn't suggesting—'

'I don't want theories, Steel, I want answers. Now the whole lot of you, get the hell out of here and find me some.'

'You don't really think this is someone trying to make a political statement, do you?' Chris asked her afterwards, when they were heading back to their respective offices.

'I have no idea. Like I said, there's a definite metaphorical overtone to the manner of death, and the posing of the bodies . . . well, there's something to that too, something we're not seeing.'

'God, I hate these mindfuck investigations,' Kennedy grumbled. 'Yeah, all the murders are weird, but is there actually anything in the evidence to connect them?'

'Nothing other than Crowe's phone number in Coffey's pocket, and we're still going through yesterday's evidence. Of course I didn't run Crowe's location – that was Gorman's.' She bit her lip. 'He won't be happy, but now I'm going to have to go down to the factory and start afresh.'

As they were no longer running each case in isolation Reilly knew she needed to look at the entire investigation from a broader point of view. Although he was a competent investigator, she couldn't take Jack Gorman's crime scene findings on trust. It was only through immersing herself in the Crowe scene, essentially walking in the murderer's shoes, that she'd be able to get a proper sense of it.

'Good idea,' Chris said. 'We're going to re-interview the wives, see if the three victims knew each other.'

Kennedy grimaced. 'I don't think O'Brien went for the golf club angle somehow.'

Reilly smiled. 'It was loose, but you're right: they're each middle-aged, upper to middle class, and by all accounts well-respected professionals. It wouldn't be at all surprising to find that they mixed in similar social circles or had some involvement with one another, however patchy.'

'Well, to our killer, they're very closely involved – with his plans at least,' Chris said. 'Could be that he's punishing them for something.'

Reilly pictured afresh Tony Coffey's sewage-steeped corpse, Crowe's frozen form, and Dr Jennings with his innards spilling out on the tree.

She exhaled heavily. 'If punishment is his motive, he sure has a unique way of dispensing it.'

CHAPTER 15

It was a crisp, dry day, a touch of frost still clinging on the ground, the sky overhead the pale blue of coming winter.

Reilly switched on her torch and slowly pushed the door open.

Even with the uniformed officer waiting for her outside, the abandoned meat-packing plant where John Crowe had been found was a creepy place.

Simply knowing that this was where a cop had died was disconcerting, but there was something more. The old building wore an air of sadness, as though the souls of all the animals who had been killed and dismembered there were haunting the place. The residue of killing lingered long after the bloodstains had been washed away.

The building had been closed for ten years, and the pale concrete wore an air of decay, as though time itself were eating away at its fabric. Teenagers had daubed the gray concrete walls with graffiti in bold reds and blues, letters two meters tall proclaiming their various allegiances. The windows had all been smashed, relentless years of target practice leaving the edifice looking like a toothless old hag, weak and defenseless.

Reilly shoved against the broken door, and it yielded slowly, creaking loudly and scraping across the bare concrete floor. A chill raced up her spine and cobwebs brushed her face in moldering welcome.

She stepped inside what had once been the reception area. The filing cabinets had been ransacked long ago, the papers strewn across the floor like confetti from a distant wedding. There were still musty old office chairs at the desks, their seats ripped apart by sharp teeth and the stuffing evidently stolen by enterprising rats to line their nests.

Reilly found herself distracted, fascinated by the pictures on the walls. One showed the plant when it was newly built, a concrete symbol of Ireland's burgeoning economic prosperity. Another was of the plant's founder, William Kelly, splendid in a dark suit. The pride in his eyes was touching, a sad contrast to the faded tones of the photograph now, tiny black dots of insects crushed between Kelly's picture and the broken glass.

The early afternoon light streamed into the office from the broken windows, slanting beams that danced on the dust motes stirred up by Reilly's feet.

She shook the cobwebs off her hair and flashed her torch around, looking for footprints in the dust, handprints on the counter, any signs of recent activity that might indicate the presence of Crowe's killer. Nothing stirred, the thick dust yielded no clues. According to Gorman's report, he was pretty certain the killer had not brought Crowe in this way, but Reilly wanted to approach it afresh, and tried to banish any preconceptions she might have picked up from her colleague's initial sweep.

She crunched gingerly across broken glass toward the back of the room, her footsteps echoing loudly on the bare concrete floor as she approached another broken wooden door, leading from the office into the plant itself.

She hesitated a moment, listening. It was deathly quiet, but once her ears became attuned to the lack of noise she was able to pick out background sounds. From behind her there was the rumble of a car passing on the road outside. The wind could also be heard playing in the branches of the trees, whipping the last of the autumn leaves free to scatter them on the damp ground. And finally one other noise, coming from inside the factory, a gentle cooing, which at first sounded creepy and a little out of kilter . . .

Then Reilly smiled.

Of course. Pigeons in the rafters, chattering back and forth to one another.

She pushed through the door from the reception area, and stepped into the plant itself. It was a large open space, crammed with mysterious machinery, illuminated by a row of skylights high overhead. She gazed at the derelict machines, iron skeletons from another time, like the remains of ancient beasts. She could only imagine what function they had served – hooks and blades and scoops for tearing, cutting and separating meat into neat little plastic-wrapped packages, ready for consumption.

The light streaming through from above illuminated parts of the plant, but left others in darkness so that strange levers, bars and blades seemed to appear suddenly out of pockets of deep shadow as Reilly progressed through the room. A cloud passed overhead and the plant was plunged into gloom, the machines once more hiding their secrets. Then, just as suddenly, the cloud passed and the rusting hulks were again revealed.

Some of the equipment seemed to have been stripped down, the valuable parts carried away by scavengers to be sold as scrap metal, leaving a maze of half-dismembered machines, the floor strewn with the discarded debris.

The cooing was louder here. Reilly looked up, and saw thirty or more pigeons roosting in the vaulted metal rafters. They would have seen it all; would have seen how the murderer had managed to get Crowe, a seventeen-stone ex-cop, into a bath of freezing water.

Stepping over the discarded parts and broken glass, Reilly picked her way carefully to the back of the vast work space, past the skeletal machines, toward the industrial freezer room where the body had been found.

She was usually composed around murder scenes – it went with the job – but right now she felt uneasy. Beneath the dust the smell of death lingered in the air. This had been a place of blood and guts, of animals being sliced and diced, flesh separated from bone and gristle. Even ten or so years after the place had last seen a carcass, the scent of blood still lurked in the dark corners. But there was another smell too: heavy and alkaline, yet sweet . . .

Reilly stood still, every one of her senses alert. It was that smell again, she realized – the same one she'd come across in the church tower. Her heart galloped.

Not exactly tangible, but it was a connection . . .

She bent down and sniffed the ground, trying to pinpoint the smell's exact location. Was it the wall . . . the ground? The scent was so pungent here it was impossible to tell exactly where it was strongest. Swabbing an area of the floor closest to the wall, she bagged the sample.

Moving on, Reilly made her way toward the rear of the building, her mind racing with this important find.

The same smell at two different murder locations. It couldn't be coincidence. She didn't believe in coincidence. Crowe had been dumped in a bath of water and frozen to death in a heavy-duty freezer, Jennings strung up on a tree and left for dead and

136

to the mercy of the elements. Her thoughts then turned to Tony Coffey, how the journalist had been kidnapped, bound, then dumped in the septic tank. It was all too weird . . .

Trying to stop herself from getting distracted, and reaching for connections where there may well be none, she brought her focus back to this particular scene.

There were so many unanswered questions here too. The first was the simple matter of logistics. How had the killer got Crowe into the plant in the first place?

He was a big man, and an ex-cop who knew how to defend himself. Subduing him would not have been easy, let alone getting him into a bath of icy water.

The pigeons cooed softly. They weren't revealing their secrets.

Reilly had reached the far end of the processing room, which was dominated by a large loading dock, metal shutters rolled down. Broken packing cases littered the floor, several of them scraped together into half-burned remnants of bonfires.

The door to the freezer room was just ahead. Reilly shone her torch beam across the floor, all around the doorway, trying to separate out visually the footsteps of the police and the investigators from the older marks.

A sudden noise startled her, a movement half-glimpsed in her peripheral vision, something closing in fast on her.

Giving a little squeak of surprise, she dropped her torch as she instinctively put her hands up to protect her face. She turned quickly, and flinched as a pigeon flew past, its wings so close she could feel the draft. The bird swooped past her, and soared up into the rafters to join its companions. They jostled for position for a moment before settling down again.

'Dammit!' Feeling stupid, Reilly glanced around to see where her torch had landed. She scanned the floor, with only beams of daylight from above to help her. The torch was nowhere to be seen.

She bent down, and peered under the conveyor belt that ran past her. It was broken, the belt hanging down creating deep shadows and pockets of darkness, but she could see no sign of her torch. She turned the other way, toward the doorway to the freezer, her eyes gradually adjusting to the gloomy half-light. Then suddenly something caught her eye that she hadn't seen before.

There were faint tracks in the dust leading into the freezer room. Around the doorway they disappeared under footsteps, but there was no doubt that something had been wheeled in from the door toward the freezer.

Reilly stepped over, bent low and examined the tracks, then followed them visually toward the back door of the building. They were narrow – but not a bike or anything like that; maybe a trolley? She looked again at the track impressions – no, not a shopping trolley; there were only two wheels.

138

Suddenly an image popped into her mind. She knew exactly what had left the tracks: it was one of those hand dollies, the sort that delivery drivers used.

Significant?

Reilly followed the tracks as they disappeared into the footprints around the freezer door, and finally saw her torch. It had rolled into the shadows that crept out of the freezer, as if telling her where she needed to go next. She went over, picked it up, and directed it toward the dust at her feet as she tried to pinpoint the faint tracks rolling into the freezer.

The freezer room itself was almost completely veiled in darkness. No outside light came in except a faint beam through the doorway, illuminating a short strip of ground. The alkaline scent was in here too. What the hell was it?

Using her torch, Reilly followed the wheel tracks into the darkness – they kept appearing and disappearing until they were obliterated by all the footsteps around the area where Crowe had been found.

Reilly shivered, despite knowing that the freezer was turned off. Yet still she felt cold. There was something personal, intimate about this space. The killer had been in here with Crowe, one on one, just the two of them, their breaths steaming in the small, frozen room.

What had Crowe been thinking? Had he known his killer? Had he known he was going to die? We spend our whole lives avoiding death, eating the right foods, not smoking, going to the gym, kidding ourselves that we will live forever – but what is it like when we suddenly know, with absolute certainty, that we are about to die?

Reilly shone her torch around the freezer. The beam of light spotlighted parts of the room as she moved around. The shelving was still in place and, at the back of the room, the bath in which Crowe had been found.

Reilly stepped over to the bathtub. It was certainly not a place she would choose to die. Crowe's last glimpse of life would have been this dirty, abandoned room, and perhaps the face of his killer leaning over him as cold water slowly turned to ice around him.

Trying to picture it threw up more questions for Reilly. How had the bath got there? It would have taken some effort to get it in, but the place had been abandoned for so long that the investigators were unable to determine if it had been there when the plant was open. Maybe the bath had been wheeled in on the trolley?

Then there was the electricity. Whoever had killed Crowe had known how to hook the electricity back up to the freezer. In fact, he had turned on the electrics for the whole plant. It was the lights suddenly blazing from the long-abandoned works that had attracted attention and led to Crowe's discovery.

She thought back to the Coffey scene. The

140

blockage in the septic tank, which iSPI had initially revealed, had turned out to be a piece of brick that was incongruous to the limestone surroundings of the drained tank.

Similarly, the killer here had gone to great lengths not only to execute the murder, but to make sure that the body was found quickly. A fresh chill ran down Reilly's spine and she turned and headed out of the freezer.

Simply being back out in the main plant made her feel better. The tight space and intimacy of the freezer had been disconcerting, and out here the alkaline smell seemed less cloying. Walking at a low crouch, Reilly followed the faint wheel tracks with her torch as they rolled toward the rear of the plant, all the way to the back door.

The door was old metal. Reilly gave it a shove but it didn't budge. She took a step back, raised her right leg, and gave a powerful kick. The door flew open, the rusty hinges screaming in protest. As it did it let in a gust of fresh air that was welcome, blowing Reilly's hair back from her face. The sound of metal screeching echoed through the cavernous space, startling the pigeons and sending them flying in a flash of wings, swooping up and out through the broken skylights.

Reilly stepped outside and breathed in a lungful of the cold November air.

She wrapped her coat around her, enjoying the breeze and the sunlight on her face after the cold claustrophobia inside. The pigeons swooped and circled together, a tightly knit pack dark against the pale blue sky, then broke apart, and one by one slipped back in through the broken roof to resume their positions on the rusting metal beams.

Reilly looked around. The back of the plant opened onto an overgrown car park, the grass and weeds thrusting up through the broken tarmac. The wheel marks ended here, lost on the hard ground, but it seemed obvious to her that this would have been where the killer had come in, the shortest, easiest route to the freezer. He would have known that, would have scoped out his territory, had his plan ready long before he seized Crowe and brought him here.

She walked across the uneven ground to the back of the property, picking her way though the tall weeds and the potholed tarmac. About fifty yards away from the plant there was a wire fence, tired and sagging, several holes punched in it where kids had broken in since the business had floundered.

Was this where the killer had scouted the building initially? There were several trees, a line of shrubs, plenty of places for someone to hide out for a while, check out the layout of the building, make sure it was truly deserted.

She turned and looked back at the building, understanding the layout. Deliveries and shipments would have come in and out through the front gate – where Reilly's uniformed companion currently sat warm in his car – down the side of the building, to the loading dock at the rear.

A picture appeared in her mind of Crowe, bound, trussed and bundled like an oven-ready turkey, being wheeled inside, possibly on a handcart. Then Jennings, also bound before he was hoisted up into the tree. What about Coffey?

Reilly pulled her phone from her pocket, and quickly touched and scrolled.

From the GFU office, Jack Gorman's deep tones filled her ear. 'What can I do for you, Ms Steel?'

She spoke quickly, hoping she wasn't already too late. 'Tony Coffey's body – is it still in our custody?'

'Let me check.' The older investigator sounded irritated, her questions clearly unwelcome to him. 'It's due to be shipped off later this afternoon,' he informed her after a few minutes' wait. 'Apparently the funeral is Wednesday.'

'Can we delay it?'

'And what would be the point in that? Oh, let me guess, off on yet another one of your cat and mouse games?' Gorman's tone barely disguised his contempt.

Reilly wished that for once he would take her seriously. She knew well how much Gorman disliked her, considered her an upstart – young and female as well as a scientist, not his favorite combination.

He'd been almost apoplectic this morning, upon learning that she planned to rerun the Crowe scene, one he insisted he'd combed to the last. But his report mentioned nothing about wheel tracks or an alkaline smell.

'Humor me, Gorman. Can you meet me at the morgue with a copy of both Crowe and Coffey's autopsy reports?'

He sighed wearily, annoyed by her intrusion into his orderly schedule. 'I'm very busy today, Steel. Unlike you, I really don't have time to waste—'

'I won't take up too much of your time,' she interjected. 'Please. It's important.'

CHAPTER 16

It was less than thirty minutes' drive from the city out to rural Drogheda where Crowe had lived for the past few years, but seemed much further.

The landscape changed quickly as Chris and Kennedy headed north, becoming flatter and more windblown with each mile, the greens turning to a dull brown expanse. The winds whipped up and the sky closed in, a November shower falling from a leaden gray sky.

Chris gazed out across the windswept shore. A lone gull battled the wind, making almost no progress, before finally seeming to quit and dropping quickly down into the long grass. He shivered, and thrust his hands deep into the pockets of his coat.

'I think I'd go crazy living out here.'

Kennedy was perched on the bonnet of the car, his cigarette cupped in his hands as he tried to light it. The flame from his lighter flickered and danced before finally catching the end of the cigarette. He inhaled deeply as the red glow devoured the white paper. 'I guess it's like anything – you'd get used to it.'

Chris shook his head. 'Not me. I'm too much of a townie.' He turned to take in the dull brown riverbanks that extended in either direction, the only sound the mournful wail of the wind as it whipped past them. 'Why would Crowe want to retire out here in the sticks?' He looked at Kennedy, genuine bafflement on his face. 'Wasn't he a Dubliner?'

'Born and bred. Always used to boast about being a barrow boy in Moore Street when he was a kid.'

'That's what I mean.' Chris turned back toward the car, pulling his coat collar up high around his ears. 'Would you ever hurry up and finish that bloody thing? We need to get moving.'

His partner took a deep drag. 'Yeah, yeah, calm down. This isn't going to be the easiest conversation, you know.'

Crowe had a place on a dead-end road out past the town, an old cottage he had fixed up. Kennedy eased the car down a narrow lane, splashing in and out of deep puddles and ruts, until they finally stopped in front of a large iron gate. A sign read, 'Keep Out. Beware of the Dogs'.

As Kennedy pulled up in front of the gate, Chris glanced over at his partner. 'Friendly.'

Kennedy gave a hollow laugh. 'Yep, this is Crowe's place for sure.'

Even from inside the car they could hear the barking of the dogs, and the animals soon appeared, a pair of muscular German shepherds, hurling themselves against the gate, their teeth gleaming in the dull light as they charged and threatened the visitors.

Behind the gate was a low cottage, a squat bungalow that seemed perfectly suited to the desolate location.

Now Kennedy finished his cigarette, and flicked the butt into a nearby puddle. The driveway was slick from the rain, dotted with small puddles, and the barking of the dogs grew even more insistent. He straightened and stomped over to the gate.

Up close the dogs were even scarier, hurling themselves at the heavy metal gate with primal ferocity, their furry coats rippling with muscle. Kennedy stepped quickly forward, rang the bell, then stepped back from the gate. The dogs kept up their furious assault, spittle flying from their mouths as they roared at the intruder.

Suddenly they paused, and looked behind them. A voice cut through the air. 'Brutus! Caesar! Away!'

The dogs gave the detectives one last look, then trotted silently away. A woman appeared from the side of the house, wearing wellingtons and a heavy, mud-stained rain jacket, her gray-peppered hair pulled back in a tight bun. She stopped about five yards from the gate, and eyed her visitors suspiciously. 'What do you want?'

Kennedy fixed his best smile in place. 'Hi, Maggie.'

Mrs Crowe squinted in confusion.

'Pete. Pete Kennedy?' he prompted her.

She reached the gate, and peered through the dark metal rails at him. 'Oh, it's you.'

Chris smiled. It was the sort of greeting his partner usually commanded, but at least she remembered him.

'Sorry to bother you, Maggie,' Kennedy continued. 'I wondered if we could have a few words.'

She peered past him at the car where Chris sat huddled up. She set her hands on her hips, exuding obvious suspicion. 'Who's in the car?'

'That's my partner, Detective Delaney. He's a city boy, doesn't like the countryside much.'

Maggie looked at the barren sky above, the rain clouds whipping past. 'Can't say I blame him. I'm not terribly keen either.'

Bloody hell, Chris thought, this was like pulling teeth. He wished Kennedy would hurry up and get on with it. 'We'd like to ask you a few questions if you don't mind,' he said, leaning out of the window. 'Just a couple of loose ends to tie up about your husband's death.'

Crowe's wife looked back at him, noncommittal. 'I've already answered a lot of questions. There's nothing more to say.'

'I understand, but—'

'Do you?' Her words were harsh, reflecting the heavy lines in her pinched face. 'Do you understand what it's like when your husband is found dead, frozen in a block of ice? And then everyone wants to know the most intimate details of your life, as if that's going to help anything.'

148

She half turned away from them, and for a moment Chris thought she was about to leave, but she stayed still, gazing out past them at the fields that surrounded the house. A line of geese worked their way toward them, their powerful wings holding their perfect V formation as they passed overhead, honking intermittently.

Mrs Crowe suddenly turned back toward them, and now she seemed to have let her guard down a little. 'I do remember you, Detective Kennedy. John always spoke well of you, said you were all right, one of the lads.' She looked up and met his gaze. 'I guess that's a compliment, isn't it?'

Kennedy shrugged. 'I hope so. Who knows with John?'

'It means he trusted you.' She fell silent, her hands playing with something in the pocket of her jacket.

Kennedy reached into his own pocket, and pulled out his cigarettes. Her eyes followed him hungrily as he slipped a cigarette from the packet, lit it, and inhaled deeply. He peered at her through the smoke. 'Want one?'

Her gaze was still fixed on the cigarette. 'I've given up,' she said quickly.

'Me too. It's a pain, isn't it?' Kennedy inhaled again, then held the cigarette out toward her.

For a second she hesitated, then suddenly her hand reached out through the gate, and took the cigarette. The first drag was slow, deep, almost ecstatic as she drew the smoke deep into her lungs.

'God, I miss that,' she said. She took another drag, and looked at the cigarette thoughtfully. 'The doctor says I was slowly killing myself with these, but hey, with the way things have worked out, who cares?'

'Yeah, my quack says the same thing, but the bastard smokes himself.' Kennedy shrugged. 'It's the little things like this that make life worth living, isn't it?'

Mrs Crowe said nothing, and simply savored the cigarette.

'Who's your doctor, by the way?' Kennedy asked with a casual air that impressed Chris. His technique mightn't be the smoothest, but he had his own ways all the same.

'Excuse me?'

'Your doctor? I was just wondering if you have one down here or use the same guy you went to back in Dublin.'

'No, it's a local. Jack Davis. Why do you ask?'

'Just making conversation.'

Mrs Crowe looked skeptical. 'Detective, please, I've spent most of my life married to a cop, and I know that when it comes to you lot, there's no such thing.'

'As I said we're trying to tie up a couple of loose ends in the investigation and—'

'What investigation? Into John's death? Because I don't remember either of you being involved in any of that at all until today.'

She was sharp, no doubting that, Chris thought. A by-product of years spent as a cop's wife.

'OK, Maggie, I'll be straight up with you,' Kennedy said sighing. 'We're not a hundred percent convinced that it was a payback murder and—'

'Well, it's about bloody time,' she interjected, and the detectives exchanged looks. 'I never once suspected that it was.'

Chris was watching her closely.

'What was your husband into, Maggie?' he asked suddenly.

She said nothing for a moment and Chris wondered if he'd jumped in too quickly, pushed his luck too soon.

She glanced back toward the house, thinking, deciding. 'John was into a lot of things,' she said eventually. 'I didn't ask and he didn't tell . . .'

Chris nodded. 'Best way. Any ideas?' He fired the words at her, trying to force her to admit what it might be that her husband had got involved in, and how it might tie in with the other two victims.

Maggie wouldn't meet his gaze. She sucked greedily on the cigarette, and let out a deep breath of smoke that was whipped away on the wind. 'People who cross the line always need someone to watch their backs – be there if things go bad,' she said finally. 'John was good at that.'

Kennedy nodded. 'He ran a security firm.'

'He had a few contracts for local businesses, but some of the characters he met weren't the kind who needed a night watchman for their office building, if you understand me,' she said meaningfully. 'People would come to the house late at night, dodgy-looking characters, I thought. They'd sit at the kitchen table talking . . .' Now that she'd opened up, Chris thought, she seemed keen to get it all out. 'I stayed out of the way, didn't want to know what he was doing. I'd make them cups of tea and then go and watch TV, pretend they were talking about football or the dogs.'

'But,' Chris prompted her gently, 'you knew something wasn't right?'

'John was always in a good mood afterwards – he'd have these big envelopes of cash, give me a couple of hundred to go shopping. "Treat yourself," he'd say, and give me that smile of his . . .' The sadness of her loss flashed across her face for a moment, but she quickly reeled it back in.

Kennedy nodded. 'He could be a real charmer when he wanted to be . . . Do you have any names for us, Maggie?'

She shook her head. 'Like I said, I stayed out of it.'

They'd got this far, and Chris wasn't going to go away empty-handed. 'What about a pub, or a bookie's maybe, somewhere he might hang out and meet people?'

She nodded. 'To be fair to him he kept most of his "business" away from home. His office was Brown's Bar on Sheriff Street.'

Kennedy gave a grunt of recognition. 'That's a rough spot.'

Maggie finished her cigarette, dropped the butt into a small puddle, and stared at it thoughtfully for a moment. It looked like their conversation was over.

Kennedy reached for his packet and held it out for her. 'Want to keep them?'

She thought for a moment, her eyes not wavering. Finally her hand shot out and grabbed the packet, like a child reaching for a bag of sweets. 'What the heck. We all have to go sometime.'

CHAPTER 17

Gorman looked less than pleased to see Reilly. Indeed, he barely looked up when she met him at the entrance to the city morgue – a modern, purpose-built place on the opposite side of the city from the GFU.

'The autopsy reports you asked for,' he grunted, grudgingly handing her the files. 'I'm sure they both say the same as they did last time you looked at them.'

Reilly took a deep breath, and forced herself to relax and not be wound up by him. Why was he always so uptight, so bitter?

Get what you need and get out of here, she told herself. Humor him, do whatever it takes to get what you want . . .

'Jack, just to be clear, I'm not undermining the efficiency of your findings,' she began. 'And the reason I went over the Crowe scene again this afternoon is because we have strong reason to believe that this murder may relate to Tony Coffey and George Jennings.'

Gorman paused for a moment before carefully

removing his glasses, folding them and slipping them into his jacket pocket.

'I'm aware of that, Steel, yet you don't see me questioning your own rather . . . slim findings at the site where the journalist was found.'

His tone was smug, and Reilly knew that the man must have been rubbing his hands with glee that he hadn't been the one to have had to wade through the stinking mess that was the Coffey scene.

'I'm not questioning anything, Jack, just trying to look at each murder with a fresh eye. The thinking before with Crowe was that it might be one of his old collars taking revenge, and with Coffey, someone or something he wrote about. Now, it looks as though there may be much more to it. The manner of their deaths—'

'I agree that the manner of their demise was atypical, to say the least, as is this most recent incident,' he admitted. He gave her a sharp look, and peered out from beneath his thick, gray eyebrows. 'However, I remain unconvinced that there is anything to link these deaths, other than their bizarre execution. And unlike you, Ms Steel, I've been in this business long enough to have encountered just about everything, and try not to be swayed by an overwrought imagination.'

He scratched at his stubbled chin with his nicotine-stained fingers, while Reilly fought the urge to tell him to take a hike. This wasn't a figment of her 'overwrought imagination', it was the direction the investigative team had been ordered to take.

She ran her fingers through her hair, and looked him straight in the eyes. 'What do you want me to do – ignore Inspector O'Brien's orders?'

'Of course not. It's the reason we're both here, isn't it? So are you going to enlighten me on why you want to see Mr Coffey's body? I'm sure Dr Thompson will be pleased to learn you are questioning her professionalism as well as my own.'

Reilly sighed. This guy was seriously hard work. 'I'm not questioning anyone's professionalism, Jack,' she said wearily. 'There's just something I need to check.'

Reilly didn't know which she hated the most – the smell or the cold. Although the morgue building was brand new, the autopsy room itself was sparse, functional, and designed for only one purpose – the efficient examination of corpses.

A wall of huge steel doors on one side housed the bodies, keeping them cold until the ME was done with them. In the center of the room were two examination tables, cold stainless steel, with hoses and drains to wash away the blood and associated gore when the autopsy was complete.

The mortuary assistant in attendance just then was a former summer intern who had stayed on as a part-time volunteer when the college season started up again. He was still young, in his early twenties, but extremely well read and intelligent for his scant years, a nice young kid who was a favorite of Reilly's, mostly because she could never be sure what sort of crazy getup he would be wearing.

Today he was dressed as a goth. His usually fair hair had been dyed black, and his face was powdered whiter than his bleached white lab coat. His hands coming out through the cuffs of the coat were covered in black fishnet fingerless gloves, and beneath his black jeans were a pair of brilliantly glossy black and white striped boots.

'Doc told me you wanted to check out the journo?' he said, handing them gowns, gloves and face masks as they entered the autopsy suite.

Reilly nodded. 'Yes, Luke. Thanks for coming out at such short notice.'

'No problemo.'

Both suited up, Gorman and Reilly waited as Luke pulled open one of the large metal drawers, and rolled out the gurney before slamming the door shut with a heavy metallic thud that echoed round the cold room.

Coffey looked bad – he was a heavyset man, with pale, hairy skin and a huge protruding belly. Death had done him no favors, either. His skin was pasty white with an almost purple sheen, his chest a cross-work of stitching where his internal organs had been removed during autopsy.

Luke rolled him under a bright overhead light, and then left them to it.

Gorman looked at Reilly. 'So what, specifically, are we looking for that you think might have been missed first time around?'

Reilly ran her gaze over the corpse. She collected her thoughts. 'Remember we were speculating about how anyone would have gotten Crowe in the freezer or Coffey in the tank – alive, especially?'

Gorman nodded, and went to pull a packet of cigarettes out from beneath his gown before remembering himself. He tucked them away. 'Neither is a small man, and nothing turned up on the tox screen, so no drugging.'

'I think they were both bound, then not dragged, but *wheeled* onsite.' Thinking back on those narrow impressions on the grass approaching the tree yesterday, Reilly was willing to bet money on it that Jennings had also been transported across the extensive grounds of the church by the same method.

Gorman scowled. 'How – like on a stretcher?'

'No. I'm thinking something more along the lines of those two-wheel dollies delivery drivers use.'

His expression was dubious but he said nothing.

Reilly looked over Coffey's body, paying close attention to the wrists.

'No ligature marks on Crowe either,' Gorman said quickly. 'We checked.'

'What if the killer didn't use rope but something else to bind them?'

'Like what? Duct tape?'

158

Reilly nodded and held up one of Coffey's hands, peering closely at his wrists. 'It is an effective way of binding someone, and it wouldn't leave the marks we typically see from ropes.'

Gorman was standing back, watching but reluctant to participate. 'Well, if that's what you're looking for, I would check the clothes. Chances are the tape might not even have touched the skin.'

Reilly set Coffey's arm back down on the gurney, and walked round to the other side. 'Coffey's clothes were such a mess it was impossible to get anything at all from them. But if any tape did touch the skin, then . . .' She lifted his other hand and again examined the wrist. 'There.'

Gorman put his hands behind his back and leaned forward toward the point Reilly was examining. He scowled. 'What exactly am I looking at?'

She turned the underside of Coffey's arm toward the light. There was the faintest gap in the dark hair around his wrist. Perhaps removed by adhesive from duct tape? Reilly looked up at Gorman. 'See it? He must have been bound, just like Jennings, and I'd be willing to bet that Crowe was too.' Such a shame he was already six foot under, and they couldn't check.

Gorman straightened up. 'What I see is wishful thinking,' he said gruffly, stepping over to the line of metal doors. 'Are we finished? I'm sure Mr Coffey's family would like to bury him sometime soon.'

Ignoring him, Reilly peeled off her gloves and

159

threw them in the bin. Pulling a camera from her kitbag nearby, she pointed the lens and zoomed in on the area around Coffey's wrist.

Gorman opened the door, and looked impatiently back toward Reilly as the flash of her camera lit up the room. 'Luke, we're finished here, or one of us is at least.' He stood in the doorway, muttering away to himself. 'If I don't get some nicotine soon I'm going to get really cranky.'

Like we'd notice the difference, Reilly shot back silently.

She took five photos in quick succession before finally standing up. 'I'll have Julius go over both sets of clothes again for traces of adhesive or resin,' she told Gorman. 'See what we have.'

Gorman looked at her, a dour expression on his face. 'Whatever you like, Steel. Fool's errands are, after all, your speciality.'

The pub in Dublin's Sheriff Street was dark, unwelcoming – not a woman in sight and no background music. A football match played on the big-screen TV in the corner. When Chris and Kennedy walked in a few locals glanced up and gave them suspicious frowns before returning to the morose contemplation of their pints.

Chris looked around, and nudged his partner. 'Remind me never to bring a date in here.'

Kennedy grunted. 'You could bring Miss Baywatch, no problem,' he chuckled under his breath. 'I'm sure she'd love this place.'

They made their way to the bar, and slid onto two empty stools. The barman was a big guy in his late fifties, with the face of an ex-boxer, or maybe a prop forward – flattened nose, thick eyebrows, enlarged ears. He looked as though he'd probably started (and finished) many a pub brawl. He gave the detectives a disinterested glance as they sat down, and wiped listlessly at the bar with a grimy tea towel.

Chris met his eye. 'Two pints of Guinness.'

The barman slowly levered himself off the bar, and wordlessly filled two pint glasses, before setting them in front of him. Chris slid across a tenner. The barman took it, rang up the sale, and flipped the change onto the counter top.

'Who you looking for?' he asked suddenly.

Kennedy shook his head, and turned to Chris. 'Told you we should have left our shiny badges in the car.'

'Nah,' Chris replied. 'It's the caps and truncheons that gave us away.'

The barman was not amused. 'You two could come in here dressed like Ronald McDonald and I'd still know you were cops. So, who are you after?'

Kennedy took a sip. 'Old mate of mine, Johnny Crowe, retired cop, spent a lot of time here.'

The barman nodded. 'I knew him.' He leaned his meaty forearms on the bar, picked idly at a cigarette burn in the wood with his thick fingernails. 'What about him?'

'We just want a little help from you,' Chris said. 'Some basic information.'

'Like who did he drink with?' chipped in Kennedy. 'This was his home away from home – who were his mates?'

The barman looked thoughtful for a moment. 'Can't say there was anyone in particular. He just liked to have a drink, watch the game . . .'

'He didn't have any mates here – any regulars?' Chris asked. 'Just liked to have a drink—'

'And watch the game. That's right.'

Chris nodded slowly and sipped at his beer. 'I get it.'

He looked around, pointed to a group of teenagers sitting in the corner also drinking beer and watching the game. 'I'll bet that at least half of those are under age . . .' He indicated two more youngsters at the far end of the bar, drinks in hand. 'And if those two are eighteen I'll eat your tea towel.'

The barman looked down at the blackened rag in his hand. He wiped it gently across the bar. 'We've been together a long time, I'd hate to see any harm come to her . . .' He looked up, and tilted his head slightly to the far side of the room where two men sat talking quietly. 'Those would be the closest to what you'd call friends of Crowe's.' Chris looked over Kennedy's shoulder at them. 'The small one is Micky McCarthy,' explained the barman. 'Corkonian git who fancies himself as a ladies' man. The big fellow – don't know his real name – he's a Russki or something. Everyone calls him Ivan.' He thought for a moment. 'Nasty piece of work. You might want to watch yourself with that one.'

Kennedy glanced over at them. 'They were Crowe's mates?'

The barman shrugged. 'Closest thing he had to mates around here.'

Chris picked up his pint. 'All right then, let's go mix with the locals . . .'

The one the barman had referred to as Ivan looked up as they approached, his radar instantly on high alert. He had a brutal face, with a mass of dark hair swept back from sharp Slavic cheekbones. He started to stand but Chris moved quickly and blocked his path, his badge in his hand.

'Have a seat, Ivan, we just want to have a little chat.'

Micky McCarthy looked up and smiled. 'Cops? Nice one.' He had a singsong Cork accent, was small and wiry, and dressed in an Adidas T-shirt and shiny blue track suit bottoms. He smiled, showing several missing teeth.

The two men sat across from one another in a corner booth. Kennedy and Chris slid in, one either side, blocking them in. Ivan looked back and forth between them, his dark eyes weighing up the situation. Despite the smoking ban, he sucked on a cigarette, a haze of smoke wreathing his face.

'What you want?' His accent was strong, his grammar imperfect, but he had a presence, and an air of menace hung on his words.

163

'We just want to ask you a few questions,' Kennedy began. 'About Johnny Crowe.'

Ivan furrowed his brow. 'I don't know no – what was his name?'

'Crowe,' Chris informed him, 'John Crowe.'

McCarthy chipped in, 'Sure you do, Ivan. Cracker – Johnny Crowe was Cracker's real name.'

Ivan nodded slowly. 'Ah, Cracker. Big guy, used to be cop?'

Kennedy nodded. 'That's the ticket.'

McCarthy gave a little laugh. 'Poor fucker wound up in a freezer, last I heard.'

'That's right.' Chris looked between the two of them. 'Any ideas why?'

Ivan shrugged, flicked ash from his cigarette onto the table. 'Why should we know that?'

'Because you did business with him.'

Ivan shook his head. 'Beer, yes. Business? No.'

Chris was seated next to Ivan. He turned and stared at him from close range. Ivan met his gaze, unblinking. 'You know it's illegal to smoke in a pub, don't you?'

Ivan kept his eyes on Chris, took another drag on his cigarette and blew the smoke out toward him. 'So arrest me.'

Chris felt a trickle run down his back – there was something almost feral in Ivan's gaze. This was a man capable of murder. In fact, Chris felt certain that Ivan had killed already, and would have no qualms about doing so again. Was this their guy?

164

'Boys, boys . . .' The tension seemed to be making McCarthy uncomfortable. He reached across the table, and tugged at Chris's arm. 'Hey, we liked Cracker, and we don't know anything about his death. It was a shock to us too, wasn't it, Ivan?'

Ivan's eyes bored into Chris's soul. Finally he smiled, a cold twist of his mouth that left his eyes unmoved, and stubbed his cigarette out on the table. 'Sure. Big shock.'

Chris finally looked away, and glanced across the table at Kennedy. 'Well, if you don't know anything . . .'

'I might know,' Ivan growled.

They all looked back at him in surprise. 'But you just said—'

'I said I don't do business with him. But I know Cracker, I know the shit he was into – some bad stuff,' added Ivan. He gave his twisted smile again. 'I would know if someone wanted him out of the way.'

'Bad stuff . . . like what?' Kennedy asked.

Ivan shrugged noncommittally. 'Just, bad stuff. But . . .' he let the word hang, making sure he had their attention, '. . . his death? It was nothing to do with his business.' He smiled suddenly. 'But he was ex-cop, yes?'

Chris nodded.

'I hear not all cops are same.' He smiled again. 'You guys are cops.' He looked back and forth between them. 'You do good job mostly, but not always?'

Kennedy looked at him. 'I don't get you.'

Ivan leaned in, conspiratorial. 'Cracker, he tell me one day, there were some peoples who asked him not to be such good cop . . .' He pulled a cigarette from his pocket, tapped it on the table.

'You implying he was taking kickbacks?' Chris looked across at Kennedy, who shrugged.

Ivan shook his head. 'He never say.' He sat back, looked from one detective to the other. 'But if I was you? That's where I would look. Not dirty pub in Sheriff Street . . .' Ivan suddenly looked past Chris, and gave a slight shake of the head.

Chris followed his gaze – four large men stood by the door, watching carefully what was happening at the table. They were all well dressed, with dark looks that matched Ivan's. At the big man's gesture they seemed to relax.

'So, you are busy men, yes? Busy being good cops,' Ivan was suddenly jovial, but it was also a clear signal that the interview was over. He flicked his lighter open, and held it just in front of his cigarette. 'Happy investigation, yes?'

Chris glanced at the four men, and back at Kennedy. 'Right, happy investigation.' He stood up, and his partner did the same. Then he held his card out to Ivan. 'If you think of anything else that might be helpful . . .'

Ivan looked at it for a moment, then nodded to McCarthy, who took the card.

The detectives turned and walked slowly out of the pub, passing the four men on the way. They

166

were clustered by the door, and moved only slightly as he and Kennedy passed, forcing them to weave between all four – close enough to see their hard eyes, smell the beer and cigarettes and sweat.

Not until they were outside the pub, the fresh wind on their faces, did Kennedy let out a deep sigh of relief. 'Jesus Christ, I haven't felt like that since my first week on the beat,' he gasped. 'What kind of shit was Crowe into?'

But the real question was, Chris thought, was it the man's dodgy dealings or his law enforcement past that had landed him in ice?

CHAPTER 18

Reilly never felt comfortable going into bars by herself. Something about the way men leered, like there was this automatic assumption that a single woman in such a place was available. She tried to ignore the staring faces and looked around for Chris and Kennedy. They were seated at a table in the corner, beers in hand, in animated discussion about something.

She had to admit she was a bit taken aback when earlier that evening she'd phoned Chris's mobile to give him an update on yesterday's sweep of the factory as well as her findings at the morgue, and he'd suggested she come down and meet him and Kennedy at a pub not far from the station.

It wouldn't have been her choice of location for a work-related get-together, but they were all working crazy hours these days, and she figured it was better than going home to her empty flat. As it was, she didn't get to experience enough of the local culture, and figured this as good an opportunity as any to soak up the world-famous atmosphere of an Irish pub.

Reilly made her way through the crowd and

slipped into an empty chair, shedding her coat as she sat. She looked back and forth between them.

'What's going on?'

Kennedy smiled at her. 'O'Brien's latest press conference – did you see it?'

She shook her head. 'I try and avoid those things.'

'It should be on YouTube,' he informed her. 'A comedy classic.'

She raised an eyebrow. 'Do tell.'

'There's really not much to tell, you just have to see it.'

'Pure waffle,' Chris explained. 'How to say nothing but look really important while you do it. O'Brien is an expert.'

'What's that phrase he always uses?' Kennedy chuckled. '"Our enquiries are proceeding with the full co-operation of the public."' He snorted in derision. 'Which really means we don't have a fucking clue . . .'

Reilly grimaced. 'If this one was good, the next should be one of the don't-miss events of the year.'

They both looked at her, intrigued. 'You found something?' Chris asked.

'Well, there's some interesting new evidence . . .' she began slowly.

'"Interesting",' Kennedy repeated. 'One little word that usually means a host of big problems.' He grimaced. 'Why do I have a bad feeling about what you're going to say next? Anyway, hold your horses for a second.' He stood up. 'What are you drinking?'

'Oh, I'm not staying—'

'You can't sit in an Irish pub without a drink in front of you – it's the law.'

Chris nodded sagely. 'Very true.'

Reilly looked from one to the other, stupidly unsure as to whether or not they were kidding.

'OK then . . . I'll have a soda.'

'Grand job.' Kennedy waddled off and she looked at Chris, who winked at her.

Feeling stupid, she colored. 'Well, you Irish and your drinking . . .' she said sheepishly, 'you just never know.'

'Aren't you here long enough now to have got over the stereotype?' Chris jibed.

'Honestly, I don't think I've even scratched the surface . . .'

He laughed, and Kennedy duly returned with the drinks.

'So – get it over with then, what's the news?' He sounded impatient as he put the drinks on the table.

She smiled and picked up her soda. 'Matching trace samples from Crowe, Coffey *and* Jennings. Well, there are a couple of links, actually.' She went on to tell them about the wheel tracks at the factory the day before, and her theory that all three victims had been bound and transported to each site on a handcart.

Kennedy nodded. 'Makes sense, I suppose. I saw those tracks in the grass around the tree myself – crossed my mind that they looked like they came

170

from a wheelchair or something.' He chuckled. 'Lucky I'm in this job and not yours, isn't it?'

'You got that from when you went back and redid Crowe's location yesterday?' Chris asked, and she nodded. 'I'm sure Gorman is pleased.'

'He wasn't over the moon about it, but this time I was actively looking for a connection, rather than going in blind. Anyway, we got a result, that's all that matters.'

'So what's the common trace?' Chris asked.

'Horse feed,' she announced proudly.

'Horse . . . and that helps us how?' Kennedy looked at her as if she was mad. 'You want us to start looking for a bogyman who has a thing for horses?' He grabbed his pint, and took several deep gulps. 'Not forgetting the Chinese food too, which got us where, exactly?'

Reilly remained calm. Perhaps neither find gave them much to go on in terms of catching the murderer, but it was still something.

Chris seemed to be thinking hard. 'Does it tell us anything new?'

She nodded. 'Well, chances are our guy works in or lives near stables, or someplace that keeps horses on the property. Dust from pellet feed is exceptionally fine, so even though he's going out of his way to be careful, he wouldn't be able to budget for this stuff. He could be bringing in residue on his clothes, his hair . . .

'Lucy found it at the Coffey scene originally, but we didn't jump on it because of Mrs Coffey's

171

hunting connection. It was also picked up from the ground surrounding Crowe's bathtub, but the components were listed as unidentified on Gorman's report. It was only today, when we compared the listings side by side, actively looking for a crossover, that we spotted it.'

'Any sign of it on Jennings?'

Reilly frowned. 'There may well have been, but thanks to that idiot groundsman, the area beneath the tree was a nightmare. Julius is working on it as we speak.'

'Anything else interesting from that site?'

'Not especially. The back door of the church showed signs of forced entry like you said – I'd guess a pry bar, something similar. Old lock, old wood, it would have opened pretty easily.'

Chris nodded.

'And despite the risk of blowing the electrics, Gary checked to see if the lights worked – nothing.'

'So Jennings' killer must have come and gone during daylight hours?'

Reilly nodded. 'It's such a quiet area – well chosen, just like the others.'

Then she reached into her handbag, opened a file and slid it across the table, pointing to a small hand-drawn map. 'There's access there, so he could have driven up the side and parked almost outside the rear door.'

Kennedy looked up, optimistic. 'Tire marks?'

'Nope. The driveway is gravel, and it was raining the night before the body was found. And seeing as Jennings had been there a few days, anything would have been washed away.'

'Christ, what do we have to do to catch a break on this thing?' the older detective spat.

'Anything new from your end?' Reilly asked.

'We followed up on Crowe yesterday,' Chris told her, 'checked up on some of the rumors.'

'And?'

He chuckled. 'Well, for starters, some big Russian bloke scared the life out of Kennedy.'

'Hey!'

Reilly raised an amused eyebrow. 'Tell me more.'

'Crowe's wife pointed us in the direction of one of his hangouts here in the city. He was definitely mixed up with some unsavory characters, there's no doubt about that, but whether they had anything to do with his death . . . My gut tells me no. Again, this whole thing is too elaborate a setup for a small-timer.'

'The wife didn't seem to know Jennings or Coffey either,' Kennedy added. 'She'd heard of Coffey, of course, but didn't know him personally. Says Johnny didn't know either of them.'

Reilly was thoughtful. 'You mentioned something yesterday,' she said to Chris, 'about punishment. And I can't help wondering if this is what it all comes down to. He is punishing them, and in a very specific way. But for what? Never mind why such a manner.'

'Well, Coffey's wife is convinced that his death

173

has something to do with his work, rather than his affairs. Maybe if Coffey was a gun for hire, ready to dish the dirt on anyone for the right price, and someone didn't like what he wrote . . .' Kennedy slurped his pint. 'We know the guy could be vicious, and he went after a lot of high-profile people. That's an easy way to make enemies and piss people off.'

'Still,' Chris said, 'it's a big leap from making enemies to having someone stuff you in your own septic tank.'

'And while both Crowe and Coffey clearly made enemies and plenty of them,' Reilly continued, 'the care and planning involved in these killings, these punishments—'

'Not to mention the way they were killed,' Chris interjected.

'Yes – Jennings especially – all point to a more meticulous killer.'

Reilly looked at both of the detectives. 'This couldn't be someone who simply got the hump over an article in the newspaper, or a speeding ticket from Crowe.'

'Or that Jennings charged him sixty euro for a prescription and told him to come back next week if he wasn't feeling better,' Kennedy added dourly.

'There's something more, something bigger,' she said, trying to figure out what these men could have done to deserve such a graphic form of punishment. 'There's something familiar, symbolic even, about the posing, too. I just can't figure out what.'

Reilly looked levelly at them, biding her time before she told them the rest. 'Which brings me to the next item on the agenda. I just had a meeting with Gorman.' Despite his initial misgivings, the older GFU investigator was on side once Reilly had pointed out the common evidence, and he'd duly updated Inspector O'Brien on their findings. 'He reckons the top brass are mulling over bringing a profiler in.'

'For football's sake . . . !' Kennedy was instantly on full alert, his fleshy face turning red. 'Not your FBI mate again, flying in and flouncing around like he's the greatest thing since sliced bread. Anyway, I thought he was retiring?'

Unable to resist a smile at Kennedy's description of her former mentor who she was sure would be tickled pink by the observation, Reilly shook her head. 'He is, and there's no question of that. Daniel only came over last time to keep an eye on me, you know that now.'

'Still . . .'

'Who's O'Brien thinking of bringing in?' Chris asked. 'Someone from the UK?' As the Irish force didn't have a behavioral unit, they sometimes worked with psychology specialists from Scotland Yard if a case required such input.

'Yes, and I told Gorman that I agreed. These murders are well beyond our range of expertise – the deliberate staging, religious overtones . . .'

175

Kennedy was almost spitting blood. 'Jesus, I hate those fuckers, always so smug, smarmy and up their own arses.'

Chris nodded thoughtfully. 'I agree, though. This case is going to need that kind of intervention sooner or later.'

'Yeah, well, I'd sooner it was later.' His partner drained his pint, stood up, and hitched up his trousers. 'I need another. Reilly, same again?'

'I'm really not staying . . .'

He gave her a look. 'No way, missy. You don't come in here, drop this bombshell, then just bloody walk out.'

She smiled. 'OK, you win – on the drink at least.'

Kennedy waddled off to the bar, and Reilly turned to Chris. 'What *are* those guys like? The ones from Scotland Yard, I mean?'

Chris raised an eyebrow. 'Pretty much exactly how Kennedy just described them: smug, smarmy and—'

'Up their own asses, I get it. Still, we need every bit of help we can get.'

A drink appeared on the table in front of her and Kennedy sat down heavily, handed Chris his pint, and set his own down on the stained wooden table. 'Help, yes. From those guys, no.' He drank deeply from his beer.

Reilly could see she was at an impasse. She picked up her drink, rolled the ice cubes around. They clinked gently against the side of the glass

176

as she raised it to her mouth. Then she gulped and immediately went to spit it out. 'Hey, what the hell did you put in here? I thought I said just a soda.'

Kennedy shoved his pint against Reilly's small glass. 'You can't sit in an Irish pub and not drink alcohol. It's the law.'

CHAPTER 19

Two days later, the task force consisting of Reilly from the GFU and Chris and Kennedy from Serious Crimes, assembled at Harcourt Street Station where Inspector O'Brien had scheduled another briefing.

Chris looked up wearily from his desk as Reilly approached with her quick, neat steps, her walk betraying much of her personality – controlled, disciplined, always slightly on her guard, aware that people were watching her.

Utterly different from the woman he'd seen ride a surfboard with wild abandon, her blond hair wet and plastered to her face as she attempted to conquer the kind of waves that would give the bravest man jitters. Despite Reilly's best efforts, surfing still wasn't one of Chris's strengths, but he wouldn't mind giving it another try when they both had some free time. The way things were going currently, this was unlikely.

He stood up and pulled a chair over from an empty desk. Reilly removed her coat and sat elegantly, crossing her legs. In the harsh light of the fluorescent strip lights he noticed that her eyes

178

looked tired. The strain was starting to take its toll on all of them.

'Rightio,' said Kennedy, 'if we're being gentlemanly I suppose I'd better organize the coffees.' He stood up, and shouted across the open-plan office, 'Hey, you, skulking in your cubby. Jenkins, isn't it?'

A pimply-faced young officer popped up from behind one of the cubbyholes, an eager expression on his face. 'Yes, sir?'

Kennedy grinned broadly. 'Don't you love it? He calls me sir.' He turned back to Jenkins. 'Three coffees, please – you know by now how we like 'em.'

Jenkins saw Reilly sitting with the detectives and his face flushed a little. 'Of course . . . pleasure . . .' He scurried out from his cubicle, and headed toward the coffee machine.

'Is that really part of his job description?' Reilly asked.

Kennedy grinned. 'Coffee, sandwiches, shoe cleaning . . . he'll do the whole lot now he knows *you're* around!'

She smiled uncomfortably.

Chris leaned forward. 'So now that we're all here . . .' he indicated down the hallway to the conference room, '. . . anything new for O'Brien? As far as I'm concerned this whole thing is still going nowhere.'

'Mr Optimistic,' Kennedy said. 'Maybe our blue-eyed boy from the UK will help us out,' he added, glowering. 'Word is, someone flew in this morning. Chances are that's why O'Brien called us in today. Wants us all lined up like good boys and girls to greet the new class pupil.'

Just then Jenkins arrived with their coffees, doing his best to avoid staring at Reilly.

'Good man, set 'em down here,' Kennedy commanded, pointing toward the edge of the desk.

The younger officer did as he was bid, but handed the third cup to Reilly directly. 'Here you are, Miss Steel. Black, no sugar, the way you like it.'

She took the coffee, and gave him the benefit of her best Californian smile. 'That's right. Thank you very much.'

He flushed brightly before hurrying away.

'Why so suspicious?' Reilly asked Kennedy. 'He could be great. Or she, even.'

Chris couldn't help but grin. 'Jesus, do you want to give him a heart attack altogether? It took him long enough to get used to having you around.'

'You're telling me.' She rolled her eyes. 'I don't know,' she added mischievously, 'I quite like the idea of another girl to even things up around here.'

'I give up,' Kennedy said, standing up and bringing his paper coffee cup with him. 'Come on – O'Brien's waiting. Let's get this over with.'

They were barely through the door of the conference room before Inspector O'Brien started the introductions. 'Meet Reuben Knight from the Scotland Yard Behavioural Unit,' he said, before introducing each of the task force members in turn.

Reilly's first impression was that the profiler was undeniably attractive, in that well-bred, English gentry kind of way, being clean-cut, tall and slim. Reuben Knight's build was similar to Chris's, but with a more refined fitness to it, and she guessed he was slightly older too, perhaps mid-forties.

He was dressed in a dark green corduroy suit, an extravagantly patterned silk scarf around his neck. It was something that might look ridiculous on another man, yet Knight carried it off perfectly. His hair was set with a Superman-style quiff at the front, his nails clearly saw the regular service of a manicurist, and as he moved across the room to greet them, he trailed the scent of high-end aftershave behind him.

'Ah, the dynamic trio . . . So pleased to meet you,' he said, unleashing a thousand-kilowatt smile that put Reilly's best Californian grin in the shade. He turned and looked directly at her. 'And the famous Ms Steel, or should I say infamous?' he added cryptically, while Reilly tried to figure out what he was referring to, hoping it was merely her professional reputation. The guy was blissfully unaware of the reaction his impending arrival had been getting, and while she returned his effusive handshake, she noticed how Chris and Kennedy both took their time sizing him up before acknowledging him.

'How's it going?' Chris said eventually, while Kennedy just nodded stiffly and continued to look suspicious.

Greetings dispensed with, Reuben flung himself down into an empty chair in the large conference room – at the head of the table, Reilly noted – and looked around.

'Let's get this over with,' O'Brien commanded. 'Now we all know why Mr Knight is here, don't we? To help us get on with catching the madman who's giving us sleepless nights.'

'Indeed.' Reuben inched his chair closer to Reilly's. 'I know it's ungentlemanly to say so,' he muttered softly, 'but I couldn't help but notice the dark circles beneath those iridescent blue eyes.'

She shifted in her seat. 'Erm, thanks, I think.'

'Steel, can you give Mr Knight an overview of the investigation so far?' O'Brien directed.

'Of course.' She withdrew her laptop from its case and set about connecting it to the overhead projector.

'Wait just a moment.' Reuben quickly patted down his jacket. Then reaching beneath his chair, he picked up a leather Mulberry manbag and began rummaging through it. Reilly saw Chris and Kennedy exchange glances.

'Need a pen?' she asked, handing him a plastic Bic.

Reuben looked at it as if she'd just offered him a stick of dynamite. 'No, thank you, I'm sure my Mont Blanc is in here somewhere . . .' He continued

182

to search for a little while longer until finally locating the elusive fountain pen, a look of deep satisfaction on his face as he produced it. 'Aha, here we are.' He nodded at Reilly. 'Please proceed.'

She turned to her laptop, and tapped the mouse to bring the screen to life. A photograph appeared on the screen at the far end of the room – Crowe, frozen solid in a bath full of ice. His face was flecked with white, arms resting on the sides of the bath as though he was relaxing at the end of a hard day.

Reuben grimaced. 'Oh my goodness, that's awful, unforgivable . . . Why on earth would anyone think of wearing a turtleneck with that jacket?'

'You might want to show a little respect there,' Kennedy scowled. 'Crowe was an ex-cop, an old friend.'

The profiler raised an eyebrow. 'Well, I suppose that explains the awful dress sense then,' he added, and Reilly glanced toward O'Brien, wondering what the older cop was making of Knight. However, the chief seemed unaffected by the profiler's comments, and was obviously much more interested in making headway in the investigation.

Knight was certainly like no profiler she'd ever met before. Most of them, like Daniel, were more solemn, brooding types, whereas Reuben seemed as flamboyant as a Mardi Gras parade.

She smiled to herself. This guy and Kennedy . . . it was bound to be fun.

They all turned back to look at the screen. A

succession of shots of the abandoned meat-packing plant scrolled across it: the skeletal machinery, the dusty floors. Reuben scribbled some notes on a pad as he watched the photos. 'Any idea how the killer got him in the bathtub?'

Reilly shook her head. 'Not for sure, but I have a theory.'

'Do tell,' Reuben smiled winningly at her, and winked. 'I hear you have great ideas.'

'The second victim—'

'Wait!' He held up an imperious hand. 'I only want to hear about one victim at a time. Just tell me what you think happened to this . . .' he peered down at his notes, '. . . this Crowe.'

Reilly nodded. 'OK. As you can see, he was a big guy – at least seventeen stone – so it would have been quite a struggle to get him in there.'

Reuben nodded, and gestured for her to continue.

'We found some wheel tracks in the dust at the plant, leading from the back door to the freezer room. I believe Crowe was bound with duct tape, then wheeled in on a trolley – like the loading trolleys delivery men and house movers use.'

'Good find, Steel,' O'Brien put in.

'Yes. Genius,' Reuben agreed, but Reilly couldn't be sure if he meant it or was merely poking fun at her observations. He scribbled some more notes, then looked up again. 'Then the killer dumped him in the bath, filled it with water, and left him to freeze to death?'

'That's what it looks like.'

He nodded, wrote something else. 'Tell me about the plant. How long had it been closed?'

'Ten years,' Chris said.

Reuben turned his gaze toward him. 'Ah, Detective Delaney. A "just the facts" detective, I take it?' He thought for a moment. 'Tell me, Detective, was the power to the building switched off?'

Chris nodded. 'Apparently so.'

'So the killer had to reconnect the power in order to get the freezer working?'

'Yes.'

'Quite a lot of work . . .' He gazed at his notes for a moment. 'And I suppose that when the body was found, every light in the building had been turned on?'

Kennedy scowled at him, suspicious. 'How did you know that?'

Reuben gave an unctuous smile. 'I deduced it by thinking, Detective Kennedy. You should try it.' Reilly's mouth dropped open, and just when she expected Kennedy to launch himself at Reuben, he turned back to her. 'OK, bored with number one. What about the second one?'

'Ah . . .' She hesitated distractedly, waiting for Kennedy or even Chris to kick off – she guessed they were both silently fuming at Knight – but the presence of O'Brien seemed to be keeping them in check. She guessed that the profiler didn't actually intend to be disrespectful; it was merely another facet of his rather strange character. Ironic

185

that those who were experts on the technical aspects of human psychology often had little grasp of the most basic social niceties.

'The second victim was an investigative journalist, Tony Coffey,' she told him.

'Show me.'

The picture on the screen changed – images of the abandoned building replaced by Coffey's bloated, purple face, floating on a bed of brown effluent.

'Ugh, even more disgusting than the first one,' Knight shrieked, aghast. 'Where was this?'

'Family home, septic tank,' Kennedy informed him flatly. 'Drowned in his own shite, how about that?' He clearly took relish in Knight's expression of disgust as he looked at the picture of Coffey's bloated corpse.

Reilly tapped her laptop again. Coffey's face was replaced by several shots of the house, the garden, and the turned-over ground around the septic tank.

Reuben resumed writing, then looked briefly at Reilly. 'Secluded rural location?'

She nodded.

'And he was missing for a couple of days before the body was dumped?'

'Two days,' Reilly informed him. 'But no one knew because he was supposed to be away on a business trip.'

Reuben made another scribble. 'And the day the body was . . . deposited in the septic tank – where was everyone, the family, whoever?'

'Wife was at her regular Wednesday afternoon bridge club, the PA has Wednesdays off,' answered Chris.

Reuben thought for a moment. 'So everything was very predictable, everyone kept to their schedule, and the house was empty?'

'That's about the sum of it.'

'Again, the killer made sure he was found quickly,' Reilly said, explaining about the pipe blockage in the tank, although she decided not to mention iSPI's assistance in helping her uncover this. Something told her Reuben wouldn't be impressed.

Reuben nodded thoughtfully. 'What about the bobby?' he asked. 'How long from his disappearance until the body was discovered?'

'We're not sure about Crowe,' Chris admitted. 'The wife said he came and went at odd hours; she often didn't know when he'd be back.'

'But she hadn't seen him for a day or two when he turned up dead?'

Chris nodded. 'Right.'

'Show me the third one.'

Reilly obliged, shuddering afresh at the grim tableau that was Dr George Jennings hung from a hawthorn tree with his innards hanging out. Reuben Knight seemed suitably affected too.

'We think the perpetrator used a hoist to get him up there, then slashed open his torso and let the crows and magpies do the rest.'

'Magpies?' Reuben looked pensive, and Reilly looked at him.

'Yes, is that significant?'

He nodded slowly. 'Perhaps, perhaps, but let's not run away with ourselves just yet. First, just let me observe – digest, if you will – these first broad-stroke impressions.'

The room fell silent as Reuben sat there, and Reilly resisted the urge to smile. This guy really was something.

Finally Kennedy spoke up. 'We're still working on the idea that all the killings may be connected but—'

Reuben gave him a look that was beyond condescending; it was almost one of pity. 'My dear Detective, they are as inextricably connected as Tristan and Isolde, as Anna Karenina and Count Vronsky, as—'

Kennedy stared back, baffled. 'Who?'

The profiler gave a deep sigh, as again Reilly tried to stifle a grin. 'Never mind . . . Yes, Detective, the killer is definitely one and the same person.'

Kennedy furrowed his brows. He wasn't going to give up without a fight. 'How can you be so sure?'

'How can I be sure?' Reuben looked almost insulted. He raised an eyebrow and turned again to Reilly. 'Ms Steel, tell me your brain is as sharp as your looks are exquisite.'

Ignoring his flattery, she nodded slowly. 'Meticulously planned murders, no effort too great, lots of research on the victims needed, the method of dispatch excessive, grotesque even? And in all three instances he ensured the body was found quickly after the murder.'

Reuben gave a little round of mock applause. 'Bravo for the lady in the very sexy McQueen skirt.' He gave her a little wink that made her skin break out with goosebumps, and then turned back to look at the others. 'Gentlemen, we do indeed have a serial killer in our midst.'

He leaned forward, his eyes fixed on a point in the ceiling, gently stroking one hand across the other, as though conducting an imaginary orchestra in his head.

Despite herself, Reilly couldn't take her eyes off of him.

He rolled the cap back onto his fountain pen, and slipped it into the inside pocket of his jacket. 'He has struck three times, but there will be more, I'll wager.' He paused for a moment, making sure his audience were coming along with him. 'These are intricately planned murders, all calling out for attention. He wants us to know he's killing these people.'

'But does he want to be caught?' O'Brien grunted.

'Good point.' Chris sat forward. 'These guys enjoy their games of hide-and-seek, don't they?'

Reuben gave Chris a gentle smile, the kind you give to a child when they have made a good effort to master something that's way over their heads. 'Don't believe everything you watch on TV, O Brooding One.' He sighed. 'If he wants to kill more people, do you really think that he wants to be caught?'

Reilly could tell that Chris was quietly seething. *O Brooding One?* Priceless!

'What he wants us to figure out,' Reuben explained patiently, oblivious to the daggers look Chris was giving him, 'is *why* he's killing these people. And the clue to that will come from . . .?' He left the question hanging, like an encouraging teacher trying to bring the class along with him.

'The extravagant way he's killed them?' Kennedy offered.

Reuben turned a beaming smile on him. 'Bravo, Detective.'

'In each case, he's kept the victims for a time before killing them,' Reilly put in. 'Any particular reason why he'd do that?'

'Miss Steel, your reputation does indeed precede you.' He turned his smile on all of them. 'Why indeed is our man keeping his victims for a while? What does he want from them?'

'Maybe he wants them to suffer before he kills them,' Chris said, and to Reilly it sounded like he was gritting his teeth as he spoke.

Reuben shrugged. 'It's possible. Were there any signs of physical torture?'

She shook her head.

'Psychological torture then,' Chris said.

'Letting them understand their predicament, lording his power over them? That's possible, Detective Delaney.' Reuben scratched thoughtfully at his chin. 'But I think there's more than that.'

'Such as?'

190

'That's his little secret right now and what *we* have to try and figure out.' He stood suddenly, picked up his notepad, carefully buttoned his jacket and straightened his scarf. 'This has been truly educational for you all, I'm sure, but I'm afraid I have to be on my way – I've got a hotel to check into. My dear man, will you get copies of these files sent over as soon as possible, please?' he said, addressing Inspector O'Brien as if he were the hired help rather than the most senior person in the room.

Reuben turned and headed for the door, then paused with one hand on the handle. 'Be warned, it won't be long until he strikes again. I think he's working quickly, working his way down a list of some sort. The only way to get ahead of him is to figure out the link between the victims.' He opened the door, smiled brightly at the three of them. 'And that, my dears, is what we are paid to do.'

Reuben flounced out of the room, the scent of his aftershave lingering heavily behind him. *Tom Ford*, Reilly noted distractedly.

She turned back to look at the detectives and O'Brien, expecting them all to be affronted by Knight's behavior. But, much to her surprise, they burst out laughing.

'I take it all back,' Kennedy chuckled. 'Working with this peacock should be a right barrel of laughs . . .'

CHAPTER 20

Alan Fitzpatrick was not a man who usually felt fear. As a former trade union leader he had come to politics the hard way, working his way up from the shop floor to the negotiating table and then on to local issues. Having served his time as a local councillor, he made his way into government, and found that the wheeling and dealing that had served him so well in his former careers were even more of an asset there. He quickly became one of his party's go-to men when difficult deals needed to be made, and was someone who had a reputation for getting anything done if the price was right.

In keeping with his carefully groomed image as a man of the people Fitzpatrick liked to dress down, preferring an open-necked shirt and sweater for everything but the most formal of occasions. He had lost count of how many times little old ladies had patted his arm and told him how much they trusted him at his local constituency surgeries – 'not like those other fancy Dans up in Dublin with their expensive suits'.

Right now, however, his open-necked shirt and

light gray sweater were soaked with blood. It oozed from a nasty gash on his head, and ran down the side of his face, neck, and onto his clothes.

'Head wounds do bleed quite profusely,' the other man in the room said in a soft voice. 'But don't worry – there's no danger of you dying from that little scrape.'

Fitzpatrick looked around, trying to figure out where he was, and how he might get out of this. He was in an old barn, long abandoned. There were several stalls along one side, but it was the feeding trough that kept drawing his eyes, the trough and the drum of hot tar that the man stood over, stirring slowly with a long stick. The flame beneath it was gradually warming it, making it more and more liquid, easier to work with, easier to pour.

'What's that for?' demanded Fitzpatrick. 'If you're planning on reroofing this place you'll need a lot more than that.'

The man still had his back to him. 'Don't you worry, Mr Fitzpatrick, I have more than enough for my purpose.'

Fitzpatrick squirmed in his chair, strained against his binds, but he was securely tied. There was no chance of getting away. 'So what's this all about, anyway? Who are you? What do you want from me? No one will pay you a ransom, you know.'

The room was lit only by the glow of the flame beneath the oil drum. 'Let's just say I'm an old acquaintance – one of the many faceless people you have wronged in your time.'

'Wronged? What are you talking about? I've never wronged—'

'No? You don't think anybody suffered from your deals and bribes and backhanders?'

'What are you talking about? Who the hell are you? Show me your face!' demanded Fitzpatrick, his features turning red with anger as he struggled against his binds.

The man gave a quiet laugh. 'Oh, no, I can't do that. You wronged me without ever knowing I existed. Now you can make it right under the same conditions.'

Fitzpatrick stared at the man's back. 'But how can I fix anything, *do* anything to help you, if I don't know who you are?'

The man turned round, pointed the stick at Fitzpatrick, hot tar dripping from it onto the floor. 'By being a good boy and doing what you are told.' Just for a second it seemed he was angry, but he immediately calmed himself. He dropped the stick back into the barrel of pitch, then walked to a video camera on a tripod and switched on a bright spotlight that stood beside it.

Fitzpatrick flinched, and blinked as the bright light glared into his face. 'What are you . . . what are you going to do now?' he asked nervously.

The man checked the camera and approached Fitzpatrick. He was tall, his long shadow running high up the wall in the glare of the spotlight. 'It's not what I'm going to do. It's what you are going to do.' He held a damp cloth in his hand, and

194

began gently to wipe the blood from Fitzpatrick's face.

At the first touch Fitzpatrick pulled away in fear, but when he realized what the other man was doing he calmed down, and held still while the blood was slowly cleaned from his face and neck. He looked up, trying to catch a glimpse of the man's face, but with the glare of the light in his eyes, he could see nothing.

'That's good enough.' The man threw the cloth down and inspected his handiwork. 'You'll do.' He stepped back behind the camera. 'Now, it's time for you to do what you do best, Mr Fitzpatrick – talk.'

Fitzpatrick looked confused. 'Talk? About what?'

He could feel the sweat beading on his forehead, running down his face. It stung where it trickled into the wound on the side of his head. 'I don't know what you—'

'You used your influence to affect the outcome of a recent parole board hearing.' The statement was delivered in a calm, flat voice, but was all the more chilling for the sudden change in tone.

Fitzpatrick tried to bluster. 'The parole board is an independent body—'

'That you paid off to ensure that a prisoner was released.' The voice was harsh, challenging. There was no mistaking the threat and venom in it.

Fitzpatrick stared defiantly at the camera, blinked through the sweat as it ran into his eyes. 'You can't prove that,' he said finally.

The other man continued softly, 'No, I can't. But you can.' He turned the camera on. 'Tell the truth.'

Fitzpatrick stared back. 'No way. You're full of bluster. Even if it was true – which it isn't – you can't make me confess to it.'

The man gave a deep sigh. 'I wish you would just make this easy, for both our sakes.'

Fitzpatrick snarled at him. 'I've got nothing to say to you or your fucking camera!'

'Very well.' Leaving the camera still running, the man stepped over to the trough of boiling pitch. He gently took hold of the stick, rolled it around until it was covered with the thick, boiling liquid, and walked back across to where Fitzpatrick sat struggling against the tape that bound him. 'Are you sure you won't reconsider?'

Fitzpatrick stared up at him, defiance etched across his shrewish face. 'Fuck you.'

The man slowly lifted the stick, held it above Fitzpatrick's face, and watched impassively as the boiling pitch trickled down, beaded at the end, then dripped in thick, glutinous drops onto Fitzpatrick's cheek as he struggled.

The scream filled the small barn, a ragged cry of fear and pain that was repeated as the burning pitch continued its slow drip, drip, drip . . .

'Do you know, I think Knight would be the kind to dance on your grave after you were dead,' Kennedy muttered. 'And what sort of a name is Reuben, anyway?'

196

Reilly couldn't help but smile, despite being tired and stretched thin by her workload. 'You really have a thing against psychologists, don't you?' she laughed. 'Why? Are you worried he might get inside your head, get to the bottom of what's really going on in there?'

'Huh, you might like him a lot less if he wasn't always making eyes at you.' Kennedy repositioned himself in his seat. 'Jaysus, my back really aches. I fell asleep on the couch in front of the telly last night. Josie said she tried to wake me but I was out cold.'

'She should have put you over her shoulder and carried you to bed.' Chris nudged open the door of the conference room, and set a tray of coffees on the table. 'Then again, she'd probably need a forklift to do that.' He handed a cup to each of his colleagues, and set one in front of his own seat, before putting the fourth in front of a vacant chair. 'So have we heard from Prince Charmless yet? He called this meeting, the least he could do is be on time.'

'Punctuality is boring, and soooo predictable,' Reuben announced, breezing into the room. He slipped into a seat beside Reilly. 'Especially ravishing this morning, my dear.'

'Actually, I thought punctuality was supposed to be the politeness of princes,' Kennedy piped up.

Reuben raised an eyebrow. 'You mean to tell me you can actually read, Detective Dinosaur?'

'Hey—'

Reuben picked up his cup and peered into it. 'Ugh! Coffee? How disgustingly American.' He set the cup down and continued without pausing for breath. 'The actual quote is *"L'exactitude est la politesse des rois."* Punctuality is the politeness of kings. It's attributed to Louis XVIII. He was a king of France, in case you're wondering.'

Kennedy took a quiet sip of his coffee. 'Nope, if anything I was wondering how you get through each day without someone punching your lights out.'

Reuben flashed his most ingratiating smile. 'Must be all down to my effortless charm – isn't that right, Miss Steel?'

'Testosterone versus aftershave – does anyone mind if I open a window? It's getting kinda hard to breathe in here . . .'

Chris pointedly clattered his cup down on the table. 'You called this meeting, Knight, said you had a breakthrough for us?'

Reilly looked up quickly, studying Chris's strained face and the dark circles under his eyes. Yes, their workload was punishing, but she couldn't help but wonder if there was something else going on with him at the moment. Typically good-humored, now he seemed testy. And it certainly wasn't like him to be rude.

Completely unaffected, Reuben nodded, the smile still on his face. 'And I do, I do.' He glanced mournfully around. 'I don't suppose there's any chance of a cup of decent Earl Grey?'

'Nope, no chance at all,' Chris replied impatiently. 'So what's this amazing breakthrough you think you've made?'

Reuben looked at him in horror. 'Think? *Think?* My dear man, I don't merely think. I—'

'Ah, will you just get on with it,' Chris commanded roughly.

Reuben gave him a huffy look, before turning and addressing Reilly instead.

'I was thinking, my dear, about one man found drowned in his own excrement, another frozen to death encased in ice, and a third hanged on a tree and feasted upon by birds. If they were each the work of the same man – which I believe they are – what is that person thinking? What is he trying to tell us? There's got to be a message, something behind such macabre methods. So what is the theme that unites such disparate—'

'Cut to the bloody chase,' Kennedy growled, having long since run out of patience. 'Some of us have work to do.'

Reilly thought she had better intervene to smooth the waters. 'I'm sure any insights you have would be helpful, Reuben. What can you tell us?'

'Give me just one moment.' He reached into his pocket and withdrew his fountain pen. 'Ah, here we are,' he continued, looking lovingly at the pen as if it was some kind of talisman. 'Well, from the outset, the elaborate tableaux and high classical elements immediately suggested that we were dealing with an artist of some kind, someone gifted

199

with a consuming creative fire, and unbalanced by the banal evil of the world around them.'

'Rightio . . .' Kennedy looked at him blankly.

'A vigilante?' Reilly said. 'Yes, we'd considered that. Well, the punishment aspect, at least.'

Chris was immediately dubious. 'We're blue in the face from working the revenge angle on Coffey. Granted Crowe would have had an enemy or two, but Jennings?'

An in-depth search of the doctor's background and connections had turned up nothing untoward, at least nothing that would make him the target for such a violent death.

'Yes, but these aren't your run-of-the-mill revenge killings; this is something on a higher plane, a work of art, if you will,' Reuben continued, waving his beloved pen in the air. 'Our killer is undoubtedly well read, obviously highly agile, and will have a very domineering demeanor; will appear to be an definitive alpha male to those around him. There will have been a trigger, a recent event that acted as a significant stressor for our man and set him off on his destructive path.'

He paused for dramatic effect. 'My belief is that we're dealing with someone who is fashioning for themselves the very thing they see lacking in the moral architecture of this world, but which they have found in the fantastical world of a medieval manuscript.'

Reilly's head shot up. 'Medieval manuscript? You're thinking he has some kind of blueprint for this?'

Yet all along the theatrical setup of the manner of death for all three killings had been niggling at her. She'd sensed the symbolism was familiar. Had she seen . . . read about such a setup before?

'Absolutely.' Reuben paused once again to heighten expectation. 'I believe our killer is casting himself in the role of Minos, one who judges and dispenses the divine retributive justice of *The Divine Comedy.*'

Reilly gasped. 'Dante . . . of course . . .'

And all of sudden, everything began to make sense.

CHAPTER 21

'Dan who?' Kennedy asked.

'Dante Alighieri. The author of a famous medieval poem called *The Divine Comedy*,' Reuben explained. 'The part called *Inferno* is about a journey through Hell. There are nine different levels, and in each one, sinners are punished in various ways for various sins. OK . . .' He picked up a nearby cup and went to take a sip, then remembered it was coffee. He set it down quickly and turned back to the team. 'Let me explain further. The *Inferno* opens with a description of the process of judgement, whereby souls are categorized according to their particular transgression, judged and sentenced to their allotted place in perdition. Responsibility for this awesome task fell on the shoulders of a mythical demi-god known as Minos, who is often represented in the poem as a humanoid somewhere between a Minotaur and the sea god Neptune. As I said, I believe our killer is casting himself in this role.'

'Huh. Doesn't sound like much of a comedy to me,' Kennedy commented.

'A common misconception, my good man. The

conventions of fourteenth-century Italian literature required that works be sorted into two major groups: tragedy, high literature; and comedy, low literature. Tragedy was written in formal Italian and did not end well for the protagonists – there was no happy ending. Comedy, on the other hand, was written in the local dialect, or vernacular language – the Florentine Tuscan dialect, in this instance – and typically had a happy ending. Dante, as a political statement in a time of great local upheaval, used the common Florentine Tuscan dialect to write what he then called simply *The Comedy*. So because the work ends with the highest achievement of the ultimate level of heaven, it has, of course, a happy ending. Common language and a happy ending therefore met the contemporary literary definition of "comedy".'

'Right.'

'Coffey was a journalist,' Reilly spoke quickly, her words trying to keep up with her brain, as all at once the pieces began falling into place. She'd studied Dante's *Inferno* at college and had a half-decent recollection of it. 'He used words to exploit people. In one of the circles, flatterers are steeped in human excrement – Coffey was dumped into his own septic tank . . .'

'The Eighth Circle, Bolgia Two, to be precise.' Reuben continued. 'Steeped alive in their own excrement, which is supposed to represent the filthy lucres with which their tongues polluted the world.'

'Or just, journalists are full of shit?' Kennedy said, putting it somewhat more succinctly.

Reuben gave him a dismissive look. 'Now the policeman. When we apply the same coding scheme to your friend Mr Crowe, the second victim, we get round one of the Ninth Circle, or Caïna. In this mythical realm, those who betrayed their state were frozen in ice up to their faces. So yes, the number fits the punishment, but does the punishment fit the "crime"? Is the killer trying to intimate that the trusty policeman was somehow traitorous to the people of the state?'

Chris looked at Kennedy. 'That guy Ivan was right. Crowe must have been taking kickbacks.'

'Maybe. This guy certainly figured he was up to something,' he replied. 'We'll get on to it, talk to Maggie again.'

Reilly fixed Reuben with a quizzical expression. 'What about the doctor? What was his transgression?'

'It seems this too has yet to be discerned, but, again, the manner of death should give us some clue. The Seventh Circle has three rings, the middle one inhabited by the suicides. According to Dante, these poor souls are transformed into thorny bushes and fed upon by harpies, winged spirits that are half woman, half magpie. We had birds feasting on the corpse in the hawthorn tree. I'll wager that this is the scene the killer was attempting to evoke.'

'Meaning that Jennings actually killed himself?'

Chris was confused with how the explanation was unfolding.

'No,' Reilly replied. 'We know from the ME that he was put there alive, and I doubt he would have slashed his own torso.'

'So was our good doctor actually a bad one?' Reuben wondered. 'Maybe a little too willing to help distressed patients shuffle off this mortal coil?'

'It's an angle, if nothing else,' Chris admitted reluctantly. 'We'll put in a request to see if we can get access to his disciplinary record. Maybe it might help shine some light on anything like that.'

Reilly shuddered, remembering all the times she'd considered how irreparably morally damaged the human race could be, and how much easier it would be if God acted as a punisher, and just stood up and started punishing sinners. Now some lunatic was taking that very calling to heart, taking it upon himself to be the punisher. But instead of finding it reassuring, she found it bone-chilling.

'So what's the pattern?' Chris asked, as though expecting further explanation. 'OK, so you say they're all connected to this poem. But what's their connection to each other? I mean, there are shysters and criminals all over the place. Why single out these guys for punishment, and why this way? There's more than just the poem in the message the perpetrator's sending us. It's got to be deeper.'

Reilly shook her head. 'Deeper, Chris? I think it's pretty deep already, isn't it?'

'No,' Reuben replied with a sideways glance at Chris. 'It isn't very deep at all. Actually, it's ridiculously shallow. Detective Delaney is right. This isn't the real message, it's simply part of the delivery. He needs us to know that this is about the *Inferno*, and that the Circles are somehow important. It's like we've found the bottle, but we still have to smash it open to see the note inside.'

Reilly looked at Reuben. 'Good work on the symbolism. I think you've nailed it.'

'Don't mention it, but I really must go now,' he announced. 'I have important work to do.' Putting his pen in his inside pocket, he buttoned up his jacket, and straightened his tie. 'Naturally, I shall continue to apply my considerable talents to the resolution of this case. Rest assured, though,' he warned, his tone grave, 'there may well be more bodies before you catch this particular perpetrator. A single, dedicated individual, obviously technically adept, who's determined to be judge, jury and executioner for all he considers to be morally compromised.' Reaching the doorway, he flicked his scarf around his neck. 'And if he's styling himself as Minos then I fear he's only just getting started.'

Gary and Lucy both appeared in Reilly's office that afternoon.

Reilly put down the notes she was reading. It had been years since she'd studied the text, so she'd printed out Dante's entire poem from the internet. But it was lengthy and the translation complex, and she wasn't entirely sure what she should be looking for.

She looked up at the lab techs. 'I'm guessing from your faces that you have some good news for me.'

Lucy grinned and nudged Gary. 'Told you she'd guess. When I was a kid my dad always knew exactly what I'd done just from the expression on my face. Still does, actually,' she added wryly.

'Bet that was hell when you'd just had a hot and heavy date,' Gary chuckled.

'Are you insinuating that I was promiscuous?'

He blushed. 'No . . . I just meant—'

Reilly smiled. 'Why don't you two just tell me what's going on, before Gary digs himself an even deeper hole?'

Shooting a mock glare at her colleague, Lucy headed down the corridor while Gary waited to hold the door open for Reilly. 'Cheers, boss,' he whispered as she passed.

'Don't mention it.'

The lab was brightly lit, a faint smell of chemicals in the air. Reilly followed Lucy over to her workbench. 'You were working on the Coffey soil samples again? The ones with the horse feed trace.'

Lucy nodded.

'What did you get?'

The younger woman held up two sheets of paper. 'This is the chemical profile for the soil samples we took – minus the feed trace.' She pointed to

207

the second sheet of paper. 'I referenced it against some soil database samples from around the country. This is the closest match.'

Reilly looked at the two sheets – the spiky lines illustrated the values of certain key organic chemicals in the soil: carbon, hydrogen, oxygen, nitrogen and sulfur. 'That's a pretty close match – where's this sample from?'

'The whole area around Kildare has similar soil.'

Thanks to her rudimentary knowledge of Irish geography, Reilly knew Kildare was an adjoining county within fifteen miles or so of Dublin.

'And even better,' Lucy added enthusiastically, 'Kildare is horseracing country. Lots of studs and horse farms down that way.'

'Interesting.' Another gaping hole in Reilly's grasp of local knowledge.

'I thought I might take a trip down that way soon,' Lucy said. 'Take some comparative samples, and see if I can narrow down the ones we have any further.'

'Good thinking.' She turned to Gary. 'What do you have?'

'Well, I've been examining trace from Jennings' clothes. Take a look at this.' He indicated a slide on the electron microscope.

Reilly held her hair back from her face, bent down and peered through the eyepiece.

'Duct tape is fabric tape with a rubber adhesive for waterproofing,' he explained. 'Of course, these days they use synthetic rubber.' He changed the slide.

'Synthetic rubber is made from the polymerization of a variety of monomers including isoprene, butadiene, chloroprene, and isobutylene.'

Reilly straightened up. 'Where's this from?'

'The sleeve. There were no physical traces, but last night, as we were packing the evidence away I noticed a slight discoloration, a whiter patch on the sleeve. I swabbed it, and bingo.'

Reilly smiled. 'Good work.'

Things were looking up. Now they knew for sure that both Jennings and Coffey had been bound with duct tape – and that their killer probably lived in or worked in stables in the Kildare region. Not forgetting, of course, that he styled himself as some form of medieval vigilante.

Reilly just wished she could figure out the source of that skunk-like smell she'd picked up at the factory and the church tower.

'You definitely don't have skunk or coon in Ireland?' she asked the techs again, despite having been told already that neither species was native to the country.

'Not unless they're kept as household pets,' Gary told her. 'Although I can't see why anyone would want to. Disgusting things.'

Still, the only comparison Reilly could think of for the foul pee scent she'd been getting was skunk spray. Was there a chance their killer was keeping skunk as a pet? Domesticating such animals was common in the US, despite being illegal in the majority of states, but most people who did this usually had the mercaptan-emitting glands removed so as to disable the defensive spray.

Even if the killer didn't do this, how could he not be aware of the pungent odor he was carrying around? Or was he leaving it behind on purpose? Reilly made a mental note to ask Reuben if there was anything symbolic or significant in the *Inferno* about a foul-smelling scent.

Wading her way through the translation of the medieval Italian text, she found it difficult to make sense of it. Her brain was wired for science not literature these days. Interpretations of Dante's allegorical references were varied and many, and she couldn't determine anything that would ultimately help them catch the man who was acting as punisher, or, more importantly, help identify his next victim.

CHAPTER 22

That night, Chris lay wide awake in the darkness, wondering if he was losing it. On his way home from work earlier, he'd passed by a bridal shop and for some reason had stopped outside it, staring mindlessly at the window display – for how long he wasn't sure.

Melanie was getting married at the end of next week.

He tried to pretend he hadn't remembered, or it didn't mean anything to him, but his subconscious wasn't getting the message. He could still clearly visualize that invitation. Lately, when he did manage to sleep, his dreams were fitful, full of images of him and Melanie as they tried – no, Chris corrected, as *he* tried – to piece their lives back together in the aftermath.

Four years earlier

Chris trudged wearily up the path to Melanie's front door. He paused, looked at the overgrown garden, and kicked at the weeds growing by the side of the path. He knew that Melanie expected him to tidy the garden regularly, but when did he have the time? It was weeks since he had slept more than five hours at a stretch, he was so busy at work.

Chris shifted the bag of groceries into his right hand, reached up and rang the bell.

'Who is it?'

How can she sound so nervous, Chris, wondered irritably, when she knows it's me?

'It's Chris,' he replied, his voice strained. He really didn't have the time and patience for this today.

'Chris who?' came the predictable reply.

Deep breath. Play the game. 'Chris Delaney.'

'Show me your ID.'

Chris started to reach into his pocket for his badge, then stopped suddenly. Despite his best efforts, he simply couldn't keep up this charade any longer. 'Mel, it's me – you know it's me, you can see me. Please just let me in.'

There was a long moment of silence. Finally her voice crackled again through the intercom. 'I said, show me your ID.'

Chris sighed, held up his badge. Some battles just weren't worth fighting.

The chains and bolts rattled noisily and the door edged open. Chris squeezed through the gap and into the dark hallway. As he reached the kitchen she turned on him, her slim eyebrows knitted together in consternation.

'What were you thinking, Chris?' she cried. 'You used my name! Anyone could have heard you. Now they'll know my name, they'll know I live here!'

Chris set the bag of groceries on the table, and stared at her back. He couldn't go on like this, couldn't support her paranoia, visit after visit, week after week, year after year. 'Everyone around here knows who you are, Mel. They're your neighbors – of course they know.'

She poured some hot water into the teapot to warm it, emptied it into the sink, then filled it, clearly pretending he hadn't spoken.

Chris tried again. 'You were born here – you've lived here all your life.'

He stared at her mute back. Don't give up, he told himself. Whatever you do, you can't ever give up on her.

'Melanie, if you don't let me help you – let someone help you – you're going to die here too.'

Her reaction was explosive – the teapot flew across the room, just missing Chris's head, and smashed against the wall, sending the hot brown liquid splashing across the floor and staining the wall.

She spun round, and stared at him. 'I watch the news, Chris, I know what's out there!' Her voice was high, on the edge of an hysterical scream. 'You do, too! On the news today, a man was shot, right on his own front step . . .' She searched for the right words. 'That world out there . . . that's where you want me to go?'

He took a step toward her. 'No, I just—'

'You know what it's like out there, better than anyone. You know what people do to each other . . .' Her face was flushed, hands clenched into fists as she tore at her apron.

213

'Honey, I—'

Suddenly the dam burst and she dissolved into sobs, her hands reaching up to cover her eyes. Her body slumped, and she slid down along the kitchen cupboard to sit on the floor, her knees tucked to her chest, arms wrapped tightly around them to protect herself.

Chris crossed the kitchen floor in two strides, sank to his knees and wrapped his arms around her. 'I'm so sorry, I didn't mean to—'

She rocked against him, sobbing raggedly, gasping for breath. Finally she managed to tear a few words out of her gasping throat. 'Don't make me do it, Chris. Don't make me go out there . . . not yet. I'm not ready yet.'

Chris held her close, his face a mask of pain and frustration, his eyes hard and cold. 'Don't worry, I'm right here.'

She clutched at him with desperate hands, almost tearing at his jacket with her thin, bony fingers. 'Don't leave me, don't leave me, don't leave me . . .' She repeated it over and over, like a mantra that could protect her from harm.

Chris sighed, held her tight. 'Don't worry. I promise I'll always be here.'

Later that same night, Reilly, too, lay wide awake, her mind churning. She glanced at the clock beside her bed – the red lights told the story of her insomnia: 2.27.

She rolled over onto her back, closed her eyes

214

and focused on breathing slowly. She had studied yoga for many years, knew enough about breathing techniques and meditation to understand that by controlling her inhalations she could relax and help herself find her way back to sleep.

Take a deep breath in, pause, hold it, empty the mind . . .

She exhaled deeply, breathed in again, and as her breathing slowed she felt herself beginning to relax. Her eyes felt heavier, her limbs began to sink into the bed. Her breaths became slower and deeper, her eyes closed, the lids feeling too heavy to open. A warm wave washed over her, taking her closer and closer to sleep.

Just as she slipped over the edge, a stray thought crossed her mind, an intrusion from deep in her subconscious.

It was too late. Reilly had found sleep, but still her nightmare had found her. She was back in the house – her mother's house – right back where her world had changed, forever. There she was, tiptoeing slowly along the hallway, knowing instinctively that something terrible had happened, but there was no getting away from it, no turning back.

The difference was that this time, Reilly knew well what horrors awaited her. She'd walked this path many times over in her dreams, turned the corner into the kitchen, caught sight of the bloody mess on the floor . . . then her mother, the knife sticking out of her beloved mother's chest. And then her sister, Jess and the expression on her face as—

Reilly's head shot up off the pillow. Her cellphone was ringing, the shrill tone cutting through the darkness and her memories. Her heart pounded, as she stared at the alarm clock. Three fifteen.

'Reilly?' It was Chris and by his weary tone she could guess he wasn't just calling for a chat. 'We've found another one. And if this is punishment, I'd really like to know what this poor guy did to deserve it.'

The location, a farmstead just on the outskirts of the city, wasn't hard to find – the flashing blue lights could be seen from half a mile away. Reilly turned the GFU van into the narrow farm lane, showed her ID to the uniform at the gate, and pulled into the yard.

She climbed from the van, wrapping her coat tightly around her, and pulled the collar up. The driveway was already full: there were a couple of cars from the local station, their blue lights flashing, an ambulance, and Chris's silver Ford.

A sudden squall of rain blasted into her face. Reilly locked the van and picked her way quickly through the puddles toward the barn on the far side of the yard.

A barn . . . horses . . . This wasn't Kildare, but clearly they were on the right track.

There were two uniformed officers outside, the lights from the police cars and ambulance illuminating the doorway.

Reilly hurried into the barn and found a cluster

of people standing just inside. Chris looked round when she entered, and she couldn't help but notice how haggard he looked.

She resolved to try to get him on his own soon – when things calmed down a little – and find out what it was that was making him so jumpy and irritable, the complete opposite of his usual composed, rational self. Was it a return of the pain in his joints, or something more?

She tapped two young uniforms on the shoulder. 'Hey, could you boys move out of the way?'

The men reluctantly stepped outside, and cleared a space that allowed the flashing ambulance lights to shine through the doorway to the back of the old barn, illuminating the scene. Any nighttime chill that Reilly felt was immediately intensified by the sight that greeted her.

A middle-aged man, his face harrowingly contorted in pain, was slumped back against the side of a battered trough – a trough filled with glutinous, shiny black pitch.

'Bloody hell . . .'

Chris nodded slowly. 'Exactly.'

Reilly looked around, her mind racing, the acrid smell of the tar filling her nostrils. 'I need this area cleared. Immediately. '

There was some grumbling from the officers – they preferred being at the sharp end of a good juicy incident – but eventually they shuffled outside into the rain.

Reilly strode across the yard to the van, not

217

bothering to avoid the puddles this time. She needed to examine the place now, as soon as possible, while the scene was still fresh. The smell of hot pitch and the color of the victim's skin had made her realize that this was probably the freshest crime scene of the four. Even accounting for the heat of the tar warming the body, it was obvious that the victim hadn't been dead for long.

She slipped into the back of the van, and wriggled her way into her dustsuit, her mind a mass of questions. There was no doubt that this was again the work of the punisher – the MO was too bizarre to be anybody else – but who was the victim, and what was the crime that led this particular man to be killed in this way? She reached over and grabbed her forensic kit, then took a deep breath to compose herself. Only one way to find out.

When she returned to the barn, Chris and Kennedy were still standing in the doorway, sheltering from the rain, which had become more persistent. The other bystanders had all retreated to their cars. Reilly turned to the detectives. 'When I said I wanted the room cleared, I meant everyone.'

'We were just going,' said Chris. 'We're going to try and find out more about this place – who owns it, when they were last here . . .'

'This scene still seems pretty fresh – it will be good to have a look around in some peace and quiet.' Reilly slipped on her booties and shone her flashlight to the back of the barn. 'Do we have any idea who the vic is?'

Kennedy nodded. 'There we can help you. You're looking at the remains of Alan Fitzpatrick, TD.'

'TD?'

'Member of our government,' Chris explained.

'Are politicians mentioned in that poem?' Kennedy asked.

'Absolutely.' In fact, now that Reilly knew the victim's occupation, she could recognize the reference. '"Barrators immersed in a lake of boiling pitch."' Difficult for the killer to organize a lake of the stuff, so clearly the trough was the next best thing.

Kennedy nodded when Reilly quoted the line to him. 'God knows, it wouldn't be the first time someone thought about boiling one of those lads in oil . . . Where does he go next?'

She shrugged.

'Look, all this Dante stuff is fine and well, but we still don't know the guy's agenda,' Chris added, sounding frustrated.

But Reilly couldn't think about the killer's agenda just then, she was too anxious to get going on the scene.

'You two go and do your thing, talk to people, beat up a couple of suspects, whatever. I'll have a look around here while I wait for the others, and we can compare notes later. Oh, and can you get the local guys to cut the flashers?' she called out as the detectives turned to leave. 'I know they think they're being helpful, but it's actually making it harder for me to focus.'

219

She'd have to make do with her torch until the rest of the team arrived with a lighting rig.

While the detectives hurried out into the rain, Reilly stood still, breathing deeply, relaxing, preparing her mind for the job ahead. She needed to be clear, focused, all her senses alert to whatever she might find.

First she sniffed the air to seek out the foul ammonia-like smell she'd identified before, but the smell of burning tar and flesh completely overpowered everything.

The majority of the emergency vehicle lights were duly switched off, plunging the barn into an inky darkness lit only by the ghostly blue glow of one remaining from the ambulance.

Reilly flicked on her torch, and pulled the barn door closed behind her to block it out. She moved the torch slowly around the room.

It was hard not to be drawn immediately toward Fitzpatrick, set firm in a trough full of black tar, his face an horrific death-mask. Even if their deaths had been violent, most murder victims actually looked quite peaceful, but Fitzpatrick's face bore the full horror of what had been inflicted upon him.

Reilly tore her gaze away, and directed the torch elsewhere. There was plenty of time to look at the victim, but right now she needed to work her way methodically through the room, missing nothing, taking in every detail, no matter how trivial it might seem.

She began right at her feet. There were muddy footprints aplenty, leading from the door to the trough – those of the cops, whoever had found the victim, the usual procession. She sighed. Nothing she could do about that. Move on . . .

Reilly's gaze scanned the room. It was clearly an old tackroom. There was a line of horse stalls along one wall, hooks and nails along the other, and several old halters still hanging there. She sniffed. Even above the smell of tar, and of the scorched flesh, she still got the distinctive aroma of horses, of straw, feces and leather. It wasn't all that long since animals had been kept here.

The walls were bare wood, the floor probably concrete, though it was covered with such a thick layer of dirt and old straw that it was hard to be sure. In fact, everything was what one would expect to find in an old abandoned barn – except the trough full of pitch, and the tar-spattered oil drum beside it.

Straw and dirt, straw and dirt . . . the floor was covered. Reilly opened her kit, pulled out her camera, and slipped a handful of evidence bags in the pocket of her suit.

Slowly, following the beam of her torch, she made her way across to the right side of the room. The beam of light made strange patterns across the floor, light and dark, shadows taking on unusual shapes, oversized, stretching and running up the walls ahead of her.

She moved slowly, taking in everything. Normally

she would be paying closer attention to her nostrils, but, as with the stench from Coffey's septic tank, the acrid smell of pitch and scorched flesh was filling the room, so she was trying her best to disable this particular sense.

Would iSPI be any good here? In truth, now that she'd seen the software in action, Reilly was slightly afraid of it. Working in a virtual world would surely dull the instincts she'd spent so many years honing, dilute the experience of being right there at a murder scene, walking in the killer's shoes. No, much better to save iSPI for the trickier locations.

Not that this one was any walk in the park.

As Reilly approached the wall, she paused. The exaggerated shadows cast by her torch illuminated some strange indentations in the mud and straw. She shone the torch back and forth, trying to find the pattern. One group suddenly revealed themselves to her – four indentations. They looked to be from the legs of a small table, and behind them was a smaller set, deeper, four again – presumably a chair?

Reilly swung her camera round, took several shots from different angles to capture the shadows that revealed where the table and chair had been. She checked the screen quickly. She loved digital cameras – could always make sure she had a good shot. Satisfied, she turned her attention to the other cluster of indentations.

These were smaller, three close together in a small

triangle pattern. Reilly looked at the position –
beside the table – and scrunched her face up in
thought. Suddenly an image popped into her
mind – three small legs, close together. A tripod?
Was the killer taking photos, or perhaps videotaping
the killings?

She quickly snapped another group of photos, a
slight smile on her face.

It was a small detail, but she knew from experi-
ence that, little by little, eventually everything
came together to reveal the bigger picture. Keep
collecting the pieces, and soon the pattern would
be revealed.

The indentations of the table and chair gave her
a good focus for her search – the killer might have
sat at the table, taking photos or a video of his
torture.

Reilly moved on toward the wall, her torch
leading the way, revealing the details that she
would miss without its relentless focus.

As she ran the beam along the base of the wall,
a tiny flash caught her eye. Something bright,
possibly metallic, was hidden in the crack between
the floor and the wall.

She leaned down, and peered closer. Half
hidden beneath the straw was a narrow wooden
cylindrical-type object. A pencil. She carefully
lifted it up by the tip, keeping her gloved hands
away from any possible fingerprints. It was a pale
shade of orange, the initials LFI embossed in silver
on the wood.

Reilly straightened up, thoughtful, and dropped the pencil into an evidence bag. It looked to be good quality, and in pristine condition, which meant it couldn't have been there longer than a couple of weeks . . . days, even.

A sudden flash of inspiration hit her as she remembered the tiny rubber shavings she'd found in the church tower. Those, taken with the pencil, had to mean—

'Have you missed me?' A distinctive plummy male voice cut right through Reilly's concentration.

A young police officer stood in the doorway behind none other than Reuben Knight. 'Sorry, Ms Steel, I tried to keep him out . . .'

The profiler was silhouetted by the vehicle light behind him, the blue casting a blinking ghostly glow over the scene. He was wearing a burgundy jacket with a paisley scarf carefully arranged at his neck, and looked dramatic standing in the doorway, his exuberantly coiffured hair silhouetted by the lights.

'Go on then, flash your torch around and let me see what our little friend has been up to this time,' he requested.

Reilly shook her head in irritation. 'This isn't some freakshow, Reuben. I'm working here.' She stood up and shone her torch directly at his face.

He threw a hand up to block out the blinding light. 'I know that – and for heaven's sake get that blasted light out of my eyes.'

Reilly dropped the beam toward his feet. 'You stay there, in the doorway – I've already had enough people prancing around in here.'

'Of course, of course.' Reuben sounded impatient – impatient and excited. He immediately began rummaging through his pockets, as if looking for his pen, and Reilly idly wondered if there wasn't a touch of OCD about their esteemed profiler.

'It's not a pretty sight . . .' she said, shining her torch toward the back of the room. As she did so, the oil drum, the trough and finally the victim came into view.

Knight gave a sharp intake of breath.

'I warned you,' Reilly said quickly. 'Ugly, isn't it?'

'*Au contraire*, my dear,' he replied breathlessly. 'This . . . this is a work of art.' He took a step forwards, then remembered himself. 'Do you recall your Dante, Reilly?'

She nodded. 'A lake full of pitch – corrupt politicians.'

'Precisely!' He sounded so gleeful, Reilly half expected him to rub his hands together.

'So, what's this all about, Knight?'

They both turned back to the doorway where Chris and Kennedy, who had obviously been made aware of Reuben's arrival, now stood.

'Well, for those of you whose education stopped at puberty . . .' the profiler began, with a mischievous glance toward the detectives, '. . . in the

225

Inferno, Dante wrote that the Eighth Circle, Bolgia Five, was reserved for corrupt politicians. They were immersed in a lake of boiling pitch, which represented the sticky fingers and dark secrets of their corrupt deals.' Reuben dabbled his own fingers in front of him, as though playing in a messy bowl of food.

Chris looked as unimpressed as ever. 'Wonderful. I'm sure Fitzpatrick's family would be delighted to know that you are so gleeful about his demise.'

Knight waved him off. 'Nonsense, Detective. I am merely showing professional respect for a worthy adversary – one, I might add, who is showing a remarkable flair for constructing original crime scenes for his chosen victims.'

Reilly was beginning to realize what an enthusiast Reuben was at heart, despite all the bluster.

Chris looked disgruntled. 'So he's following the script. What does that tell us about him that we don't already know? Will this make it any easier to find him?'

Knight gave him a dismissive look. 'As usual, Detective, no foreplay, always straight to the point. That won't woo the heart of a maiden like Miss Steel, you know.'

Reilly flushed, but before Chris could reply, Knight turned quickly back to her.

'When you spoke just now, there was a definite tremor in your voice. Is it just the thrill of the crime scene, the proximity to the rather over-done Mr Fitzpatrick, or do you have something to share with us?' He coughed. 'Have you found something?'

She was faintly impressed. Knight might be unorthodox but he was good. She nodded in acknowledgement. 'I think I'm getting a better idea of how he works.'

'Please enlighten us.'

Reilly directed her torch to the ground at her feet. 'Over here, there are some clear indentations in the straw.'

'And?'

'I'm thinking that there was a small table here, and possibly a chair.'

Reuben nodded, looking thoughtful. 'So our killer is a voyeur; he likes to sit back, relax and watch his victims die?'

'There's more than that.' Reilly pointed to the floor again. 'Here, there is a smaller set of imprints. I think it could be a tripod, for a camera, maybe a video camera.'

'I see.' Reuben fiddled idly with the fountain pen. 'So not only does he like to watch, he likes to record the details too?'

'Perhaps not just with a camera,' Reilly said, Reuben's comment suddenly putting her recent finds in perspective. 'I picked up some fragments of rubber at the Jennings scene, and here I've found a pencil. I'm now thinking the fragments could perhaps have come from an eraser.' Which indicates that the killer may have been drawing or sketching the Jennings scene in the tower with his pencil. He'd made a mistake, corrected it, and absently brushed the rubber detritus onto the floor, little suspecting that someone would find the almost microscopic traces'.

Knight clapped his hands together, and turned back to the detectives, triumphant. 'What did I tell you? An artist at work, I said!'

'Lucky guess,' Kennedy mumbled.

'Pshaw! No such thing!' Reuben ran his hand across his hair. 'Well, my little investigators, I can see you have a long night ahead of you.' He straightened his scarf. 'I have a date waiting. You continue doing whatever it is you do, and I shall return to my beau. Why don't we reconvene first thing tomorrow? You can tell me what you found here, and I'll present you with a detailed portrait of our killer.'

He flashed Reilly a smile, then pushed past the detectives and back out into the damp night. He unfurled a large umbrella and disappeared across the muddy yard.

'I swear, one of these days I'm going to strangle that guy,' Kennedy growled.

'You'll be easy to catch,' Chris joked. 'Motive, opportunity . . .'

Reilly smiled, absently trying to figure out if Reuben's date was male or female. It was all too easy to assume him gay, but from the way he flirted so relentlessly with her she couldn't be sure.

She rolled her shoulders and neck, tired from both lack of sleep and the intense concentration. 'Are my guys here yet?'

228

Chris nodded. 'Just saw them outside getting changed.'

'Good. I'm itching to have a proper look at the body before the doc gets here. They can finish up the rest of the room.'

She cracked her knuckles, then looked back and forth between the detectives, an impish smile on her face. 'Come, gentlemen, come!' she said imitating Reuben's distinctive manner. 'The game is afoot. Not a word! Into your clothes and come!'

Chris gave her a look of deep suspicion. 'Are you quoting Sherlock Holmes at us?'

Reilly grinned. 'Yep, the night is young, the trail is still hot. This is what we live for, why we do this, right?'

He scowled, and looked outside at the dark, wet night. 'Knocking on doors of unsuspecting neighbors in the middle of the night in the rain? Your trail may be hot, but ours looks distinctly damp.'

'Well, actually I think Reuben is right,' she said, thinking that now that they could recognize the killer's MO, they'd figure out more about him from this scene than the other three put together. 'We are making progress – I can just smell it, can't you?'

Chris turned his collar up, his tone unusually curt. 'At the moment, Reilly, all I can smell is toasted politician and dodgy aftershave.'

CHAPTER 23

Simon Darcy slowed as he approached the turn. The sign at the entrance left no doubt where you were, or what to expect:

Entry Forbidden
Visitors and Authorized Vehicles Only
Beyond This Point

Simon looked outwardly calm, but inside his nerves were jangling.

He drove carefully, taking his time over everything. Finding an empty space at the far end of the car park, he reversed in. He couldn't help but smile – it was almost as if he was planning a quick getaway.

The building loomed overhead, an uninspiring edifice of granite, but the tall red-brick tower and the razor wire surrounding the perimeter betrayed its real purpose. This building was built to contain, incarcerate.

Carrying his briefcase, Simon slowly approached the main door of Mountjoy Prison.

He passed through the first doors, the security barrier ahead. His briefcase went through the scanner, and was subjected to a cursory search. Simon himself went through, and was checked over with a hand scanner.

The guard was tall, middle-aged, a weary expression on his thin face. He recognized Simon. 'Who you seeing today, then?'

'Ricky Webb.'

The guard grunted. 'Good luck with that one – he's a right little shit.'

Simon nodded. 'Thanks for the warning.'

'I can't believe he's getting out,' the guard continued, scowling. 'If I had my way, a little prick like that would never see the light of day again.'

Simon looked sympathetic. 'Oh, well, we'll just have to trust that they all get their just deserts in the end.'

The guard sat back on his metal folding chair, looking at Simon from under the brim of his cap. 'I wouldn't hold my breath on that one.'

The reception desk was behind a thick glass window. Simon stared at his reflection while he waited for the officer to finish talking on the phone. He ran his hand through his thinning fair hair, and slid his passport under the glass. His heart was pounding, his palms clammy.

The guard finished up on the phone, glanced at Simon's ID, then down at his face. 'Officer Carey's gone to fetch Webb – interview room two.'

Simon felt as though a serpent had wrapped its coil around his gut. 'Thank you.'

'You know where it is?'

Simon nodded. 'I've been on that block before – end of the hall, turn left?'

The guard smiled. 'That's it. Second door on your left. Need any help?'

'I'm fine, thanks.'

The other man slid a visitor's badge under the glass. 'You know the drill – keep this on you at all times.'

Breathe deeply, stay calm . . . 'Thank you.' Simon took the badge, clipped it to his gray sweater, and turned and headed down the hall.

The hallway was long, lined with CCTV cameras. Simon tried to relax, tried to act normal, but he was sure that every camera was watching him, that sooner or later he would hear the loud angry buzz of the alarm, the pounding of polished black shoes on the linoleum, that a group of guards would come thundering round the corner, seize him, and drag him off to a cell.

He couldn't help himself; as he reached the end of the corridor he glanced up at the camera, the red light blinking insolently at him, the all-seeing, never-resting eye. Just as quickly he looked away. *Relax, try to stay calm, keep going* . . .

Simon stopped in front of the second door on the left. Interview room two. This was it. He gripped his briefcase tight – everything he needed to do the job was inside. Take a deep breath.

Simon reached out, felt the cheap metal door

handle, cold and slick against his sweating hand. He turned the handle, and went inside.

Ricky Webb lounged back in an orange Formica chair. He had a thick head of soft, dark hair swept back from his forehead. Even in his prison clothes – dark blue trousers, a white T-shirt, black trainers – he was cocky, had a presence about him. He looked up with interest as Simon entered the room, and stared him up and down, studying him.

'All right?'

Simon nodded to the guard standing against the wall, hands behind his back, then carefully approached the table, and sat directly across from Webb.

He set his briefcase down by the side of his chair, and looked up at Webb for the first time. 'Hello.'

The prisoner gave him a grin. 'So you're the artist bloke?'

Simon nodded. Keep control. Everything is going according to plan. This was how you wanted it. He breathed deeply, forced a smile to his face. 'Yes, the artist bloke.'

Webb looked up at the guard, gave him a wink, then turned back to Simon. 'So what's this all about then?'

Simon carefully folded his hands on the table in front of him, held them tight to each other to avoid them shaking. He needed steady hands for what he was about to do. Just talk to him, get comfortable around him, forget what you know about him, and gradually relax, then you'll be ready to get the job done.

233

'I'm here to draw you,' replied Simon.

Webb smiled. 'Can't blame you – I'm a bit of a picture, aren't I, Carey?' He looked to the guard for support, but was met with an indifferent stare. He turned his charm back on Simon.

'So apart from my lovely looks, how come you're drawing me?'

Simon slowly reached down, and slid his briefcase into his lap. 'I'm doing a series of drawings of offenders – some when they have first been incarcerated, others when they are about to be released.'

Webb gave a big grin. 'I'm out next weekend.' He stretched his arms wide, as if embracing the whole world. 'Women of the world, look out, Ricky Boy is on his way.'

Simon's blood went cold, but he knew he couldn't allow his personal feelings to influence what he was about to do. It was essential that he didn't do that. He opened his briefcase, pulled out a large sketchpad, and a set of artist's pencils.

'So what are you going to do with your pictures?' Despite the chattiness, Webb wasn't stupid.

Simon opened the pencil case. There were forty-eight pencils, each of a different color, organized in an elegant sequence. He blinked. Actually, no, there were only forty-seven – one was missing. He frowned in confusion.

Pushing the thought from his mind, he turned back to Ricky. 'By comparing the faces, particularly the eyes, of new prisoners with those who

234

are about to be released, I hope to see if their incarceration has had any effect on them. I believe that the pictures will show if you have been changed, rehabilitated by your experience,' Simon explained.

Webb gave him a challenging look. 'But that all depends, doesn't it?'

Simon's eyes were still fixed on his pencil case, trying to figure out which one was missing. All were present and in order, but for one – the orange one.

'I said that depends, doesn't it?' Webb repeated.

'What?' Simon was put off his stride, knocked off balance. His heart pounded. He was so careful, so meticulous. Where could he have lost a pencil? He tried to pay attention to Webb while casting his mind back – where had he last used them? 'Depends on what?'

'On whether I was guilty in the first place.'

He looked up and met Webb's gaze. 'That is of no concern to me.'

Simon's pencil moved fast across the page. First he sketched the outline of Webb's face.

'Which way do you want me, Picasso?' Ricky turned his head from side to side, gurning and grinning.

'I don't mind,' Simon replied quickly, 'as long as I can see your eyes, and as long as you stay still.'

Webb turned with the left side of his face slightly tilted. 'I think that's my best side. That do the trick for you?'

Simon nodded. 'Yes, that's fine.' He drew quickly, the pencil defining Webb's high cheekbones, his strong jaw line, dark eyebrows, the sweep of his dark hair.

'This going to take long?' Patience was clearly not one of Ricky's virtues.

Simon gave a tight smile. 'It will be over soon enough.' He took a colored pencil from the box, began adding some shading to Webb's clear skin. 'So what will you do when you get out of here?'

Webb gave a smile of deep satisfaction. 'Like you said, I've been thinking about it for a long time.' He rubbed his hands together. 'So the first stop will be The Baggot Inn to get a few pints down me, and find all my old mates – that's where we always used to meet up on a Saturday night . . .'

Simon's hands moved quickly across the page, capturing Webb's lustrous black hair perfectly.

'I'm not familiar with it,' Simon replied.

Webb cast his eye over him again, took in his gray sweater, the prescription glasses, everything . . . 'No, don't reckon you would be,' he said, smirking.

Simon managed a tight-lipped smile. All that was left to draw now were the eyes.

'Eighteen months and nothing . . . I've been saving it up – some little lady is going to be in for the night of her life.'

Simon felt nauseous as he looked up over his sketchpad, and met Webb's eyes. 'You're in for rape, aren't you?'

236

Webb looked straight back at him, a cold, hard stare. For a moment there was silence, an almost electric pulse in the room. Simon never took his eyes from Webb, challenging him to look away first.

The guard unclasped his hands, and took a half-step forward. He knew a confrontation when he saw one, had broken up hundreds of fights in his time.

Just as suddenly, Webb looked away and grinned. 'Ah, that's all behind me now. Always said I was innocent, and parole board must believe me too. They're setting me free, aren't they?'

Simon's pencil moved slowly across the page with infinite precision. He had looked into Webb's eyes, got everything he needed. Everything to capture his essence perfectly – the mocking stare, the slight hint of weakness, the predatory cast.

Simon looked at his picture, and smiled. 'Yes, I'm a great believer in justice,' he said slowly. 'True justice.'

Webb grinned, but his eyes were less certain than before. He shifted in his seat. 'Right. Like the man said, I've done my time. Justice.' He glanced at the guard again, but he had settled back against the wall, a slight smile playing around the edges of his mouth. Webb turned again to Simon. 'So, are we all done here now, or what?'

Simon nodded. He carefully packed his pencils away, closed the case and slipped it back into his briefcase.

The prisoner leaned toward him, trying to get a glimpse of the portrait. 'So is it any good?'

Simon closed the sketchpad, and put it under his arm. 'Of course.'

Webb looked confused. 'Go on then, show it to me.'

Simon snapped the brass locks on the case closed. 'All in good time.' He nodded to the guard.

Webb furrowed his brow. 'In good time? What the fuck does that mean?' He started to stand, but the guard took a step toward him, and fixed him with a hard glare. He sank back into his seat.

Simon turned toward the door. The guard stepped over, and unlocked it. 'You said you're out next weekend?' he called back to Webb.

The prisoner nodded. 'Right. Saturday.'

'I'm putting on a small gallery exhibition of these pictures soon. I'll make sure you have a personal invitation.' He turned his back on the prisoner, and slipped out through the door.

Webb stood up and took a step forwards, but the guard stopped him with a stare. He called out after Simon, 'Wait . . . how will you find me?'

Simon's voice drifted back into the room from the corridor. 'Don't worry, Mr Webb – I'll find you.'

CHAPTER 24

Reilly looked at Chris and Kennedy as they trooped into her office. They'd agreed to meet with O'Brien there, as the chief was in the GFU building that morning concerning another matter.

The detectives both looked tired but it was nothing Reilly didn't recognize. She had seen the same thing when she looked in the mirror that morning. One advantage to being a woman – you could hide the worst of it with makeup.

Kennedy set a tray of coffees on the table, and dropped wearily into a chair, glancing up at the clock. It was five minutes before O'Brien was due to arrive. 'What are the odds that Princess Reuben will be late?' he grumbled.

Reilly looked at his sour face. 'And good morning to you too.'

He met her look, and for just a moment appeared about to say something smart, but couldn't keep his irrepressible good nature under wraps. 'And how do we find you this bright sunny morning, Miss Baywatch?'

Reilly glanced out her window at the gray leaden

sky, a typical November shower hammering against the windows on the back of a cold easterly wind. 'I feel a bit like the weather,' she admitted.

Chris lifted the lid of his coffee, blew to cool it. 'So what do we have?'

'Too right, Chris,' Kennedy quipped. 'Let's just dispense with the pleasantries and get straight to work.'

'I just wanted to have all our ducks in a row for O'Brien before Knight flounces in. He's bad enough when we know what we're talking about – God knows what he'd be like if he saw we were disorganized.'

'Who's disorganized?'

Reilly looked up quickly. Reuben's tall frame filled the doorway. Today he was dressed in a dark pinstriped suit with a red tie, and matching silk handkerchief spilling extravagantly from his breast pocket.

'Come on in and take a seat, Reuben,' Reilly told him.

He looked around, ignoring the detectives. 'My first time in the castle of the fairy princess – fascinating.' He gaze circled the room, before eventually zeroing in on Reilly's bookshelf. He stood in front of it, hands behind his back, perusing the titles. 'You can learn so much about a person from their bookshelves, don't you think?'

Chris looked at Reilly, then back at Reuben. 'We really need to get this meeting started, Knight,' he said testily.

'Go ahead,' the profiler replied without turning round. 'I'm sure you have very important police work to do to get yourselves organized. I'll just stay over here out of the way until you are ready for me.'

Chris sighed. 'Fine. We'll just pretend you're not here – which is a pleasant thought, actually.'

Reilly gave Chris a reproachful look. Why was he being so rude? 'Reuben, would you like a cup of coffee?' she asked.

He turned and glanced at their paper cups on the table. 'If you mean real coffee, made from freshly ground Colombian coffee beans, I would love a cup. If you are referring to that execrable brown liquid they pump out of the machine down the hall, then no thank you. I would rather drink my own bile.'

'That could easily be arranged,' Kennedy muttered under his breath.

'OK,' Chris put in quickly. 'What did we get from last night?'

'Why don't I go first?' Reilly suggested.

Kennedy nodded into his coffee cup, while shooting a look at Reuben's mute back that would cut diamonds. 'I took a number of samples,' she informed the detectives. 'Not surprisingly, there was horse feed aplenty in that barn – but none of it is a match to the stuff we isolated before.'

Chris looked surprised. 'So you're saying that it's somewhere else he's been getting horse feed on his feet?'

'It looks that way.'

'Are you really surprised that he didn't take you straight to his home territory so early in the game?' Reuben threw over his shoulder.

Chris ignored him. 'So he's got another barn somewhere else, and just used this one for Fitzpatrick's killing?'

Reilly nodded. 'That seems to be the case.'

'It's like we said before. He gives us exactly what he wants and no more.'

'Very astute.'

'I did, however, find something interesting.' Reilly continued quickly, before Chris had a chance to respond to Reuben's taunting.

Reuben paused, his head cocked slightly, listening carefully.

'I think that Reuben's right. Our killer is indeed an artist, not just in the metaphorical, but in the actual sense. Or at least fancies himself as one. I found an artist's pencil hidden in the straw against the wall. Taken with the traces of rubber we found in the church tower—'

Reuben spun around, his eyes bright. 'He's drawing the victims, the murder scenes . . .'

Reilly met his gaze. 'So it would seem.'

The wheels of the profiler's brain were spinning fast as he absorbed the new information. 'Fascinating,' he murmured, whipping out his fountain pen. 'And understandable. The arrangement is so theatrical, so vivid.'

'There's more,' Reilly continued.

'Do tell.' The profiler was now fully engaged, his

brain working overtime to process the new information.

'I was about to – unless of course you want to carry on analyzing my books?'

He shook his head impatiently. 'I've already gleaned all I need to know about you from that particular source,' he said cryptically.

Reilly nodded toward the vacant chair. 'In that case sit down and join the party.'

Reuben sighed, but knew when he was beaten. She had something he wanted. He sat down in the empty chair next to Chris.

'In addition to the imprints from the table and chair, there was another set of imprints in the straw,' she informed them.

Reuben was leaning forward in his chair eagerly, and she took her time, enjoying the moment, relishing stringing him along for a while. 'At first I wasn't sure what they might be. Three little marks close together—'

'A tripod!' Reuben exclaimed triumphantly.

Despite herself Reilly laughed. 'You take all the fun out of it. Don't you know it's rude to provide the punch line to somebody else's joke?'

Reuben stood up again and began pacing the small room. 'If he's videoing the killings, then he's got a cause, something that's driving him onwards – an injustice – so it's vital to him that every detail is recorded.'

Chris twisted round in his chair to look up at Reuben. 'So what's he doing with the videos?'

'A good question.' The profiler gazed out of the window, his eyes far away. 'If I had to make a guess, at the moment I would say he's editing them.'

'Editing them?' Kennedy repeated. 'Like a home movie or something? Why?'

Reuben tipped his head to one side. 'You're not far wrong, Detective.' He hurried back to his seat, leaning forward conspiratorially. 'As for why . . . Imagine for a moment that you are the killer. A great injustice has taken place. You want to exact your revenge, so you kill the guilty parties – but there's more to it than that. You want – need – people to know about it, you want to inform them, perhaps educate them. So you make videos . . .'

'. . . So that you can show them to an audience.' Chris finished the sentence, his eyebrows furrowed. 'But what would be on the videos? Just him killing people in his own sick and twisted way?'

Reuben shook his head. 'No. That would show him in a bad light, make him look like a crazed psychotic killer with no discernible agenda.'

'Heaven forbid,' Kennedy said, mocking Reuben's verbal mannerisms. 'So what *is* on them then?'

The profiler looked back and forth between the three of them. 'Any thoughts? He sees himself as the punisher, remember?'

Reilly nodded slowly. 'Confessions.'

Reuben clapped his hands together in delight. 'Reilly, you really do have a brain to go with those heavenly legs!'

Their discussion was interrupted by the door flying open. Inspector O'Brien stood in the doorway, a furious look on his face, waving a newspaper at them. 'Have you lot seen this?' he demanded.

'What is it, Chief?'

O'Brien opened the paper, and held it up for them. The banner headline proclaimed: 'Serial Killer Stalks Dublin – Where Will The Punisher Strike Next?'

'The Punisher? Speak of the bloody devil,' growled Kennedy, looking at Reuben, who'd just described the killer as exactly that.

O'Brien slumped in the chair opposite Reilly's desk and rubbed his forehead. He was a small man, with short salt-and-pepper-colored hair, always immaculately dressed. Today he was wearing a dark gray suit with a purple tie – he looked more like a politician than a policeman. He tossed the paper on Reilly's desk and turned to look at them all. 'How in God's name did this get out? Tell me that.'

Reilly ran her gaze down the page – the usual lurid account, describing all four murders, with the obligatory pictures of the victims.

'Did you read the last line?' O'Brien thundered.

She turned to page two, scanned to the bottom of the column.

'Go on, read it out loud to the other eejits in the classroom,' he instructed.

She cleared her throat, and began to read. "'But as horrific as these crimes are, as demented as the killer must clearly be, the scariest fact is this: the police have absolutely no clues yet as to who this madman is, or when and where he will strike next.'"

O'Brien stared at the detectives. 'Well, is he right?' he growled.

Chris sat up. 'We are moving forward—'

'Ah, cut the PC crap, Delaney. Do we know who this bugger is or don't we?'

'Not yet, no.'

'Do we know what he wants? Do we know when he'll strike next?' The questions came thick and fast. 'What am I supposed to say to the press? They want a statement. People want some reassurance that there's not some maniac out there who's going to steal their babies from their cots while they sleep.' He threw his hands up in exasperation. 'What am I supposed to tell them? My secretary tells me there's a wolf pack waiting outside my door at the moment – all the nationals are on the story now – and they're baying for blood. Mine!'

He stood up, and paced the small office. Three strides up, three strides back. 'Can you lot give me anything, any hope, *anything* to appease the angry mob?'

'We are making progress, Chief, but we can only work with the evidence we have,' Kennedy said. 'Whoever this guy is, he's clever. He's giving us only what he wants us to have.'

'What about you, Knight?' O'Brien whirled round to face Reuben. 'You're supposed to know all about these bloody maniacs.'

'Actually I was just about to outline my theory—'

'Well, then – outline. Get on with it.'

Reuben proceeded to bring O'Brien up to speed on what they'd discussed so far, about the Dante blueprint, the drawings and the videotaping.

Reilly noticed that Chris all the while seemed to be thinking hard. 'He's going to want to make the videos public, isn't he?' he said suddenly. 'I hope to God he's not planning to put them on YouTube or something. That's all we need.'

Reuben looked at him in surprise. 'O Serious One, you really are beginning to see the way this works, aren't you?' He gave Chris his most ingratiating smile.

'Imagine that?' Chris spat. 'Only ten years on the force, and already I know what the hell I'm doing.'

'This really is splendid, isn't it?' Reuben beamed. 'All of us getting along so well and learning so much . . .'

Ignoring this, Reilly thought about what Chris had said about the killer making the videos public in order to showcase his work. She too hoped he didn't plan on sending them to the media or uploading them online. Although some press would be sensitive enough to the victims and their families not to use them, others would no doubt jump at publishing something of such a gratuitous nature. And online . . . well, there was no limit to the havoc that would cause. The public would go crazy.

'What else?' O'Brien cut in, looking impatiently at Chris and Kennedy. 'Anything to report from last night?'

Kennedy looked at Chris and shrugged. He pulled out his notebook and flipped it open.

'Oh, goody!' Reuben cried. 'I do love a cliché – a detective and his trusty little notebook.'

Kennedy ignored him. 'We asked around. Seems the property belongs to an old guy who died about seven years ago . . .' Screwing up his eyes, he peered at his notes. 'A Joseph Patterson. Locals say it's been abandoned ever since. Kids play in the yard from time to time, but other than that it's just sat there abandoned.'

'That's how the body was discovered,' Chris added. 'The killer started a big bonfire in the yard, kids discovered it on their way home yesterday evening, saw the door to the barn was open, and came across Fitzpatrick in his bath.'

'Again, ensuring the body was found quickly,' Reuben observed. 'He does like to be noticed, doesn't he?'

Chris glanced pointedly at Knight's flashy suit. 'He's not the only one.'

'It makes sense,' Reilly said. 'He's deliberately choosing out-of-the-way locations to do his work, but then drawing attention to these locations once he's finished.' She turned back to the detectives.

'I guess nobody had seen anything suspicious recently?'

Kennedy shook his head. 'He's a clever bastard – chooses his spots very well.' He sniffed, and sipped at his coffee. 'I mean, look at the place last night – it's completely hidden from the road, there are no close neighbors, but it's on a road that's busy enough that you wouldn't notice the same car passing a couple of times.'

'How does he find out about these places?' O'Brien asked. 'Did you check the estate agent to see if anyone had made enquiries?'

Chris nodded. 'Called them first thing this morning. She said no one had enquired about the place in over three years.'

'He wouldn't make a mistake like that,' Reuben said quickly.

'So what *would* he do then?' Chris demanded. 'You're the expert, the big-shot profiler, the one who is supposed to tell us about this guy. So far all I've heard is us giving you information, and you mincing around saying how brilliant you are. So how about displaying some of the genius you seem to think you have?'

Reilly stared at Chris, shocked at the outburst. He sounded as though he was completely at the end of his tether, yet she didn't quite believe that it was the investigation alone that was getting to him. They'd had frustrating cases before and usually Chris was the calm, unruffled one, keeping the rest of the team motivated with his relentless optimism. This was a side to him she had never seen before, and she really wanted to get to the bottom of what was troubling him.

But if Chris's sudden attack had taken Reuben aback, he showed absolutely no sign of it. He sat back in his chair, unbuttoned his double-breasted jacket and carefully stroked his pen. 'A good question, my good man. What does all this tell us?'

He gazed up toward the fluorescent light, and puckered his mouth. The room was silent for a while and just when Reilly thought O'Brien might spontaneously combust, Reuben spoke again.

'Our killer is a careful, meticulous, possibly obsessive individual. He's the type who would spend his weekends trainspotting, collecting matchboxes, trying to hit the highest score on his favorite videogame, something tiresome like that. He has been planning this for some time, doing the background research on the individuals involved in this miscarriage of justice, planning how each of them should be punished for their transgression according to the writings of Dante in the *Inferno*– choosing his exact locations, scouting them out, getting his supplies.' He looked around the room at the other four.

'That's one of the things that makes him so dangerous, so effective. Because he's not in a rush, he's had time to do things gradually. For example, you might consider checking around with roofing suppliers, find out if someone has bought a large quantity of pitch lately—'

'We've already got someone checking that,' Chris interjected.

Reuben nodded. 'Yet I'd wager there's no point. He would have bought the pitch a long time ago, probably even had a job he could use some of it on. That way he could experiment with it in his own time, make sure he had the ability to heat it properly, know how to work with it, to pour it, et cetera.' He let the thought settle for a moment. 'Then, when the time came, when he had his victim, he would know exactly what to do, how long it would take to reach the right temperature.'

O'Brien nodded. 'So he's a meticulous bastard. He's been planning this for a while. What else?'

'The art angle is interesting,' Knight admitted. 'From what we know of this person, he wouldn't be drawing these scenes unless he's good – he certainly wouldn't settle for something amateurish. That means he's either a professional artist or a very gifted hobbyist.'

'So why is he drawing them?' Reilly wondered. 'If he's already videoing them, he's got a record. Why the drawings?'

'A very shrewd question from the Fairy Princess.' He turned to her. 'My guess is it's how he relates to people, how he sees the world. If he draws them, he's captured the soul, the essence, the spirit of the moment. He owns it.'

'Like the Egyptians and their carvings?'

'Precisely. It's his way of seeing the world. I would imagine that the videos are without doubt

251

for public consumption, but the drawings – well, the drawings are for himself.'

O'Brien still looked irritated. 'All of this sounds fan-fecking-tastic, Knight, but are we any nearer to catching this cute hoor?' he spat. 'We don't know who he is, where his home, barn or . . . bloody spaceship is, or where and when he'll strike next.'

Reuben gave him a searching look. 'You are asking for certainty where there is only mist and fog, a real animal when all we have is a chimera . . .' Then he sighed. 'All right, here's what I think.' He waggled a finger at them all. 'Notice I said *think*, yes?'

Chris rolled his eyes. 'Get on with it, man.'

Reuben stood up, carefully rebuttoned his jacket, and gazed at his reflection in Reilly's window. He patted a stray hair back in place, then spun back suddenly to face them all. 'He will strike again soon. And I think it won't be long until he reaches his last victim, the true perpetrator.'

'True perpetrator?' O'Brien repeated.

Reuben explained carefully. 'There's been a great injustice, a crime committed, yet the ultimate transgressor wasn't effectively punished. The journalist wrote about it, the policeman covered it up, lost evidence, took a bribe, whatever. The doctor is connected in some way, how I'm not yet sure. The politician presumably pulled some strings. But someone, somewhere, committed this original crime. The true perpetrator.'

Reilly nodded in understanding.

'He wants us to know what it's all about,' Reuben continued, 'so I would imagine that the video – or videos – will appear soon. They will be cryptic, but they will give us some degree of understanding all this.' He fidgeted with his hands. 'He lives alone. He is a professional, meticulous person – calm, collected, studious even. In fact, he is probably the very last person you would suspect of such brutal crimes.'

O'Brien had his eyes fixed on Reuben. 'Will we catch him?'

'The million-dollar question.' The profiler sighed. 'Sadly, I suspect not until he's ready.'

CHAPTER 25

Lucy edged her car out of the parking space, deep in the bowels of the GFU building. The quiet thrum of the engine vibrated through the seat – the car seemed as eager as she was to escape the lab for a few hours.

She emerged from the gloom into a bright winter's day. She was planning to earn her stripes on this case, spending several days working overtime to try to isolate the soil samples, and had finally come up with a match from a small village near Kildare town. But before saying anything to Reilly, she was going to grasp the nettle and investigate the area herself. She could imagine it was what her boss would have done when she was learning the ropes at the FBI Academy. Lucy never tired of hearing Reilly's stories about her time at Quantico, which always sounded so brilliantly exciting, almost glamorous.

So much better than studying for a Forensic Science degree at boring old UCD.

The N8 was one of the better roads in the area, and Lucy felt herself unwinding as she drove, Today FM chirping happily from her radio, the gear changes crisp and sharp as she pushed her little Mini along at speed.

Some thirty minutes later, she reached the village of Clane and pulled into the car park of the pub. It was a large white painted building with a brown tiled roof. A bare cherry tree stood by the pub's wooden fence, its branches still tinged with dew.

Lucy climbed out of the car, stretched and took a deep breath of the cold, clean air. She was dressed casually, jeans tucked into brown leather boots under a heavy winter jacket, and her curly hair pulled back. She zipped her jacket up and hurried into the pub.

It was a quiet family establishment with a blazing fire burning in the hearth. Lucy unzipped her jacket, and settled onto a stool at the bar. A bored-looking teenage girl chewing furiously at a piece of tired gum sloped over.

'What are you having?'

Lucy looked around. If she wanted information this was not who she needed to talk to. 'Is your boss around?' she asked politely.

The girl maintained her air of effortless boredom. 'You mean Mr Cooper?'

'Is he the owner?'

The barmaid nodded, smacked her gum. 'Him and his missus.'

Lucy remained polite. 'Could I talk to him, please?'

The girl shook her head. 'Wednesday is Mr Cooper's day off.'

'I see. So who's in charge today then?'

'Mrs Ellis, the bar manager.'

The girl continued chewing furiously, bringing to mind a ruminating cow.

'Well, could you go and get her for me, please?' Lucy asked.

It wasn't long before Mrs Ellis appeared. She popped out through the doorway looking slightly breathless, and turned toward the barmaid. She was in her mid-forties, with short brown hair and a slightly worried expression on her face.

She bustled over. 'Hello. Can I help you?'

Lucy smiled, keen to reduce the woman's obvious nervousness. 'Hello, Mrs Ellis. My name is Lucy Gorman, I'm an investigator with the GFU.' Lucy proudly showed her ID, feeling like she was in a TV show or something. It was merely her lab access card and nothing like an official investigator badge, but the woman wouldn't know that. 'I wonder if you could answer a few questions for me?'

'The guards . . . is something the matter?'

'No, no, not at all,' Lucy smiled. 'I just wanted to ask you a few questions about the local area. Have you lived around here long?'

Mrs Ellis drew herself up to her full height. 'Born and bred here in the village.'

'That's wonderful.' Lucy looked past Mrs Ellis to the barmaid, standing just behind her and pretending not to listen. She indicated the empty table behind them. 'Could we sit somewhere quiet and chat for a minute?'

The older woman caught the glance. 'Oh, of course!' She untied her apron, tucked it under the bar, scampered out from behind it and led Lucy over to a small table that looked out over the deserted car park.

'So how can I help you?'

'It's nothing serious. I just wanted to talk to someone with local knowledge.'

Lucy opened her handbag and pulled out an OS map that covered the local area. She spread it across the table. 'Do you know of any abandoned stables or barns around here – anywhere horses might have been kept?'

'Well, you're in Kildare, honey, the place is riddled with stables! But abandoned, you say?'

'Either abandoned, or else quiet, tucked away. Somewhere private.'

'There's a few places you might want to look,' the woman informed her. She found a spot nearby on the map, pointed at it with her stubby finger – Lucy noticed that her nails were chewed to the quick. 'Bradshaw's farm would be worth a look. There's a couple of old stables there . . .' She marked the point on the map with a red pen. 'You might also look there – it's not much more than an abandoned plot of land, but we had some travellers through there a couple of years ago. Then there's . . .' her eyes scanned the map, '. . . ah, here it is.' She pointed to a spot about four miles out of town on a quiet country lane. 'That's probably your best bet.'

'Why's that?'

'It's so isolated. Just look at it. That lane's a dead end. It winds up at the estuary, and the farm has been abandoned for about seven years, since old Mr Harrington died.' She leaned in closer. 'It was hardly more than a ruin even when he lived there – can't imagine what it's like now.'

'Do you know who owns it these days?'

The woman shook her head. 'Not sure. I think some relative inherited it. It's up for sale now.'

Lucy smiled. 'That's very helpful, thank you.' She began to fold her map.

'You won't be going to these places on your own now, will you?' Mrs Ellis asked, looking dubiously at her. 'I presume you have a big strapping partner with you—' Then she put her hand to her mouth. 'I'm sorry, I know we're not supposed to say things like that these days, but—'

'It's fine,' Lucy waved her apology away. 'And don't worry, of course I'll have somebody with me.'

'Good. The world is a funny place these days, and I don't like the idea that it might be me who'd sent a little scrap of a thing like yourself off to . . . I'm sorry, there I go again. No doubt the likes of you are so well trained these days, you could kill me stone dead as soon as look at me!'

Lucy smiled. 'Honestly, I'll be fine.'

Having finished collecting soil samples from the first two farmlands, Lucy headed to the third location

Mrs Ellis had indicated on the map. As the bar manager had pointed out, it was near the bottom of a lane, with no other buildings anywhere around.

The lane was rutted, full of potholes – she had to pick her way carefully along it at barely twenty miles an hour, weaving a path around the various obstacles. The high hedges on either side blocked her view, and the farm was so well hidden that she almost missed it.

Lucy hit the brakes and looked to her right. Through a small gap in the hedge a narrow track disappeared round a curve. She backed up, then turned onto the driveway, noting a 'For Sale' sign tacked onto a nearby fence post.

The terrain was even more potholed than the road, but after about fifty yards or so it opened out into a farmyard.

Straight ahead was an old farmhouse – traditional style, two up two down, brick built, the tile roof showing signs of neglect. To her left was a low concrete outhouse. Lucy cut the engine, took a moment to look around and allow her mind to absorb what was there.

She pushed the car door open and got out.

What to do? Should she give Gary a call back at the lab just in case, let him know where she was? Then again, this was only a fishing mission, no need to overexcite anyone just yet. She was here to take soil samples, that was all.

But while she was here, Lucy figured she might as well take a look around.

She stepped over toward the rundown building, taking care to step on the drier, frostier patches of ground so that she wouldn't leave any footprints. If this was a place of interest, the last thing she wanted to do was leave prints behind.

Up close the house wore its air of abandon like an old coat. The window frames were rotten, the paint peeling, the glass covered in years of grime. She stepped up to one of them and tried to look inside, but with the bright glare of the blue sky above, it was impossible to see anything of the gloomy interior.

She glanced around the small garden – it was wild and overgrown – then paused as a noise floated to her on the still air. A vehicle was approaching.

Lucy froze. With her car sitting in the entrance to the yard there was no hiding the fact that she was there, and no way to escape if someone pulled up behind her. If someone did appear she would just have to bluff it out, say she was looking to buy the place or something.

The engine noise grew closer, sounding suddenly very loud in the quiet yard. Lucy turned, and looked toward the narrow driveway, expecting all the time to see a vehicle pull up behind hers. Her nerves were taut, the skin on the back of her neck standing up . . . then the noise started to fade as the car just carried on past the lane and further up the road.

She breathed a sigh of relief. It could have been

anyone – a fisherman, someone going to take their dog out for a walk . . .

She glanced again toward the outhouse and a sudden loud barking startled her. From inside, several dogs – large ones, from the sound they were making – had become very agitated indeed, snarling and growling ferociously. They weren't simply sounding a warning, they wanted to attack whoever was out there.

Lucy had a strong desire to leave immediately. The place was unnerving her. She bent quickly, scooped some soil into a plastic evidence bag and sealed it tight. This was what she had come for, after all.

An icy wind raced around the side of the building and whipped at her legs. She shivered. She had been here long enough, and was pushing her luck coming on her own. It was time to go.

Then she heard the unmistakable sound of a twig snapping.

CHAPTER 26

'We've turned up something on Jennings,' Kennedy said.

Chris looked up from his desk. 'The doctor? What did the wife have to say?'

It had now been over a fortnight since the first murder, and in the hope of finding so far elusive common ground between all four victims, Chris and Kennedy had arranged further in-depth interviews with the families.

Chris had just returned from the Coffey house, where Mrs Coffey had revealed she had no knowledge of Dr Jennings or Alan Fitzpatrick, nor could she think of any reason (other than work related) why her husband would be in possession of John Crowe's mobile number.

'Seems the doc has a previous conviction,' Kennedy said triumphantly.

'What?' Chris sat forward. This he hadn't expected. By all accounts Dr Jennings seemed your typical salt-of-the-earth GP. The staff at his surgery had been devastated to hear of his demise, and had nothing but good things to say about him.

'Yep. His wife brought it up, actually; is convinced his killer is someone with a grudge.'

'So what's the conviction?' Chris asked, somewhat heartened that they seemed to be getting somewhere. But he wondered why the conviction hadn't turned up in their initial background search on Jennings.

'An interesting one,' Kennedy continued. 'About a year ago, one of Jennings' patients stockpiled antidepressants he prescribed and used them to top herself.'

'Criminal negligence then?' Chris queried.

'The very one. Wife says he was really torn up about it. Seems the patient was a rape victim, and he was doing everything he could to try and help her, blah blah blah.'

Chris was silent for a moment as he tried to take in the implications. A rape victim.

He could understand why the doctor had been torn up about a patient suicide, especially if the supposed remedy he'd offered to try to ease her pain had had the very opposite effect. Or had it?

'I don't get it. How come none of this turned up in Jennings' background search?'

'Good question.' Kennedy slumped down behind an adjacent desk, and set Jennings' file on top of it. 'Which is why we need to go a little deeper where our good doctor is concerned.' He looked at Chris. 'I'm gonna give our HSE guy a call, see if he can dig up Jennings' disciplinary record.'

'Good idea.' Chris nodded approvingly. The

suicide incident would surely have been reported to the Health Services Executive, Jennings' employer.

An hour later, the detectives had their answer. Kennedy's HSE contact duly faxed over a copy of the incident report – although the name of Jennings' patient – the suicide victim – was blacked out.

'Man, they really do take this patient confidentiality thing to heart don't they?' Kennedy complained. 'Although I s'pose we should all be glad of that. Would hate for anyone to see the ins and outs of my last medical,' he joked, reminding Chris that he himself had a force medical coming up soon. Given that he was rarely without pain these days, he felt his palms clam up at the thought of what they might find.

'So what's the lowdown?'

'Aha!' Kennedy tossed the three-page fax across to him. 'Mystery solved. The wife had it only half right. Yes, Jennings was charged, but there was no conviction because the judge ordered a suspended sentence.'

'And Jennings walked away a free man?'

'Exactly.'

'Let's look at the judge then – see if he's the missing link between Jennings and the other three,' Chris suggested, somewhat heartened by the discovery but frustrated by it too.

While the finding pushed the investigation closer to the right track, insomuch as it gave them some form of motive for the doctor's murder, without knowing who the suicide victim was, they couldn't turn their attentions to any potential grudge-bearers. Like the cooking sauce, the equine soil and the pencil, it was another piece of the overall puzzle. Unfortunately, it still didn't move them forward toward completing the jigsaw.

Later that evening, Reilly looked at Chris, who sat slumped in a chair in front of her. His skin was ashen, his eyes were red-rimmed from lack of sleep, and despite having just outlined an apparent breakthrough regarding motive concerning Jennings, his defeated demeanor remained.

Not for the first time, Reilly wondered if the arthritic-like problems from last year had returned. Certainly, something was going on that was causing the normally upbeat detective to look and sound so worn down.

She glanced at her watch. It was after eight p.m. 'When did you last eat?' she asked, seizing an opportunity to get to the bottom of this once and for all.

Chris shrugged. 'Eat? What's that?'

She gave him a dubious look.

'I don't know . . . breakfast maybe?' he finally admitted.

She stood up. 'That's it. We're out of here.'

'Reilly, I honestly—'

She cut him off. 'You can't think straight if you don't get some food inside you. I'm the one with the medical background, so don't argue.'

'You're right, but—'

'I said, no arguments.' She reached round the back of the chair upon which Chris was sitting. Pulling a dark wool coat from it, she threw it at him and grinned. 'Get your coat – dinner's on me.'

Outside, she sniffed at the damp air. 'Hell, it feels like weeks since I was out in the fresh air.'

'I hear you.'

She glanced at him. Under the wash of the sodium streetlights his skin looked wan. Something was seriously taking its toll on him. Reilly now felt faintly guilty that they'd spent so little time together lately. Especially after everything they'd been through before.

Chris looked up and down the quiet manicured grounds outside the GFU building. 'Not exactly culinary central around here, is it?' he pointed out. 'Did you have anywhere in mind?'

'Of course.' She led him out of the grounds, and eventually pointed down a quiet side street. He followed along, and a little way down Reilly pointed out a sign for an Italian bistro called The Opera House. 'Here.'

He shook his head. 'I never even knew this place was here. How on earth do their customers find them?'

Reilly gave an enigmatic smile. 'Julius tipped me off about it. They're pretty new but very, very good. Not to mention convenient, especially for a quick bite to eat after late nights at the lab.'

266

Chris followed her into The Opera House. The small restaurant was tastefully decorated with just enough Italian paraphernalia to give it charm. Only two other tables were occupied.

The waitress sashayed over, having some difficulty walking in her black satin pencil skirt. She took their coats, and directed them to a booth by the window. They settled onto red velour benches that faced each other across a deep expanse of red-and-white-checkered cotton tablecloth. Reilly noticed Chris's gaze idly following the waitress as she tiptoed back to the bar.

'See something you like?' she teased.

Caught unawares, he blushed. 'Not my type.' He opened the menu. 'I was actually just wondering how she actually manages to walk in that.'

Reilly shook her head. 'Hmm . . .' She buried her nose in the menu, suddenly aware of just how hungry she actually was.

The waitress returned and they ordered their food, water, and a single glass of wine respectively as they were both driving. The drinks arrived quickly and for a moment neither of them said anything, both enjoying the cool liquid, and the feeling of temporary relaxation that washed over them as they sipped their drinks.

Reilly was the first one to break the silence. 'So if the slinky Italian waitress isn't your type, what is?' she asked suddenly.

Chris looked up at her, evidently surprised. 'That's a very un-Reilly-like question,' he observed.

She shrugged. 'Hey, I can talk about shallow stuff just as well as the next woman.'

Chris sipped his wine. 'So my personal life is shallow then?'

'You tell me.'

They both waited for a moment, but Chris didn't elaborate.

'I notice you dodged that question nicely; both of them, in fact,' Reilly grinned, looking up as the waitress arrived with their food. 'Did I hit a nerve?'

He couldn't reply immediately as the waitress was fussing around with their food, and as soon as she had gone Reilly set to her dish like a hyena, shoveling cacciatore chicken and pasta into her mouth, and pausing barely long enough to wash it down with a sip of wine.

Eventually satisfied, she pushed her plate back and dabbed at her mouth with a crisp white cloth napkin.

'As always, if I hadn't seen it with my own eyes I wouldn't have believed it.' Chris nodded at the scattered remains on the table. 'I've seen swarms of locusts do less damage than you do.'

She smiled. 'I guess you're just not used to being around a woman with a healthy appetite.'

'I've certainly never been around a woman who looked like she could eat my arm for dessert,' he countered.

Reilly sipped at her water, and looked at him. 'So,' she began, deciding to dive right in, 'are you going to tell me what's been going on with you lately?'

He looked up quickly, visibly tense. 'What do you mean?'

"Hell, Chris . . . I know this case is a bitch and it's getting us all down, but you . . . I can't quite put my finger on it.'

'On what?'

'On why you're so . . . edgy these days,' she said finally, and Chris looked away.

'I don't know what you mean.'

'Look, I know Reuben can be . . . challenging, but he's harmless really. You nearly took his head off the other day.'

He wouldn't meet her gaze. 'I'm just frustrated that's all. All these dead ends. We're getting nowhere.'

'Hey, come on – it's me you're talking to,' she said, not believing a word of it. 'Something's bugging you at the moment and I don't think it's just the case.' She glanced at his hands, clasped together on the table. 'Is it that again? The thing from last year, the tremors and stuff . . . has it come back?'

She had her suspicions; especially as more than once recently she'd noticed him put both hands in his pockets, as if trying to hide them.

'What? No, everything's fine.'

'Yeah, and I'm Miss America,' she said drolly.

'You are according to Kennedy,' he joked, but his heart wasn't in it and she knew it.

She reached across the table and put her hand on top of his. 'Chris, let me help you. I can run some more tests, maybe get Julius to take a look at—'

'It's fine, Reilly,' he interjected, his face shuttering. 'Honestly, it's nothing. I'm just a bit stressed out with this case, that's all.'

'If you say so,' she replied automatically, stung by his obvious stonewalling.

It felt like a slap in the face. She'd trusted him, confided in him, and he knew all of her deepest, darkest secrets.

Was that part of it? she wondered, trying to figure out how the closeness they'd developed in the early days had all but disappeared lately. Did he blame her for last year – hold her responsible for what had happened? After all, he was the one who'd ended up in hospital, bleeding from his injuries. Who could blame him if—

'It's nothing, honestly,' he continued, his voice softening a little. 'I'm just stressed out, we all are.'

'I don't know, Chris,' she said, her eyes downcast. 'Sometimes, you can be a bit like Area 51, a big no-fly zone, full of mysteries.'

Chris looked up and met her gaze for the first time. He seemed to be thinking hard, as if weighing something up.

At last, he exhaled, and cleared his throat. 'Remember last year, when you were doing your analysis of me in the restaurant, using your Jedi mindspell, or whatever weird thing you do,' he said, referring to a dinner they'd shared in the early days of working together.

She nodded. 'What's that got to do with anything?'

'You said something about my not being married because I'd been—'

'Burned in the past. Bigtime burned,' she finished, recalling the conversation almost word for word. She raised an eyebrow, seriously wondering where he was going with this.

'Well, you were right.' There was a brief pause. 'I was . . . was engaged once.'

Reilly looked up, surprised, her eyes boring into his. 'You were?'

He looked down at the table. 'Yes, it ended a few years ago – almost three years now. I'd just graduated from training college when I proposed to Mel. Melanie, her name was Melanie Adams.'

'Melanie, that's a sweet name,' Reilly mumbled, unsure what to say, her voice echoing Chris's somber tones. *Was?* Had his fiancée died? she wondered, horrified, her mind racing. If so, why hadn't Kennedy ever said anything?

'I'm sorry to pry,' she mumbled quickly. 'It's just I never knew you were actually engaged to someone. You never mentioned . . . So what . . .? Did something happen?'

He paused again. 'It's difficult to explain really,' he said, and she breathed an inward sigh of relief. OK, if the girl had died it would be easy enough; he wouldn't have to explain anything.

He looked up and saw her regarding him

271

carefully. 'It's complicated,' he continued finally. 'I've never really talked to anyone about it before.'

She nodded. 'Hey, that's OK. Honestly, it's really none of my business and—'

'When we got engaged,' he said, 'it was a good time. We were happy, had everything going for us, and I really thought we'd be spending the rest of our lives together.'

Reilly waited patiently to hear the rest.

'But then . . . not long after, something happened,' he added, his face pained, and his expression closed once again.

'I see.' Reilly figured her early analysis of him that time had been correct. Evidently this Melanie had hurt Chris deeply.

'Was there somebody else?' she asked gently, when he didn't elaborate.

His hand tightened around his glass. 'You could say that.'

'Look, Chris, this is really none of my business,' Reilly insisted, feeling unaccountably discomfited now. 'I'm sorry for pressing the issue. It's just . . . I noticed you've been kind of testy this last while and . . . is that it?' she asked, a flash of inspiration hitting her. 'Has she – Melanie – been in touch recently, or something?'

It was a shot in the dark but if the ex-fiancée was preying on Chris's mind, then maybe she'd come back into his life recently. And maybe he still held a candle for her, which was why he was so highly strung.

He gave a short laugh. 'Not exactly. But I do know she's getting married at the weekend.'

'Oh.'

So that was it, Reilly realized. Chris had been prepared to commit his life to this Melanie, but for some reason she'd rejected him, tossed him aside, and now she was marrying someone else, perhaps the guy she'd left him for. That had gotta hurt.

She looked at him. 'Sounds like you two might have some unfinished business,' she said, trying to choose her words carefully.

'Nah'. Chris sat back in his chair. 'I know the fella she's marrying, he's a good guy. Peter – we used to be mates. Good luck to them.'

'I see.'

'I'm glad, actually – glad she's getting on with her life,' he added, and Reilly guessed he was trying his utmost to sound like he meant it.

She looked closely at him, but his expression remained inpenetrable.

Clearly a lot more had gone down between Chris and the ex-fiancée than he was prepared to admit.

And despite herself, Reilly was deathly curious to find out exactly what.

CHAPTER 27

Reilly was astonished the following day when she heard about Lucy's little adventure.

First thing that morning, Jack Gorman stormed into her office, angrier than she'd ever seen him. 'What the hell were you thinking?' he demanded. 'Sending my daughter off to remote places like that all by herself?'

'I don't know what you're—'

'Lucy was cautioned for trespassing on some godforsaken farm in Kildare yesterday. We're lucky she wasn't arrested!'

Reilly frowned. What the hell . . .? 'Jack, I have no idea what you're—'

'Collecting soil samples, she told me. Seems you wanted her to get them so you could narrow down a location for this *Inferno* madman! My daughter is not your personal slave, Steel, nor should she be a sacrificial lamb!'

Reilly's head spun. When had she asked Lucy, or indeed any of the techs, to go off and do something like that?

'Jack, honestly I would never ask any one of my staff to—'

'She may be only "staff" to you, but she's my daughter,' Gorman fumed, but the tremor in his voice betrayed to Reilly just how worried he'd been about Lucy, and rightly so. They might have a difficult relationship, but there was no doubting how much the older Gorman cared for his daughter.

'I know that, and believe me when I say—'

'She was wandering around an abandoned farm in the middle of nowhere,' he blustered. 'A local who knew the place was unoccupied passed by and saw the car in the driveway, reporting it as suspicious. Thank God he did. Who knew what dangers she might have walked into?'

'Jack, honestly, I had absolutely no idea that she'd taken it upon herself to go and investigate. I knew she'd isolated the samples to a particular area, and we were discussing looking into it further, but only in a general sense. I would never, ever ask something like that, let alone agree to it.'

He shook his head. 'You and your fancy FBI career, making it all sound like some sort of snazzy Hollywood movie. It's a tough fucking world out there, Steel, full of sick bastards who are only looking for an opportunity to—'

'Where is she now?'

'At home. Where I want her to stay until I get to the bottom of this. Can you imagine my horror when I got a call from the sergeant in Kildare yesterday evening? Can you just imagine?'

Reilly could imagine only too well the kind of terror Jack had felt, and the scenarios he'd been envisioning. Such nightmarish thoughts would be even more vivid for someone in this business, who knew only too well the dangers that lurked.

'Let me just say again that I'm as surprised and upset about this as you are,' she persisted. 'Lucy is one of the most valuable members of my team, not to mention how much I admire her personally. I would never, ever, knowingly put her in harm's way, Jack. If you feel I'm responsible for this, then I will happily take responsibility for it, but also for ensuring that it never happens again. Let me talk to her.'

The color on his face receded somewhat. He looked at Reilly. 'It's all very well to show them the fun side of things, Steel, but we also need to remind them that fighting crime is nothing like it is on TV. All this virtual reality stuff too; they're so focused on that that they're completely ignoring the reality. You've been around the block long enough to know that they need to be aware of the dangers.'

Reilly nodded. Gorman had a point. She guessed she did have a tendency, particularly in training sessions, to lead the team toward the more interesting, sometimes more glamorous side of forensics. iSPI was a case in point.

But perhaps it was her way of shielding them in some small way from the harsh realities of the job. Hell knew she found these tough enough herself to deal with at times.

'You're right and I'm sorry,' she conceded again. 'I'll talk to Lucy, and I promise that nothing like this will ever happen again.'

'Good enough.' Gorman seemed satisfied. He looked away into the distance. 'Because believe me, Steel, dealing with an angry parent has nothing on dealing with a grieving one.'

Chris sat up, bleary-eyed and shivering. He was on the couch, a thin blanket half draped over him. The insistent ringing of his mobile phone had finally woken him.

'Chris, where the hell are you?' Kennedy growled.

'I'm . . .' He glanced up at the clock on the wall. It was ten a.m. 'I'm running a bit late this morning.'

His partner sounded surprised. 'Well, you picked a great day for it. A package arrived last night. I think we have a present from our man.'

Chris eyes widened. 'The Punisher?'

'Don't you start . . .'

Chris snapped his phone shut, and rubbed his hand across his face.

He felt like he'd taken a pounding from a group of hammer-wielding dwarfs the night before. Last night, he'd enjoyed the glass of wine in the restaurant so much that he'd picked up a bottle on his way home, hoping it would relax him, help him sleep a little. The wine bottle sat on the table; it was about empty.

There was no doubt that the alchohol was exacerbating the joint pain too. He looked at his hands, which were trembling as usual, and felt his bones ache as he sat up. He stared at the wine bottle.

Maybe he should have a quick one before he went to work, just to take the edge off?

Kennedy looked up as Chris hurried in. He'd shaved and put on a clean shirt but by his partner's expression Chris figured his face still showed the ravages of the pain he'd been suffering the night before.

'I thought *I* looked bad this morning.'

Chris forced a smile, hoping he wouldn't push it. 'Cheers . . .'

'Hey, I was just kidding. Seriously, are you all right?'

'I'm fine. What have we got?'

Any lethargy he felt was quickly dispelled by the note Kennedy handed him from Inspector O'Brien's office: 'PRIORITY. Package received. Possibly relevant to current Inferno investigation.'

'So when do we get it?' he asked.

His partner shrugged. 'You know the protocol – it will be hours before we see anything.'

Since 9/11, all incoming packages to law enforcement had to be checked carefully – first of all for explosives – then by the GFU for fingerprints or trace. It would be a considerable while before either of the detectives found out what was in the package.

The explosives check took time. First the main package was checked for chemical traces, then the small padded envelope inside was X-rayed, confirming that there was a DVD inside. Only once those checks were completed could the GFU lab team access the package to examine for fingerprints, trace – anything that might help them find the sender.

It was early afternoon before the package finally sat on the gleaming counter top in the GFU lab, the bright lights shining down on it.

Reilly stood in the lab with Julius, Gary and Rory. The run-of-the-mill-looking envelope, fresh from its explosives check, lay innocently on the workbench.

'OK, first of all – thoughts?'

The team studied the workbench. 'We could check out the envelope itself?' Gary suggested. 'See who makes these, sells them.'

Reilly nodded. 'Great, that'll be your job then. Thanks for offering.'

Ignoring his look of disappointment at being handed such a mundane task, she looked again at the envelope.

Julius was peering at it. 'The handwriting looks interesting.'

Reilly followed the older tech's gaze. It was interesting – very elegant, a flowing script, almost like a distinctive font. 'Those in charge of Punisher investigation, Harcourt Street Station,' it read.

'What does it tell you?'

'Knight said that we were looking for an artist – this is the handwriting of someone who is artistic, creative.'

'Agreed, Julius. Anything else?'

'The fact that he refers to himself as the Punisher means he must read the newspapers, so he knows exactly what they're saying about him,' Gary said.

'And that he's comfortable, almost proud of the nickname,' Julius continued.

Reilly nodded. It had been her first thought upon seeing the envelope.

'Self-adhesive stamps,' as always Rory seemed less interested in the psychology than in the evidence, 'so no saliva for DNA.'

'Unfortunately,' Julius agreed in a rueful tone. 'And it's simply postmarked Dublin, so no clues there that might help us narrow our search. He's thorough, isn't he?'

'Yep.' Reilly reached out and flipped the package over with her pen.

'No return address either,' Gary joked. 'There's a surprise.'

She turned to Julius. 'Dust it for prints, then we'll open it and see what it is he *has* decided to share with us.'

As expected, there were lots of prints on the envelope – it would have been handled by several people on its passage through the postal system – but as the sender hadn't left a single, or even partial fingerprint at any of the crime scenes, the prints they obtained were of little use. That didn't stop them checking any they did find against the database, but as Reilly expected, nothing came up a match.

So far, so little . . .

Finally the team carefully pried open the envelope, which had been sealed with its self-adhesive flap, and no additional tape. They carefully examined the adhesive, but again, the sender had been meticulous – there was absolutely zero trace on the adhesive surfaces.

Eventually, they were ready to see what was inside.

With Rory's assistance, Reilly carefully slid the contents out: a single DVD in a clear, plastic jewel case. The lab tech recorded the particulars of the products – a standard Sony DVD, a no-name jewel case – and again they went through the likely fruitless ritual of dusting the case and the disk itself for prints. There was no paper, no accompanying note, or anything written on either the DVD or the case to identify what might be on the disk.

'Nothing but minuscule traces of latex,' Rory muttered as his efforts once again came unstuck.

Reilly nodded. 'Gloves, of course.'

At last – hours after the package had first been delivered – all the checks were complete, and they could finally see what had been sent to them. The sense of anticipation around the lab was rife.

'You know, we could all be making a big assumption here,' Gary said, as Reilly picked up her tweezers and prepared to release the disk from its case.

She looked at him, puzzled. 'About what?'

'Well, we don't even know if this is from the killer, do we?' He laughed. 'It could just as easily be Rory's holiday snaps.'

Rory looked embarrassed. Stories of the holiday he and a couple of his rugby mates had taken in Majorca a few weeks back were legendary and had spread all throughout the GFU. 'I really don't think—'

'Don't mind him,' Julius said. 'When do you think we'll be able to watch it, Reilly?'

'As soon as the detectives are done with it, I promise.'

Chris and Kennedy were already en route to the GFU building to see exactly what was on the disk. Reilly had tried to contact Reuben too, but his mobile went straight to voicemail and he wasn't in his hotel room.

She had plenty of work to distract her while she waited.

Soon the detectives arrived, and they all settled into the chairs in the conference room.

Reilly slipped the disk into the DVD player. The drawer slid shut, she hit 'Play' and the room fell silent as the DVD player hummed softly into life. They would soon know if this was the breakthrough they had been waiting for.

'I really hope this is what we think it is,' Kennedy grumbled. 'If it's just some guy's home movies I'm not going to be a happy bunny.'

'That would make a change,' Chris muttered.

As Reilly took a seat, an image filled the screen. It was a printed sheet of white paper, bearing the following typed words:

Law and order exist for the purpose of establishing justice, and when they fail in this purpose they become the dangerously structured dams that block the flow of social progress.
Martin Luther King, Jr.

It was quickly followed by another sentence, that read:

I am simply unblocking that flow to social progress . . .

Reilly pressed the pause button on the remote control. She nodded toward the screen. 'Once again, he's careful – those are simply A4 sheets printed off a computer – nothing distinctive or characteristic about them.'

'No doubting his motives either,' Chris commented.

'Let's see what else he's got.' She hit the play button again and the white sheet of paper dissolved into video footage.

'That's Coffey,' Kennedy pointed out, quickly recognizing the man on screen.

The journalist was sitting at a small table, his feet bound to the legs of the chair. He was writing something and occasionally he looked up toward the camera. Reilly was busy studying the background, trying to figure out where Coffey was being held while the footage was filmed.

It was clear he'd suffered. There was a streak of blood down one cheek, his hair was dishevelled and his clothes dirty. Although sadly for him, Reilly thought, shuddering at the memory of Coffey bobbing about in putrefying sewage, they were about to get a whole lot dirtier.

After about a minute or so Coffey looked up. 'I've finished.'

The screen flickered in what looked to be a sharp edit. In the next shot Coffey was holding up a sheaf of papers. He looked directly at the camera.

'This is my confession,' he said, his voice cracking. He looked to be on the verge of tears, fearful and psychologically weakened by his experience, dark circles beneath his eyes as he stared uncertainly toward the camera. He paused to catch his breath and wiped his face, trying to compose himself.

'Although I was brought here against my will, what I have written here is the truth – nothing has been added or changed.' He set the papers back down on the table, and slowly signed each page with a trembling hand. 'There . . .' He held them out to the unseen person behind the camera and the image faded to black.

Chris turned to look at Reilly. 'You didn't get anything else in the package – some papers, Coffey's confession?'

Reilly shook her head. 'Just the disk.'

They both looked back toward the screen as more typed words flashed into view. These read:

Inferno Eighth Circle: Bolgia 2: Flatterers
drown in their own excrement
Tony Coffey – the dam unblocked

'Well, there's certainly no question now that Reuben's correct,' Reilly stated. 'Our killer is indeed re-enacting the punishments from Dante's *Inferno*.'

'Flatterers?' Chris queried. 'How was Coffey a flatterer?'

'He used words to flatter some and exploit others,' Reilly explained. 'The excrement represents the words he produced.'

'Or again, journalists are full of shit,' Kennedy said flatly.

The white sheet on the screen faded away, and was once again replaced by more video footage, this time of ex-cop John Crowe.

He was a giant of a man, the kind you'd want on your side in a fight, Reilly noted, and definitely the kind of guy you wouldn't want to cross. His face was hard, with short-cropped gray hair and flinty pale blue eyes. But however tough Crowe might have been, right then he was a prisoner, entirely at someone else's whim, at someone else's mercy, and he knew it.

He was looking around, analyzing, assessing, but there was a hint of fear in his pale eyes, the realization that his fate was out of his hands. In the narrow focus of the video it was also difficult to make out where he was – the background was dark and featureless.

Crowe was sitting on a chair, his hands couldn't be seen, but from the way his arms disappeared behind his back, it was clear that they were also secured firmly.

Unlike Tony Coffey, though, Crowe's face showed no sign of defeat. He may have realized that he was in a tight spot, but he was determined not to show it. He was defiant, staring straight into the camera. 'This sick fucker is making me talk,' he growled.

'That's Crowe for you,' Kennedy commented. 'He wouldn't kowtow to anyone.'

'He wants me to make a confession,' Crowe continued in his coarse Northside Dublin accent. 'I've got nothin' to hide, nothin' to be ashamed of. I did what I did, that's the way it was; everyone who was smart did the same. You did what you were told, kept your mouth shut, no questions asked, then the perks and the promotions came along.' He paused for a minute, as though thinking. 'The guy—'

There was another sudden sharp change, as yet again the footage was edited and when the video resumed, Crowe was still talking.

'I didn't think anything of it; it wasn't unusual for someone to make a request like that. You lose a bit of evidence, misplace a file, can't remember a name . . .' Crowe stopped, and shrugged. 'I wasn't totally happy about it,' he admitted. 'Guy was a nasty piece of work, an arrogant little fucker, if you asked me, but the top brass turned the heat up, so I did what I was told – and a week later ten grand in cash turned up in my locker.'

'So he *was* taking kickbacks,' Kennedy said, his tone filled with disdain. 'Stupid bastard . . .'

'Hold on . . .' Reilly paused the video. 'What's that – on Crowe's shoulder?' When the others looked confused, she pointed at the screen. 'There on the jacket, on the right-hand side.' She wasn't sure at first if it was just the shadows in the barn, but was almost certain she could make out a distinctive light-colored mark on the cop's dark jacket.

Chris screwed up his eyes. 'Looks like it's just dust of some kind. That horse feed, maybe?'

'I don't think so. It looks very powdery and too light in color – not something you'd get in a farmhouse or barn.' Had Crowe brushed up against something when being moved to the site, in the unsub's van perhaps?

It could be nothing, but she'd get the tech guys to zoom in on the footage later, see if they could ascertain what the mark was. If they could do that, perhaps they might also be able to work out where it had come from – and thus add another piece of physical evidence to the pile.

Kennedy looked thoughtful. 'Listening to that, whatever Crowe did – destroyed evidence or whatever – it sounds as though somebody higher up in the force was in on it too.'

'Look, let's not jump to conclusions,' Chris said.

'The last thing we want is O'Brien and the suits getting even more involved in this.'

Reilly shared Kennedy's concerns. 'But what if one of them is on the killer's list? We have to say something.'

'I don't think so.'

She looked at him with interest. 'You sound pretty certain. What makes you say that?'

'I may be wrong, but this guy is so careful, I don't think he'd tip us off before he got to someone – he's too determined to administer his own form of justice. Either he didn't pick up on it, or else he didn't know what Crowe was referring to.'

'Why don't we just keep watching?' suggested Kennedy. 'Maybe we'll find out?'

Reilly resumed 'Play'.

There was another quick edit before the footage continued with Crowe still talking. 'You didn't usually ask those questions, but in this case, I was pretty sure where the money had come from.'

Again the footage jumped abruptly.

'Damnit!' Kennedy exclaimed.

'It stood to reason,' Crowe went on. 'I knew who his father was, so it didn't take much to add two and two together and come up with four.'

'Whose father?' Chris asked. 'Bloody hell, none of this is making any sense.'

There was another quick cut, and when they saw Crowe again, he looked more downcast. 'Of course it made a difference. If I'd presented all the evidence there's little doubt the fucker would have got what was coming to him.' He looked directly at the camera. 'Most of the time what we did was neither here nor there, but in this case, yeah, it made a big difference . . .'

The screen faded, and yet another title card appeared:

Ninth Circle: Round Two: Traitors
Betrayers of community ties encased in ice
John Crowe – the dam unblocked

Reilly recalled a recent reading of the *Inferno* in which traitors were mentioned. A dishonest policeman would certainly fall under the description of a betrayer of community ties.

Once again the punishment was designed to fit the crime.

Kennedy grunted in frustration. 'This guy really knows how to leave his audience hanging.'

'He's certainly a tease,' Chris agreed. 'Knows just when to lead us on, then makes a cut just at the pay-off.'

The picture morphed into a shot of Alan Fitzpatrick's face.

Looking at the background, the politician was in the barn where they had found him, which led Reilly to assume that Crowe and Coffey's footage had been recorded there too. This was good; it meant that they had information on a primary crime scene for at least three murders.

Like the others Fitzpatrick was bound to a chair. A streak of black pitch ran down his face, the skin at the edges of the pitch appearing red and angry.

Reilly grimaced. This one seemed more brutal – there was no doubt, Fitzpatrick looked scared, much more so than the other two had been. He blinked at the camera, clearly in pain from the burns on his face. 'I'll say whatever you want . . .' He blinked, gave a little sob. 'Please don't hurt me again.'

There was another edit, and when the picture returned, Fitzpatrick looked more composed, the black pitch had been removed from his face, and the tar cleared off it. 'We'd been friends for a long time—'

'Friends with who?' Kennedy muttered, irritation evident in his voice. 'Who the hell are these guys talking about?'

'It certainly sounds as though they're all referring to one person in particular,' Chris agreed.

'To be honest, he owed me.' Despite the circumstances, Fitzpatrick was still unable to keep a faint note of pride out of his voice. 'Lots of people owe me . . .'

He glanced up at the camera, as if quickly remembering where he was and what he was supposed to be doing. 'All it took was a quick phone call to be sure that we got the result we wanted.' He gazed at the camera lens, gave a wan smile. 'I scratch your back, you scratch mine. That's the way it works, isn't it?'

He was obviously discussing his abilities to wheel and deal, bend the rules, make things happen, Reilly mused.

'It was almost a formality getting early release approved . . .'

Early release. They had to be talking about a prisoner . . . perhaps the perpetrator Reuben was referring to?

Once more the screen went black, but was soon filled with another caption card.

Eighth Circle: Bolgia 5:
Barrators Immersed in Boiling Pitch
Alan Fitzpatrick – the dam unblocked
once more

Again the screen went dark and all that could be heard was the sound of heavy, ragged breathing. Then Fitzpatrick's voice cut in.

'When you do these things, you never think about the consequences, how it might affect someone else . . . I'm sorry.' Fitzpatrick was sobbing, tripping over his words in fear and remorse. 'You're going to kill me, aren't you? Please don't kill me . . .'

A final caption appeared:

Two more to go until the Dam is fully unblocked
And true justice will be served . . .

The screen went black for a long time. Finally, the recording was finished.

Reilly gave a deep sigh – she was unsure how to feel. They now knew for sure that they were dealing with the same killer, one with a Dante fixation. They also had a better sense of the perp's motive – he was a vigilante, someone who had been failed by the system and was dishing out his own form of justice in his own unique way. And clearly his chosen victims had somehow helped bring about this injustice.

The light mark she'd noticed on the ex-cop's jacket deserved further investigation, but that could well turn out to be nothing. She felt deep frustration . The killer was, as Kennedy had observed, a tease – a clever, motivated, meticulous tease. She glanced across at the detectives. Their faces seemed to be registering the same emotions as her own.

'Thoughts?'

Kennedy scowled. 'He's a clever little fucker.'

'Let's include that in our next press conference, why don't we?' Chris said drily.

'Might as well – nothing else we're doing is getting us any closer to finding him.' Kennedy stood up and stomped over to the far side of the room where the coffee pot stood steaming. 'He holds all the cards, doesn't he?' He poured himself a cup and looked over at the others. 'You lot want any?'

Both Chris and Reilly nodded, and Kennedy kept talking while he poured. 'So he tells us it's all about justice – well, we'd kind of figured out that much. He tells us there are two more to come – but how do we know who they are, or how to stop him?'

'I hate to say it,' Chris admitted, 'but Knight is right. Until this guy fucks up, we're still just pissing in the wind.'

Kennedy scowled. 'And from where I'm standing, the wind is blowing straight toward us.'

CHAPTER 28

By the time Reilly got home it was after eight, and she felt exhausted – worn out but at the same time wired too. She warmed some leftover pasta in the microwave, found a half-bottle of wine in the fridge, then collapsed in front of the TV to chill out . . .

Some time after midnight she woke up to find the half-eaten bowl of pasta had slipped off her lap and spread itself across her couch. The TV was muttering away to itself. Reilly shivered – the heat had been off for a couple of hours, and the room was now bitterly cold. She scooped the leftover pasta back into the bowl with the spoon – cleaning the couch would have to wait until tomorrow – then headed straight for bed.

She slipped off her skirt then burrowed deep under the covers, still wearing her blouse. Trying not to shiver, she curled herself up in a fetal position and wrapped the covers all the way up around her neck, cocooning herself in a deep layer of goose down and Italian linen.

Little by little she began to warm up, and was able to start to relax her muscles. But though she was tired – exhausted, even – sleep refused to come. Her nap on the couch had done just enough to take the edge off of her tiredness, and now sleep was as difficult to catch as a butterfly on a summer's day.

Every time she started to relax, her thoughts turned back to the investigation. The arrival of the video footage had given them a brief moment of optimism, but in the end it had produced more questions than answers.

Was the barn they could see in the background the same one where they had found Fitzpatrick, or was there another location – the region where the samples of horse feed and cooking sauce had come from? And, more pertinently, who were the next two victims? And where and when would the killer strike next?

Reilly had sent the disk on to the tech guys to analyze the footage itself, and to focus in on the dust mark she'd spotted, but she didn't expect much; the killer was skilled at covering his tracks, and giving them nothing.

In fact, the only thing they had so far that she suspected he didn't mean to give them was the orange pencil, which dovetailed with Reuben's suggestion that he was an artist, sketching each individual scene for his own enjoyment.

Was that something to follow up on? And if so, how? All they knew about the guy was that he most likely worked or lived in an area frequented by horses, could have a taste for spicy food and liked to sketch.

Her thoughts then shifted to last night's conversation with Chris, and his surprising revelation about his ex.

He obviously still held a candle for Melanie too, and her forthcoming wedding was clearly the reason for his recent short temper.

Reilly was also somewhat taken aback by how much the idea bothered her.

She lay in the darkness, unsure what to think. She and Chris had some kind of . . . connection, she was pretty sure about that; she just couldn't tell if it was solely down to what had happened earlier this year, and the closeness they shared throughout that investigation, or was it something more, something deeper?

One thing for sure was that she trusted him, felt safe around him.

And as she'd learned last night, there was so much more going on behind the calm, easygoing façade he presented to the world.

Now Reilly wanted to find out much more, wanted to know exactly what made Chris Delaney tick, besides work, of course.

She smiled, thinking about Pete Kennedy and his beloved Josie. She didn't think she was made for quite that kind of domestic bliss, but maybe a piece of something similar might be good?

It would definitely be nice to have someone to share things with, someone to have breakfast with in one of those nice little cafés down by the canal at weekends, or a stroll through St Stephen's

Green on a sunny afternoon. Someone who understood the demands of the job, but could help her forget about them too.

Reilly rolled over, feeling annoyed at herself for even going there. Who was she kidding? In this job, there was barely time for sleep, let alone play.

Notwithstanding that, Chris had never given the slightest indication that he was interested in anything more than the findings of Reilly's electron microscope, and clearly he was still nursing a broken heart. So how had she gone from thinking of him in terms of a good working relationship to almost comparing them to an old married couple?

When Reilly woke the next morning, she didn't feel at all refreshed.

For just those few short hours in front of the TV she had been able to relax and forget everything about work, the murders (and Chris), but with the dawn of a new day it all came rushing back to her, along with the nagging feeling that there was something about this investigation she was missing.

Down on her knees scrubbing the couch in the gray light of a December morning, she wrestled with the idea, but whatever it was that had momentarily surfaced, was once more hidden in the depths of her subconscious.

For a brief moment she considered talking to Reuben Knight about it – he was a qualified psychologist, after all – but the thought of him snooping about in her subconscious . . .

The last thing Reilly wanted was his lascivious mind probing her darker thoughts. Sometimes, the way he looked at her, it was like he knew everything about her. Her family – what had happened with Jess . . .

Arriving at the GFU headquarters sometime after eight, she flicked on the light in her office and almost jumped in surprise: the devil himself was sitting in her chair in the dark, gazing up at the ceiling with his dark, thoughtful eyes.

Reilly stared at him in surprise. 'Goodness, Reuben, what are you doing?'

He looked entirely comfortable behind her desk, fingers steepled together, lips pursed in thought. 'I find the dark is much more conducive to creative thinking, don't you?'

Reilly dumped her handbag on the floor, and sat in one of the chairs facing the desk. If he wanted to play the mysterious profiler, she was quite happy to humor him. For all his eccentricities – and there were many – there was no denying that he'd come up with the goods. 'Really? So has your nocturnal cogitation produced any radical break-through?' she teased, mocking his own way with the English language.

Reuben was pensive. 'Breakthrough? I wouldn't go so far as to claim that, but I am rather impressed with our little serial killer.' He gave a wicked smile. 'He has quite the sense of style, doesn't he?'

'Yes, I suppose he does have his own distinctive way.'

Reuben leaned forward, his face full of enthusiasm. 'I watched the video several times last night. I'm so sorry I missed the premiere but I was otherwise engaged,' he added mysteriously. 'Anyway, I couldn't help but notice how our man set us up, then knocked us down several times.'

'Detective Kennedy made the same comment.'

Reuben arched his eyebrows. 'Detective Dinosaur? You deduced that from his grunts?'

Reilly did her best to resist a smile and kept her cool, steady gaze on Reuben.

'Also,' he added, leaning forward in a conspiratorial way, 'did you catch the potential reference to the upper echelons of the force?'

She nodded. 'I was going to ask you about that – do you think the killer noticed it?'

'What you mean is, do I think that another lawman is at risk? Perhaps one of the two remaining victims he mentioned?'

'Yes, because if there's even the slightest suspicion—'

Reuben grinned wickedly. 'How delicious that would be . . .' Then his expression turned suddenly serious. 'I don't think it's a serious threat, no. I think our unsub included it as another tease, possibly another wind-up to send us off in a different direction.'

Reilly thought for a moment. 'So if the police are not a target then who are the remaining two? We'd have to assume that the final one will be

299

what you talked about before – the perpetrator himself?'

Reuben nodded. 'Once again your beguiling looks are matched by your sharp-witted mind.' He gazed at his immaculately manicured fingernails, then back at Reilly. He shrugged. 'Assuming that we believe him when he says that this is all about justice—'

'Or rather a miscarriage of justice,' Reilly clarified.

'Indeed. And given the effort he's gone to with the Dante setups, it seems unlikely he's lying.'

She thought for a moment. 'Well then, I suppose the one person we don't have yet is a judge.'

Reuben clapped his hands together in mock applause. He stood suddenly, and walked quickly round to her side of the desk. Reilly felt his warm breath on the back of her neck.

She laughed uneasily. Although she liked Reuben, there was no doubt that being alone with him unnerved her.

'Tell me, is that work ethic of yours innate – or born from a relentless drive to cast out the demons in your past?' he remarked.

Reilly whirled around to face him, her heart pounding. 'What the hell are you talking about?'

'Oh, come, my dear.' Reuben looked disappointed. 'I am a behaviorist, after all. And given your rather . . . impenetrable demeanor, but very obvious psychological fragilities, you must have known I'd be tempted by your personnel file.'

Her face flushed. 'You had no right!'

'My darling Reilly, you and I both know that what happened to your mother and sister is what drives your every move – fuels your quest to overcome evil,' he continued, as if she hadn't spoken. 'I think it's admirable, actually. After all, every brilliant investigator needs a powerful motivating factor. But what confuses me is this: are you trying to run away from your family sins, or atone for them?'

Reilly just sat there, unable to respond. It was a question her therapist back home in Cali used to ask, and one Daniel had raised the last time she'd seen him.

'In any case, I must now convene with your colleagues,' Reuben continued, dropping the subject just as quickly, and leaving Reilly's emotions spinning. 'Should be fun. And just between us, I believe O Serious One has a major bee in his bonnet about my naked admiration of your talents . . .' Again, he let the comment hang in the air, waiting for her to respond.

'Delaney?' she laughed nervously. ' I just think he's taken a serious dislike to your cologne.'

Reuben held her gaze for a touch longer than was necessary, as though he had found some way to read her mind. 'Perhaps.'

She swallowed, deciding to deflect the conversation back to the investigation once and for all. 'Just before you go . . . if our killer does have a judge in his sights—'

'"The hottest places in Hell are reserved for those who, in time of great moral crisis, maintain their neutrality."'

'Dante?'

Reuben grinned. 'John F. Kennedy, actually. In the *Inferno*, Dante and Virgil pass by a group of dead souls outside the entrance to Hell. These individuals, when alive, remained neutral at a time of great moral decision. Virgil explains that these neutrals cannot enter either Heaven or Hell because they could not choose one side or another while on earth. They are therefore worse than the greatest sinners in Hell because they are abhorrent to both God and Satan alike, and have been left to mourn their fate as insignificant beings, neither hailed nor cursed in life or death, endlessly travailing below Heaven but outside of Hell.'

'In a limbo of sorts?'

'Indeed.' Reuben looked pensive and she guessed he was having the very same thoughts as she was, namely trying to guess what punishment awaited the judge upon whom the killer had set his sights.

'So what should we expect?'

'These wretched ones, who never were alive, went naked and were stung again and again by horseflies and wasps that circled them.' Reuben seemed to be quoting directly from the text. 'The insects streaked their faces with their blood, which, mingled with their tears, fell at their feet, where it was gathered up by sickening worms.'

302

CHAPTER 29

Chris stared at the glass of vodka on the bar in front of him.

The pub was busy, full of the office lunchtime crowd looking for sandwiches and shepherd's pies on a Friday afternoon.

Chris was looking for a remedy.

The place was across the road from the station, and he'd popped in for a quick one, realizing that alchohol was doing a better number on his limbs than ten painkillers. He knocked back the vodka; unable to remember the last time he had been really, truly, shitfaced drunk.

Actually no, he was wrong. He could.

Three years earlier

Chris parked his car carefully, but still couldn't avoid hitting the kerb.

He unbuckled his seatbelt, managing to get it tangled as he stumbled out of the car. Then he made his way unsteadily up the path, rang the front doorbell, and stood swaying slightly while he waited for her to reply. After a moment the hall light flicked on, then the outside light, bathing him in a yellow glow.

'Who is it?' Her voice was edged with annoyance.

'Mel, you know it's me. Let me in, for Christ's sake.'

'You're drunk.' The accusation, though true, sounded harsh and judgemental issued from the small intercom.

Chris pushed the button to speak. 'Yes, I'm drunk,' he admitted. 'Let me in, I need to talk to you.'

There was a long silence as Melanie thought about it. 'Show me your ID,' she said finally.

'For fuck's sake . . .'

'I said, show me your ID,' she commanded, and frustrated, Chris whipped his badge out from his jacket pocket. Tonight, he was in no mood for this.

She opened the door and he stepped into the hall. Peeking outside, she caught a glance of his car. 'You drove here?' she said, her eyes heavy with accusation, and Chris automatically felt guilty.

'Yeah, I drove. I told you, I needed to talk to you.'

'But you're the one who's supposed to do things right – you're the one who's supposed to uphold the law, supposed to protect us from —'

Chris's head ached. He didn't need to hear that shit just then.

Finally she sighed, pointed him toward the living room. 'Go and sit down. I'll get you a cup of coffee.'

Chris slumped down on the couch, and looked around the small room. It looked just as it had when Melanie's parents died a couple of years ago – the ceramic ducks flying forever above the mantelpiece, Melanie's childhood photographs on the piano, the old fourteen-inch TV on its little stand in the corner of the room.

The screen flickered at Chris, but he ignored it, and closed his eyes, allowing the tiredness to wash over him while he listened to the comforting domestic sounds of Melanie pottering around the kitchen. If only everything could be normal again, back to the way it used to be . . .

'Don't fall asleep here. You can't stay here, you know that.'

Chris woke with a start. Melanie was standing over him, holding out a chipped coffee mug with a butterfly on it. He remembered buying it for her a long time ago, at the time he was away in training college, maybe? And despite its somewhat worn appearance she refused to get rid of it.

'I don't like it when you're drunk,' she said.

'I know, I know. I'm sorry.' He sipped at the scalding coffee, and tried to clear his thoughts.

Chris gazed at her. He could see the pain still lurking there, the years of loneliness, of fear. Suddenly he slid off the couch, and dropped to his knees in front of her. 'I'm so sorry, Mel. Sorry I wasn't there for you, sorry I can never make you feel safe . . .'

Melanie just stood there, immobile as he wept, when all he wanted was for her to take him in her arms, gently stroke his hair, and wipe the tears from his cheeks as he sobbed, his head in her lap.

He wanted her to comfort him, to tell him that of

305

course he made her feel safe, that she knew he was doing everything he could.

But Chris realized that the life he wanted for him and Melanie would never happen. Their future was ruined, their past forever tainted by someone who'd taken everything. And their present . . . well, this was their present. Him drinking too much and ignoring his responsibilities while she stayed locked away in this house, afraid to face the world, afraid to face him.

And with a heavy heart, he understood that neither of them would be able to bear this life much longer.

Later that afternoon, Reilly's phone rang. She answered quickly. 'Steel.'

It was Kennedy. 'Is Chris with you, by any chance? He mentioned something about calling over . . .' He sounded hurried.

'No. I haven't heard from him since yesterday.'

'Damn. There's something going on with him . . .'

Reilly wondered what Chris was up to now. It wasn't like him to go walkabout. Then she remembered what he'd said about Melanie getting married this week. Could the wedding be today?

'If I hear from him, I'll—'

'I wanted to talk to you anyway. We've found the next victim – at a quarry of all places,' Kennedy told her quickly. 'One of the workers stumbled across the body this morning. Victim's since been identified as one Andrew Morgan. And guess what – he's a district court judge.'

It wouldn't have been how Judge Andrew Morgan would want to be remembered.

'This guy really is something else,' Kennedy said, struggling to speak with his hand clenched over his face. Karen Thompson was low down in the sand, examining something, a white flag positioned nearby.

Already the smell was bothering Reilly less and less. That's the way it was with unpleasant things, she thought – at first they seemed unbearable, a great intrusion, impossible to ignore, but little by little they lost their edge, and became almost everyday occurrences.

Was that what was happening to all of them in this job? Were they becoming immune? She looked at Kennedy, who was standing on the grass just above the gravel pit, talking to the medical examiner.

Chris was still nowhere to be found. Reilly had tried his mobile but it went straight to voicemail. Where the hell was he?

She was worried. While she was glad he'd confided in her, this thing with his ex-fiancée was obviously affecting him a lot more than he was letting on.

Still, this wasn't the time or the place to worry about it.

Lifting up her kitbag, Reilly took a deep breath, and approached the small group. 'Afternoon, Doc.'

'Hey, there.' Karen nodded toward the body. 'Another little beauty for us to unravel.'

'Oh, man . . .' Reilly turned her gaze to the heap on the ground and almost immediately averted it. The setup was as hideous to behold as it was to smell.

Judge Morgan had been a large man – no, she thought, if truth be told, he was obese – and nakedness certainly didn't improve his looks.

Struggling to regain her professionalism, she looked again at the hulking mass in the sand, trying to take it all in. It was clear from the outset that he had been dead for three or four days – decomposition had already started, turning his flesh a disconcerting gray. But for Reilly, the biggest indicator that this wasn't a fresh death was the maggots.

The dead man's pasty naked form pulsed with teeming, relentless burrowing larvae. Most of his upper body, including his head, was completely enveloped by the stubby writhing mass.

As Karen went to turn the body over, handfuls of worms rained down from his nose, ears and mouth. They were devouring his flesh in a relent-less manner, and every orifice seemed to pulse with movement. The maggots had colonized so much of his face that his dead eyes stared widely upwards, the eyelids eaten away. His nose, too, was barely recognizable, most of it already devoured.

A cloud of blowflies hovered doggedly around – despite the cold December temperatures there was enough heat from the rapidly decomposing body to sustain them.

Swallowing hard, Reilly immediately recalled Reuben's words from that morning, and realized he had correctly predicted this particular punishment in accordance with their killer's twisted code.

'Any idea on the cause of death?' she asked Karen Thompson.

The other woman nodded, her saucer-like eyes peering up at Reilly as she bent over the corpse.

'If I were a betting woman, I would say that the good judge was first brought here under some kind of duress, and judging by the swelling,' she indicated a particular area on the victim's head that seemed to be wriggling more intensely than the rest, 'it looks like he was hit over the head with something. Can't say for sure until I get him on to the table and pry off all these little creatures.'

Reilly thought that this relatively fuzzy description of the maggots seemed very much at odds with their disgusting appearance.

The doctor straightened up. 'So what sin does this punishment signify?'

Reilly pursed her lips. She recalled a particular passage she'd read in the *Inferno* about the neutrals soon after her conversation with Reuben.

They swatted helplessly in the air, swatting their own bodies, while insects and flies circled their naked forms. Maggots crawled out from rotted gaps in their teeth, gathering in heaps below. These souls were said to follow a blank banner ahead of them as a symbol of their pointless paths.

Reilly looked at the white flag. Something to symbolize the blank banner?

'Neutrality,' she told Karen. 'Our man seems to have identified Judge Morgan as someone who was uncommitted.'

'But judges are impartial by definition, surely?'

'Yes, but he must have ruled some way on a case that the killer didn't like. The neutrals are portrayed in Dante's *Inferno* as those who had the opportunity to do good or evil, but choose not to do either.'

'Charming,' the ME replied flatly, and Reilly followed her gaze back to the judge, the maggots still gorging on his rapidly decomposing flesh.

If the man's crime was indeed impartiality, this particular punishment seemed unnecessarily harsh.

CHAPTER 30

The following day, Reilly stood with her hands behind her back, and watched O'Brien carefully. The team had all been summoned to an early morning meeting. The chief wasn't exactly reading the riot act – he had been in the force long enough to know that without solid leads and evidence there was little they could actually do – but he was venting his frustrations at them all the same.

Chris and Kennedy stood beside Reilly, while Reuben Knight lolled in a nearby chair, one leg hooked over the arm of it.

She looked closely at Chris, and watched him resolutely place his shaking hands in his pockets. She didn't believe him when he'd mentioned something about missing the Morgan discovery yesterday afternoon because he'd been following up on some mysterious lead.

His eyes were bloodshot, his shirt wrinkled and his tie askew, as if he'd slept in his clothes. To someone like Reilly (who, with an alcoholic father, knew the signs all too well) Chris looked like he'd spent most of the day at the bottle.

What the hell? So much for being happy for

Melanie and wishing her well. For a guy who didn't drink all that much this was a worrying development. Reilly sorely hoped this whole thing with the ex-fiancée, coupled with the pressures of the workload, wasn't the start of a slippery slope for Chris, and she resolved to confront him about it as soon as she got the chance.

'Five murders!' O'Brien thundered. He held up a national paper for emphasis, a huge headline emblazoned across it: 'Punisher Claims Fifth Victim'. 'Are we any nearer to finding this madman?'

'He's not really a madman,' Reuben drawled, fiddling with his precious Mont Blanc pen. 'That's the problem, really.'

O'Brien shot him a furious glare, but the profiler seemed impervious.

'So do we have anything? Anything at all?'

They glanced at each other like unruly kids hauled up before the headmaster, as if trying to decide how to tell their side of the story without getting anyone else in trouble.

'I'm afraid Reuben is right,' Reilly finally replied. 'It seems pretty clear that our killer had all this planned out long before he committed the first murder. So far he's made few mistakes, or has given us little that moves us forward.'

'Except,' Kennedy added, glancing at the others, 'now that we've found the judge, we might have a good chance of connecting the dots and finding a link between all five victims, and maybe figure out the original crime that it's all related to.'

O'Brien now had his back to them, and was gazing out the window. 'You mean the justice angle?' He turned round suddenly. 'Assuming it's related to an actual crime . . .'

'There is little question that all these murders – these punishments – stem from a single transgression,' Reuben said. 'As I outlined in my profile, what we have is an angry vigilante who is intimately familiar with the failings of the modern courts system, and determined to extract what vicious justice he can from those he thinks were complicit.'

'All very well and good, but how does it help us find the maniac?' O'Brien demanded.

'We're going to cross-reference any cases that Morgan sat on, where Crowe gave evidence, that Coffey wrote about, and so on,' Kennedy went on. 'We've been having trouble with the warrant for Dr Jennings' files. Identifying the suicide victim in his care could well be the key to all of this.'

Reilly couldn't help but think how the delay was a perfect example of how frustrating the law – and how slow the wheels of justice – could be.

'Well, do whatever it takes to get that, for fuck's sake!' For a moment it looked as though O'Brien was going to combust, but instead he turned and addressed Reuben again. 'So you think there's just the one more victim – "the primary perpetrator", as you referred to him in your profile?'

Knight nodded. 'Assuming he's telling the truth.'

O'Brien glowered at him. 'We're not paying you to assume – does it fit the profile or doesn't it?'

Reuben gave an easy smile. 'Based on the rigorous planning, the exaggerated theatricality of it all? Absolutely. He had a well-thought-out plan that he has executed to perfection. Dante's *Inferno* is his blueprint. There's no reason to think that he would deviate from his cause now.'

'Right. Well, let's see if we can find the bugger before he claims his last victim. That would be some degree of consolation at least . . .'

Later that morning, Chris returned to the large conference room, his head feeling like it was on fire. The long wooden table was covered in boxes of files. An administrative assistant wheeled a trolley in, laden with yet more files and folders.

He glanced around. 'Where do you want them?'

Chris looked up – in truth he couldn't care less. He pointed to the far side of the room. 'Just stack them against the wall over there.'

The assistant dutifully rolled his trolley over, and unloaded the boxes one by one.

'Is that the last one?' Chris asked.

'Yep, that's your lot.'

'Thank God for that.'

As the assistant rolled his trolley out, Kennedy strode in, his hands full with a cardboard tray of coffees and a Starbucks bag. 'Here we go,' he said brightly, 'some half-decent coffee.' He looked at the heavily laden table and his face fell. 'Bloody hell! Please tell me that's all of it.'

Chris nodded. 'Yep, this should be fun.'

There was no room on the table, so Kennedy dumped the coffees on a small filing cabinet, and dropped down into a chair. He held out the bag to Chris. 'How about a bit of sugar to get your engine started? It's going to be a long bloody day.' He bit a huge chunk out of his muffin, and slurped on his coffee. 'I got you some kind of fruity one.'

Chris almost retched at even the thought of food. 'Do you have any idea how many calories are in those things?' he said, hoping that Kennedy would think he was just worried about his health, rather than his hungover stomach.

His partner was busily cramming pieces into his mouth. 'Do you have any idea how little I care?' he spluttered through a mouthful of crumbs.

Chris cast a glance at his partner's bulging waistline and raised a smile. 'I could hazard a guess.'

Kennedy looked down at his belly, and gave it a gentle pat. 'Hey, go easy on this fella – it takes a lot of work to get a body like this.' He indicated the mountain of files. 'So where do we start on this lot?'

Chris took a mouthful of coffee, and picked up a list. 'These are all the major cases that Crowe and Judge Morgan had in common.'

'How many?'

He glanced at the bottom of the list. 'One hundred and twenty-seven.'

Kennedy shook his head. 'Unbelievable.'

'Let's sort through them first,' Chris suggested,

'get the minor cases set aside, then have a look at each of the biggies. We can make a list of those and then cross-reference them against any articles that Coffey wrote.'

Taking the new victim and the killer's motive into account, they needed to go through Coffey's articles again with a fine-tooth comb.

Reilly had agreed to take on this part of the workload, and had also suggested Rory from her office, who was a speed-reader, by all accounts, and good at seeking out info relevant to an investigation. Much to Reuben's consternation, he had also been roped-in to help with the search under strict orders from O'Brien.

Kennedy wasn't looking at all happy. 'Bloody hell, what a chore . . .'

Chris looked at the list, and then at the case number on the nearest box. 'Right, this one is shoplifting. I think we can forget that.' He pointed to one corner of the room. 'Why not put the misdemeanors over there? The sooner we create some space on this table the better.'

By midday, the task was starting to take shape: all boxes for the minor cases had been removed and stacked at the far end of the room. The remaining ones – the forty-seven more serious cases common to Crowe and Judge Morgan – formed their own pile at the end of the table.

Chris checked the list again and looked up. 'I think that's it.'

'Great.' Kennedy pulled the closest box toward

his feet. 'Then let's grab a box each and dig in. What are we supposed to be looking for again?' He opened the nearest box and looked inside at the densely packed files.

'Anything out of kilter,' Chris replied. 'Something to suggest that maybe Crowe "lost" evidence, or any possible link to Coffey or Jennings . . .'

The afternoon passed slowly, each of them poring over one case file after another, looking for links, connections, and making notes that might tie in with some article of Coffey's. Kennedy remained reasonably cheerful, but after a few hours even his enthusiasm was starting to wane.

Chris looked up from the case he was reading. This was pretty depressing stuff – case after case that was either dismissed on a technicality, or where a clearly guilty suspect was given a minimal sentence after the police had spent a huge amount of time gathering evidence.

He had learned long ago that it was best not to pay attention to what happened once the prosecution service got involved – it tended to lead to disappointment and frustration for the police and the investigators, seeing suspects they knew to be guilty either not being charged, getting acquitted, or receiving a minimal sentence.

At times like this he was half able to understand the motives of someone like their killer. After all, and despite his job, Chris knew perhaps better than most that justice was rarely served.

CHAPTER 31

Copper Face Jacks nightclub on Leeson Street was hopping on a Saturday night. The music blasted out, the drinks were flying, and the lads and ladies of Dublin were out in force on their weekend mating rituals. Drink in hand, Ricky Webb stood in the corner of the room watching it all. It was his first night of freedom, and he was determined to enjoy it.

He had been released earlier that morning. The screw had come to his cell at eight o'clock, and walked him down to the office, the other inmates all calling out to him.

Officer Matthews, a hard-faced man with a jaw like Superman, had processed him wordlessly, filling out the forms and handing them over to Ricky to sign. Finally he handed Ricky his clothes, his dead watch, and three hundred and seventy quid in cash.

Ricky looked around for somewhere to change, but there was nowhere. Matthews just stared at him. 'Oh, what the fuck . . .' He tore off his prison clothes, threw them on the table, and dressed quickly in his civvies. He glanced up, and saw

Matthews' eyes still on him. 'Had a good look? Fancy me, do you?'

Matthews said nothing, and maintained his intense glare.

'So are we all sorted?'

The guard nodded to the clothes Ricky had thrown on the table. 'Fold them.'

'Screw you.'

Matthews simply repeated his gesture. 'Fold them. Mommy's not here to clean up after you now.'

Ricky looked down at the clothes, then glanced at the door on the far side of the room. Freedom was waiting for him. What the hell . . . He picked up the clothes, carefully folded them, set them back on the desk. 'Happy now?'

The guard grabbed the clothes and flung them into a laundry hamper behind him. 'Now I am.'

'Bastard.'

Matthews simply grinned, stepped over to the door, and rapped on it with his knuckles. There was a scrape, a clank of keys, and the door swung open.

A lanky young guard held the door open for him. 'All right, let's go.'

Webb stepped through, and the smell of asphalt assaulted his senses. He paused, looked up at the gray winter sky, and grinned. 'About fucking time.'

The young officer closed the door behind him.

Ricky looked around – everything looked so normal – so wonderfully, fucking normal.

319

'Were you expecting someone to pick you up?' the officer asked.

Ricky gave a grunt. 'Who the fuck would come to get me?'

Now in the pub, Ricky sipped his drink and thought again about the question. He had spent the day chewing over it, letting his anger and frustration build. His father was dead, his mother was a cold-faced bitch, and to the rest of the family he was a pariah, the skeleton in the cupboard, the black sheep they never spoke about.

But now he was back. Out after eighteen long months, and he wanted to make up for lost time . . .

His dark eyes scanned the room. So far the night had been a big disappointment. Earlier, he had headed to The Baggot Inn, his old hangout. The place was full of yuppies, bankers and IT technicians in designer clothes, with not one of his old mates to be seen anywhere.

After a quick pint he had moved on to Coppers nightclub. At least that was still the same, still the best place to go and pick up easy women; that he could see straight away. None of his mates was there, no one recognized him, but the talent was there, and tonight, that was what mattered above all else.

Eighteen months he'd spent inside, eighteen long months of fantasizing, but tonight it was going to be the real thing. It didn't matter which girl, he wasn't fussy, and any would do so long as she was up for it. And here, they all usually were.

He nursed his pint, and watched the guys and the girls play their games. All the time he was clocking, assessing – who was with someone, who was single, who looked like they might be willing.

One by one the best-looking girls were hit on – some of them several times before they let anyone buy them a drink – and little by little the losers were left at the margins. The big girls, the ones whose features didn't quite add up, the ones with too much make-up on, too many miles on the clock and all that.

Finally, Ricky made his move.

'You all right, love?'

The girl looked up. She was in her late twenties, with bleached blond hair, heavy make-up, a bit overweight, but nothing fatal. She wore a black miniskirt and a stretchy white top that struggled to contain her ample bosom. She had spent the evening on the dancefloor, as her more attractive friends got picked up at the bar, and now she was alone – alone, drunk, and vulnerable.

She looked up and saw a handsome face staring at her.

'Can I get you a drink?'

She smiled and Ricky was sure she was thinking he was a cut above the losers who'd approached her that night. 'Sure. Bacardi and Coke.'

Ricky caught the barman's attention, no easy task in this crowd. 'Bacardi and Coke, and a pint,' he shouted over the din of the music. He turned back to her. 'So what's your name?'

'Laura.'

Ricky took her hand, and brushed it with his lips. 'Lovely to meet you, Laura. Mine's Ricky.'

Laura gave a little giggle. 'Well . . . you're quite the romantic, aren't you?'

The barman brought their drinks. Ricky flipped him a twenty and smiled at Laura. 'Been watching you for a while.'

She sipped at her drink and looked up at him through heavily mascara'd eyelashes. 'Oh, you have, have you? And what have you been watching exactly?'

'You've got quite a pair of legs, for starters . . .'

She smiled, obviously thrilled with the compliment. 'So what do you do, Ricky?'

'What do I do? Let's just say I'm a . . . private security consultant.'

'Hmm. Sounds interesting.'

'Oh, it is.'

For the next hour Ricky plied Laura with drinks and compliments, and she in turn soaked them up. At around two thirty he decided to make his move. She was nicely drunk, and he was done waiting.

'Fancy going somewhere quieter?'

She looked up at him, struggling to focus her eyes. 'Where?' she slurred.

'My place is just around the corner,' Ricky told her. 'They've stopped serving here now. We could head back there for another one?'

She gave a watery smile. 'Sounds good to me.'

Nice one, Ricky thought. As usual, it was almost too easy.

The air was bitter when they stepped outside, a blast from the east bringing a flurry of snowflakes. Ricky took off his jacket and wrapped it around Laura.

'I think you might need this.'

She looked up at his dark eyes. 'You really are a gentleman, aren't you?'

He wrapped his arm around her. 'Yep, a real gentleman, that's me . . .'

He steered her out of the nightclub and further down the street, Laura tottering along beside him on her high heels.

Their footsteps echoed on the quiet streets. 'Is it much further?' she asked as they turned onto a quiet backstreet a few minutes later. 'These heels are killing me.'

'Not long now,' said Ricky. 'My place is just down here.'

She suddenly stopped as he made to turn down a dark alleyway. 'What kind of stunt are you trying to pull?'

'I told you,' said Ricky evenly, 'it's just down here.'

She peered into the darkness. An articulated lorry passed on the street alongside them, drowning out her response.

'What did you say?'

She tried to pull away. 'I said you're crazy if you think I'm going down there with you.'

'You'd be right.'

Ricky suddenly frowned at the strange voice, and saw Laura's attention turn to someone behind him. Then, without warning, something hard smashed down onto the back of his head.

She screamed as he slumped on the hard ground beside her. The figure quickly kneeled over Ricky, and Laura caught a brief glimpse of her savior. He was dressed all in black, and wore gloves and a black baseball cap, but his face was hidden by the shadows.

'Are you OK?' he asked her.

She nodded shakily. 'Thanks, I wasn't sure if—'

'You're welcome,' he replied gently. 'You should go home now. I'll take care of your friend.'

By then, Laura was only too happy to extricate herself from whatever issue was between the two, and she duly tottered quickly away down the street.

When she was gone, the man bent down over Ricky, and carefully sat him upright. He worked his hands up under Ricky's armpits and, breathing a sigh of relief that he was a lightweight, hauled him to his feet.

For a moment they swayed forward, then the man steadied himself, bent down, and hoisted Ricky up into a fireman's lift.

With Ricky draped across his shoulder, the man staggered up the alleyway. It was hard work, but he had been preparing for this for months, working out in the gym, squatting endlessly, practicing lifting and carrying heavy things.

Like dead bodies, for instance.

He soon reached the end of the alleyway, and cautiously looked out. There was no one around. He approached a white van, anonymously parked in the pool of shadows beneath a broken streetlight, slid the side door open, and dumped Ricky unceremoniously in the back of it.

His burden gone, the man straightened up, and arched his back to stretch it out. No one was around; no one had seen him except the girl, and she was too drunk to remember much.

He climbed into the driver's seat, and slid the key into the ignition. Drive carefully, attract no attention. He had it all planned and he wasn't going to make any mistakes now.

As he pulled away, he heard Ricky groan from the back and couldn't suppress a smile of quiet satisfaction.

Better get used to pain, he thought. It's what will fill what little life you have left.

CHAPTER 32

The following morning, Reilly was in her office, poring over Tony Coffey's newspaper articles to help with the search for that elusive thread that bound all five killings together.

The answer was proving as difficult to find as anything else in the investigation. While Chris and Kennedy had advised that there were plenty of cases involving Judge Morgan and Crowe, none of them seemed controversial enough to have attracted the journalistic attention of Coffey, or the influence of Fitzpatrick. And Jennings didn't seem to fit in with anything at all.

The smell of old paper lodged in her nostrils, a musty aroma that made her think of old libraries, old offices.

'You might have warned me . . .' Reuben stuck his head round the door, a cheeky grin on his chiseled face.

Reilly looked up, glad for any distraction from the tedium of reviewing the newspapers. 'Warned you about what?'

He trotted in with a brisk step. 'Coffey's secretary.'

Reilly smiled, recalling Chris's description of Kirsty Malone with her denim miniskirt and heavy eye make-up. O'Brien had requested that Reuben re-interview some of the key witnesses in order to help with the search for a link. True to form, he had chosen to begin with the most attractive one.

He raised an eyebrow. 'I don't think I've seen so much of a woman's cleavage since I was a baby.'

Reilly grinned. 'So did you get anything out of her?'

He looked shocked. 'Reilly Steel, I'm sure I don't know what you mean—'

'Any useful information then,' she clarified, shaking her head indulgently.

'Well, yes, as it happens.' Reuben rummaged inside his manbag, and pulled out a stack of papers. 'In addition to having a delectable bosom, Ms Malone is also rather well organized. It transpires that one of the things she did for Mr Coffey was catalogue his articles all the way back to when he was writing for some socialist student rag . . .'

Reilly picked up the top article. The title read: 'Why Our Courts Are Broken, and How to Fix Them.'

'He really was quite the populist,' she commented, having briefly scanned the text.

Reuben nodded. 'Not my reading choice. The man tends toward simplistic solutions to complex problems. I ignored all the earlier ones – they were more rants than anything else – but over the past ten years or so he's written about the Irish courts,

327

sentencing, justice, parole . . . on a number of occasions.' He patted the stack of articles. 'Happy reading, my dear.'

She gave a wry smile, and indicated the massive piles of newspaper around her. 'More reading, just what we need . . .'

'You can thank me later. Have fun!' Reuben turned and headed for the door.

'Well, I'm glad you made it out with your virtue intact at least,' she called after him.

His head popped back inside the doorway and he grinned wickedly. 'My darling, whoever said I did?'

Reilly thumbed idly through the articles Reuben had mentioned. If Coffey mentioned a particular case, it could shortcut the whole process of going through the case files.

She was halfway through reading them when Lucy showed up. It was her first time seeing the younger woman since her renegade trip the other day, and Reilly noted how she knocked politely on the door, waiting to be invited in.

She stood up and stretched, amazed at how much time had passed – it was almost ten a.m. already. 'Hey there. Come on in.'

Lucy seemed reluctant to meet her gaze. 'I just wanted to apologize . . . about the other day.'

'What were you thinking, Lucy?' Reilly asked without preamble. 'Going down there by yourself?'

'I just wanted to try and pinpoint a location for the samples.'

Reilly ran a hand through her hair. 'It was very

328

irresponsible of you, sweetheart, not to mention above and beyond the call of duty. You can't take chances like that. You should have told me; I could have arranged for a uniform to go down there with you; have gone myself, even.'

Lucy still didn't look at her. 'I know it was stupid, but I thought I'd just ask around, see if there were any abandoned barns nearby, any old stables, things like that. I wasn't thinking . . .'

'And what would you have done if the killer had suddenly shown up while you were snooping around?'

'That's what my dad said. Look, I didn't mean to get in trouble and I couldn't believe it when the locals showed up. It was just supposed to be a fishing mission. There are dozens of similar farms out in that area. The chances of any of them being the right one—'

'Yet Julian tells me that the samples you brought back are a match?'

Reilly had had mixed feelings when she heard about this. It seemed that Lucy had been a lot closer to the correct spot than she'd thought.

Fantastic if it helped them narrow down the doer's location, but to think what could have happened if Lucy had stumbled across the right property . . .

Lucy nodded eagerly. 'Yes, a sample I took from one of the farms matches the others, but the same logic still applies. It just means I was in the right area.'

'Well, there's no denying that you got a result, but still . . .'

'I know, I know, I should have told somebody where I was going. But it was just a spur-of-the-moment decision, you know? We were getting so little in the case, and I thought if I could—'

'I admire your initiative, but Dr Gorman, your dad . . .'

Lucy shook her head. 'Don't mind him.'

'Lucy, he's your father. If anything happened to you—'

'I know, but you don't understand, he's so bloody overprotective of me. As if what happened to Grace will happen to me too.'

Reilly looked up. 'Grace?'

'My older sister. She went missing fourteen years ago. When I was ten.' Reilly's face must have betrayed her surprise. 'I'm sorry, I guess I thought everyone knew. Nobody mentions it anymore really, but . . .' She shrugged and Reilly struggled to get her head around this.

And here she was, always wondering what made Jack Gorman so angry, so bitter . . .

'Your sister – she's never been found?'

'Not a sign,' Lucy confirmed, her voice softening. 'It's silly really, but it's sort of why I got into this job in the first place. I thought if I knew forensics I'd be able to follow the clues, and maybe find out what happened to her.' She looked away. 'Of course, it's hard to follow clues when there aren't any.'

'It's still an open case then,' Reilly said.

Poor Lucy – and poor Jack. To think that she hadn't been aware of such a pertinent piece of information about her colleagues . . .

She resolved to dig out the missing persons file as soon as she had a free moment. A fresh eye might do some good; maybe pick up on something that had been missed?

'Yeah,' Lucy continued, 'but I think everyone knows by now, the police included, that she isn't coming back. The first twenty-four hours are crucial they say. It's been fourteen years.'

It was true. Reilly knew from experience with missing children cases back home that sadly there was little chance the girl would ever be found. 'She . . . Grace was your older sister, you said?'

'Yes. She was fourteen. Would have been twenty-eight this year.' She swallowed hard, and Reilly could tell that despite Lucy's young age when it happened, she was still very much affected by her sister's disappearance. How could she not be, when something like that would have shaped the family dynamic ever since?

She, perhaps better than most, could understand what that was like.

Jack Gorman's apparent overreaction about Lucy's behavior the other day was suddenly making a whole lot of sense. Particularly the comment about an angry parent being preferable to a grieving one. Poor Jack Gorman was that grieving parent, and had no doubt suffered the loss of his eldest daughter every day . . . that horrific limbo of not knowing if she were dead or alive.

'I suppose now you have a better idea of why Dad is on my case so much about working here,' Lucy continued drily. 'He went crazy when he heard I wanted to study forensics – and then when the new lab positions opened up here . . .'

Upon her arrival at the GFU, Reilly had indeed been taken aback by Jack Gorman's dismissive attitude toward his daughter, particularly as Lucy was hugely diligent and very capable. But of course she hadn't seen it for what it was – parental protectiveness.

'I guess it must have been tough on you, growing up?' she queried. 'I can't imagine your folks were happy about you staying out late dancing, or that kind of thing.'

Lucy smiled tightly. 'It was . . . different,' she said, and Reilly figured that family life had been one of two ways. Either the parents, crippled with grief over their missing child had (unintentionally) ignored the one remaining, or alternatively, smothered her. It was usually the way with the families of missing kids and in truth it was remarkable that Lucy had ended up the confident, well-adjusted person she was.

'It's understandable,' Lucy continued. 'After what happened to Grace, Mum and Dad have always been terrified of losing me too.' She shook her head. 'That's why Dad was so mad at me for what I did the other day. But sometimes . . . I suppose I just felt the need to break away a little and do something spontaneous, something *useful*.'

Thinking about her own family setup, Reilly looked at Lucy, realizing that the two of them had much in common. Professional lives driven by family tragedies, and perhaps in trying to overcome the helplessness of the past, they each felt the same strong desire to control the future.

Now Lucy was shifting from foot to foot, evidently anxious to end the topic of conversation. 'Anyway, I get why you're mad and I promise I won't do anything like that again.' She smiled guiltily. 'So if you're done reading me the riot act . . .'

'Of course,' Reilly said, her thoughts still all over the place as she tried to process this new information.

Lucy held out two reports. 'The lab's findings from the Morgan scene, and Dr Thompson's autopsy report.'

Reilly waved them away, trying to regain some focus. 'I've done nothing but read all morning – tell me what we've got.'

Lucy perched on the edge of her desk. 'Dr Thompson concludes that Morgan's COD was blunt-force trauma to the head.'

Reilly pictured the poor naked man in the quarry. 'Anything else of interest?'

'No. He was naked, so nothing on the body, other than the holes those maggots left behind.' She shuddered visibly. 'Disgusting. We did get some more of that capsicum sauce in the sand, though.'

'But nothing new otherwise?'

'No.' Lucy gave a sigh of exasperation. 'Seriously, what do we have to do to catch a break with this guy?'

'I don't know that we ever do,' Reilly told her. 'Most of the time, the only reason we catch these people is because of bad luck on their part, or because they do something stupid. This guy certainly isn't stupid, and so far his luck has held.'

Lucy looked downbeat, frustrated.

'Hey, don't let it get to you,' Reilly told her. 'We're doing the best we can, and despite the circumstances, you did good with the soil.'

She spread her arms to indicate the room full of files. 'I'm just hoping that somewhere in here, amongst all this paperwork, is the key that unlocks this whole mystery.'

In the end it was indeed Coffey's articles that gave Reilly the breakthrough she so desperately needed. She had waded through over twenty of his newspaper columns – he was a good writer, but his strident prose became a bit grating after reading several articles in a row – and she was starting to feel sleepy when a headline caught her eye: 'The Curious Case of Missing Evidence'.

She read the article quickly, scanning for the key indicators that might tie all the victims together, and soon found what she was looking for.

Coffey was referring to a brutal rape case that had been heard by Judge Morgan three years ago, in which the main detective, Crowe, had apparently mislaid some key evidence.

So far, so good. A link between three of their victims. But what tied it to Fitzpatrick or Jennings?

Reilly read on – the journalist was suggesting that in a case like this, where the evidence was weak, the courts should be more lenient, and the defendant should be released.

A name in the article popped out, and something that Chris had mentioned leaped into her mind. He had told her that Coffey's house – way too expensive for a humble journalist – was actually his wife's. What had he said? *Part of the hunting set.*

Reilly pulled her phone from her pocket, and quickly dialled an extension. Nobody better than Julius to seek out this kind of information.

'Hi, Reilly. What's up?'

'I need you to do some digging. Have you got a pen handy?'

'One sec.' There was a pause. 'OK, shoot.'

'I want you to check the connection between a few people for me. The first is Sandra Coffey—'

'The journalist's wife?'

'Right. But her maiden name is Webb.'

'Got it. Who else?'

'A defendant in one of Morgan's cases – Richard Webb. Call Detective Delaney for the docket number.'

'Richard Webb,' he repeated back to her. 'That it?'

'For the moment at least. Find out if they are connected, or if there are any family connections to either Judge Morgan or Alan Fitzpatrick.'

'Will do.'

'And, Julius? Call me back right away if you find anything.'

Reilly flipped her laptop open. Time for her to do some research of her own. A few minutes later, she called Chris at the station.

'I've just had Julius on the phone. What's all this about Richard Webb?' he asked her before she could speak.

Reilly filled him in on the only link she'd found between Morgan, Coffey and Crowe. 'Nothing to get excited about just yet, but can you get me the docket number?'

'Sure. Let me know if anything flies.'

'Will do. How are you two getting on?'

'Well, Kennedy seems to be enjoying himself. He's using it as an excuse to overdose on muffins.'

'Dangerous work as usual,' she chuckled, glad that Chris sounded a lot more awake and upbeat than he had the day before. Promising him that she'd keep them updated, Reilly hung up. She then logged on to the criminal court system's secure website and entered Ricky Webb's docket number.

The case soon popped up. Richard 'Ricky' Webb had been convicted eighteen months before, and had been given a three-year sentence. She scanned down the file. He was currently being held at Mountjoy Prison and – her breath quickened – he'd been granted parole by a review board earlier in the year.

Webb's conviction was for the rape and battery of a 17-year-old girl, yet his sentence was just three years?

A shiver ran down Reilly's spine. She strongly believed in intuition and had studied enough psychology to know that such feelings were often the result of processing in the deep parts of the subconscious mind. We don't know why we reach certain conclusions, and often dismiss them, but the truth is that they are correct most of the time. Now she felt, deep in her gut, that this was the case they were looking for.

She quickly opened another window on her laptop. The sentence was disturbingly lenient for such a grievous offence. And who had made the decision to parole Webb barely eighteen months into his prison term?

The names of the parole board popped up, but nothing significant jumped out.

Clicking open another window, Reilly did a search on the politician Alan Fitzpatrick. Who were his buddies, his associates, his cronies? Page after page flashed by – photos of Fitzpatrick mixing and meeting – and gradually a few names began to appear over and over again. She made a list, then checked back with the members of the parole board.

Bingo.

Two members of the same board were regulars in Fitzpatrick's inner circle, Nigel Finnegan, and Ken Howard. Had he somehow influenced them to look favorably on Webb's request for parole?

The ringing of her phone startled her. It was Julius.

'What did you find?' she asked.

He couldn't keep the triumph from his voice. 'You were right. Richard Webb is Sandra Coffey's nephew.'

'You're kidding.'

'He's her brother's kid.'

'And he is?'

'Was. He died last year. Roger Webb – founder of Webb Construction.'

Reilly scribbled on her pad. 'I think I've heard of them.'

'I'm sure you have – they're one of the biggest construction companies in the country. They're based in Meath.'

The owner of a big construction company . . . Reilly was thinking. 'There wouldn't have been a link between the father and Alan Fitzpatrick, would there?'

'I thought you might ask that. Seems Webb was one of Fitzpatrick's biggest supporters when he was an up-and-coming TD. There was speculation that he smoothed Fitzpatrick's path into politics, as a reward for convincing the builders' unions to accept some dodgy pay conditions in the mid-nineties.'

Reilly whistled. 'Very cozy.' She could feel her excitement rising. 'Julius, you know that you have to keep all of this to yourself for the moment, yes?'

'Goes without saying. Are we getting close?'

She could hear the enthusiasm in his voice. Everyone had worked so hard on this case, invested so much time, emotion and energy. 'I don't know, but what you've just told me is a very big piece in the jigsaw. Good work.'

Right away, she called the station again. 'I think I'm starting to pull all of this together,' she told Chris. 'And if I'm right, I also know who the final victim will be.'

CHAPTER 33

'So what's the big news?' Kennedy asked when Reilly joined them in the meeting room at the station and quickly explained the connections she had found linking Ricky Webb to Morgan, Crowe, Fitzpatrick and Coffey.

Chris was impressed. 'So you're figuring that the brother-in-law leaned on Coffey to write the article supporting leniency for his boy?'

'Exactly. It doesn't fit with many of his other columns – he usually takes a more populist slant – you know, "Lock 'em up and throw away the key".'

'It does sound out of character,' Kennedy agreed. 'What about Fitzpatrick? Where does he fit into it?'

'He was clearly deep into the father's pocket,' explained Reilly, 'and he's tight with two members of the parole board.'

'So you think he twisted some arms or spread some of Webb's cash around to get the parole board to grant the Webb kid an early release?'

'We can't be sure, but it's the best fit we have right now.'

'And Jennings?' Chris asked.

'It's the one that still stands out, but remember the rape victim who died in his care?'

'Yes?'

'Well, that's what Webb is in for. Or was.' She spoke quickly. 'He was released yesterday morning.'

Chris paused for a moment, trying to gather his thoughts. He moved over to the coffee machine. 'In which case, the newly released Ricky Webb would be the next victim.'

'So he needs to be found, fast,' Reilly said quickly. 'Every minute we delay now increases the chance of the killer getting to him first.'

Chris slowly poured himself a coffee, then looked back at her over the top of the steaming paper cup. 'I presume you've read his case file?'

She nodded.

'I did too, while we waited for you to come over. Let's just say it makes for . . . interesting reading.'

The brutality of Webb's rape crime had been shocking. 'You really think we should go out and find this bastard, save him from the only real justice he's ever going to experience?' His fingers tightened around the coffee cup. Webb could rot in hell as far as he cared. Maybe the killer was the sensible one after all.

'What?' Reilly frowned. 'Chris, listen to yourself. That's not our decision to make – the Court made its ruling—'

His cheeks were hot as he tried to stop himself from losing control. 'A compromised decision

341

because Daddy flashed his shagging money around!'

Reilly pressed on. 'Still, the Court made its ruling, Webb's served time, and now he's out. That's the way it works, Chris. We all know we don't get to decide who's guilty, or how long they should be inside.'

'Exactly,' Kennedy agreed, studying him carefully, as if wondering why they were even having this conversation.

Chris gulped his coffee down, crushed the paper cup in his hand and hurled it toward the rubbish bin, unable to prevent his emotions rising. 'This is fucked up. The whole case has been fucked up from the start, and now we have to go and protect some piece of shit at the end of it?'

'Talking about me again?' Reuben Knight drawled, entering the meeting room. He winked at Reilly. 'Or would O Serious One be referring to someone else as excrement, perchance?'

'Knight, we're really not in the mood for this today . . .' Kennedy began, staring curiously at Chris.

'It's nothing, just a difference of opinion,' Reilly replied.

The profiler looked dubious. 'If you say so. I got your message. Very kind of you all to invite me to the party. For once. So tell me, what's the big breakthrough?'

Chris picked up Webb's file and flung it across the table at Reuben. 'Meet our next victim. And seeing as you're the psychologist, take a look at that and give me one good reason why we should prevent some scumbag rapist from getting his just rewards.'

Shortly afterwards, Chris and Kennedy left to see if they could pinpoint the newly released Webb's current location.

Reuben looked pensive. 'Well, well, well . . . that was quite the outburst from our trusty detective, wasn't it?' he commented.

Reilly nodded. She too had been taken aback by Chris's uncommonly negative reaction toward saving Webb.

'Not that O Serious One is typically a barrel of laughs – hence the moniker,' Reuben continued, studying his nails, 'but I'm wondering if there's something else at play. Would Mr Webb's misdeeds have hit a nerve, perhaps?'

Reilly looked up, confused. 'What do you mean – hit a nerve?'

Then thinking back to her and Chris's recent conversation about his ex, suddenly something clicked into place.

Not long after we got engaged, something happened . . . She had immediately assumed that Melanie had cheated on him. But was it possible that—

'Of course, it's likely that the right-thinking Detective Delaney possesses a natural, and indeed understandable, reluctance to protect a convicted rapist,' he continued pensively. 'However, the force of his negativity suggests to me that there may be something more personal at play.'

Reilly's heart sank to her stomach. She felt completely wrongfooted now, but she also had to admit that Reuben's snapshot profiling of Chris's behavior might have some legs.

'In any case,' Reuben went on, 'as time is of the essence, I should depart for my hotel – and my Dante. With luck, my reading of the text may be able to shed some light on our killer's next move.'

With that, he left, leaving Reilly alone, unsure what to make of Chris's outburst or indeed the profiler's incisive interpretation of it.

Was Reuben right? Was there something more behind Chris's reservations about saving Webb? Or was she jumping to conclusions too quickly?

Notwithstanding the root of his anger, Reilly could, of course, appreciate Chris's misgivings about rushing to the rapist's aid.

She ran her gaze across Webb's file – the particulars of the attack did indeed make for gruesome reading. In the normal course of events, the guy should have got twelve to life; might not have seen the light of day for a decade. Instead, he was out within a couple of years.

Perhaps Chris was right on that much at least – there was no justice.

However, there was no question that trying to find Webb before the killer did was the right thing to do – on a rational and, more importantly, professional level. But on a moral, emotive one? It was hard to tell. They were now working feverishly to save a convicted rapist whose family had used their money and influence to subvert the true course of justice.

And if it turned out that Chris did indeed have some kind of personal hang-up thrown into the mix, Reilly thought grimly, that was one hell of a moral dilemma.

Chris and Kennedy sat in the car outside the gates of the Webb family residence in Meath, some fifty minutes' drive from Dublin. It could just be seen through the driving rain, a vast hulking mansion set well back from the road.

Kennedy looked toward the house through the gloom. 'It's bloody ginormous.'

'Of course it is,' Chris said testily. 'Daddy obviously has plenty money to splash around on things like fancy houses and subverting the course of justice.'

Kennedy looked at him. 'What's going on, Chris?'

'What?'

'I've never seen you so het up as you were back at the station when Reilly was telling us about Webb. Yeah, the guy's not exactly a model citizen, but that's nothing new in this business.'

Chris looked away. 'It just pisses me off, that's all. Our job is to protect innocent citizens, not pond scum like Webb.'

'Look, I can see why it would get to you,' Kennedy said, and Chris looked at him quickly. 'It gets to me too, having to waste time and resources on guys like this. But the Webb kid's been identified as a potential victim, and as such our job is to prevent this punisher guy from getting to him.' Kennedy shuddered. 'I can't even imagine what that weirdo has in store for him. Judging by what happened to the others, I'm sure it would be no picnic.'

'Maybe.' In truth, Chris couldn't imagine any punishment the killer might level at the rapist that would even begin to make amends for what he'd done to the girl he'd harmed. 'Prince Charmless might be able to give us the heads-up on that one.'

'It's not just about protecting Webb either,' Kennedy insisted. 'It's more about finding our guy and trying to secure justice for five dead men and their families.' He rolled the car window down just enough to fit a cigarette butt through it. 'Anyway, let's just get this over with.'

'Agreed.' Chris pulled up the collar on his coat. 'By the way, I know what you're doing,' he said.

Kennedy looked at him in surprise. 'What?'

'You're waiting for me to go out in the rain to buzz the damn intercom, aren't you?'

His partner feigned a hurt expression. 'Always so bloody suspicious . . .'

'Well, I don't see you getting out.' But before Kennedy could answer, the gates began slowly to open inwards and Chris slipped the car into gear and moved forward. 'Which is why I called ahead and made an appointment,' he continued.

'I figured they would have CCTV and that someone would let us in if we waited a minute.'

'God, I hate it when you come over all clever.' Kennedy said, glaring at him.

'I'd have thought you were used to that by now.'

Through the rain, they scurried from the car into the house. The front door was already open, a young Eastern European woman, whom Chris deduced was some kind of housekeeper, waiting patiently in the doorway.

As soon as the detectives were inside she closed the door behind them.

'I'll take your coats,' she said. They wiped their feet on a huge mat, shook the rain off and handed their coats to her. 'Mrs Webb is in the library.'

Chris looked around – the entryway was huge, bigger than his little flat, with a vast chandelier hanging high overhead. Their feet echoed on the polished wooden floor as the housekeeper led them to the far side of the hallway. She opened a door and waved them inside.

The room was large, the walls lined with hardback books that looked as though they'd never been handled, let alone read. Chris looked at it with some disdain. This was definitely the house of your typical arsehole Irish property developer – a library was such a typical nouveau riche touch.

A fire burned in the grate at the far end of the room. As they walked in, a woman stood up and turned toward them.

'Detectives? I'm Angela Webb. How can I help you?'

Chris, taking in the room, found his gaze irresistibly drawn to the woman.

Although now in her mid-fifties, she was beautiful, with natural poise and grace. He instantly guessed that she had been a model, actress or dancer in her younger days. Today she wore a slim-fitting gray skirt, elegant pale pink blouse, and a long string of pearls, but she would have been just as arresting in sweats and an old pair of wellies.

She stepped forward to meet them and held out her hand. Chris shook it, Kennedy right beside him. Like Chris, he too appeared to be temporarily tongue-tied. She looked at them quizzically.

'Detective Chris Delaney,' he said, finally finding his voice. 'And this is my partner, Detective Pete Kennedy.'

'You said this was about my son?' Mrs Webb continued without further preamble.

'Yes,' Kennedy replied. 'Thank you for taking the time to see us.'

'So how can I help you?' She still hadn't offered them a seat; it was clear that, for her at least, this was going to be a short conversation.

'Seems he was released on parole yesterday,' Chris said flatly.

'So I believe,' she replied without missing a beat. 'And?'

'We'd like to speak with him.'

348

She gave Chris a condescending look. 'Well, I'm sure I haven't seen him.'

'We really need to find your son,' Kennedy put in. 'We believe that someone may want to kill him.'

At those words, Mrs Webb's resolve seemed to crack. 'What? Who on earth would—'

Kennedy quickly explained about the recent murders and how they believed her son was the last name on the killer's list.

'What? But that's impossible!'

'Mrs Webb, I'm sure you're aware that there were . . . irregularities surrounding your son's conviction,' Chris said, trying his utmost to keep his tone neutral. Surely she knew that her husband had paid off people connected to the trial?

She half turned toward the fire, the orange glow casting dark shadows on her high cheekbones. For a moment no one said anything. The only sounds were the crackling of the logs in the hearth and the wind dashing the rain against the windows.

Finally she turned back toward them. 'I'm sorry, I've not been a good hostess. Please sit down.' She indicated a small cluster of chairs by the window. 'I'll get you some tea.'

They sat as instructed, and watched as she pressed the button on an intercom. 'Freya? Please bring tea for my guests.'

When she turned back toward them, she had regained her previous composure. She too sat down, legs crossed at the ankle, hands held neatly in her lap. 'I'm sorry,' she began, 'but the last few years have been . . . difficult.'

Chris's knuckles whitened. *Difficult? Imagine how difficult they've been for the parents of the poor girl whose life your bastard of a son destroyed!* he wanted to say.

Kennedy again took up the baton. 'I'm sure it must have all been very hard for you,' he said, giving Chris a surreptitious questioning glance. 'With your son . . . and the trial and everything?'

Chris took a deep breath, trying to hold it together and get back on track.

Angela turned her haughty gray eyes on him, as if picking up on his negative opinion of her son. 'Do you have children, Detective?'

'No, ma'am, I don't.'

She nodded, as though she suspected as much. 'When Ricky was little he was always mischievous, always headstrong – typical boy, really. Still, I know that he didn't . . . would *never*—'

'Are you saying that you think your son is innocent of the sexual assault charges?' Chris asked disbelievingly.

She looked up as the housekeeper entered the room, carrying a tray. 'Set it over there, please, Freya.'

The young woman scurried across the room, put the tray on the table and looked expectantly at them. 'Would you care for a cup of tea?'

Kennedy nodded and she poured three cups of

tea, handed them out, then turned and hurried from the room. Chris half expected her to curtsy on her way out.

Mrs Webb sipped at her tea. 'To answer your question, of course he's innocent. Richard is an intelligent, attractive young man who could have any woman he wanted. Why on earth would he need to . . . force . . .'

Chris was so angry he couldn't concentrate on the rest of the sentence. The arrogance of these people! 'The girl in question was seventeen years old,' he said heatedly, 'and besides raping her violently, your son also broke her nose and fractured her jaw.'

If Ricky Webb was anywhere near as patronizing and disdainful as his mother, then he must be a right little shit. Clearly, these people considered themselves completely above the law. And that given the father's wheeling and dealing had secured Ricky such a short sentence, evidently they were. It was surprising that Webb had spent any time in jail at all.

'Chris . . .' Kennedy frowned at him, then turned back to Angela. 'Mrs Webb, it's important that we know where to find Ricky now.'

'I'm sorry, but I really don't know. I haven't seen my son since his release.' She regained her closed, impenetrable demeanor.

'Do you have any idea where he might have gone?' Kennedy pressed. 'To see friends, any other family, a girlfriend, even?'

Anglea shook her head 'You must understand, Detectives, Richard is a free spirit, always has been,' she said fondly.

A free spirit? Overindulged little prick, by the sounds of it, Chris thought bitterly.

Given everything he'd heard today, he was coming to the conclusion that if the killer got to Webb before they did, he certainly wasn't going to lose any sleep over it.

CHAPTER 34

Back at the station, Reilly tried to put aside her concerns about Chris's state of mind, and refocus on the investigation. She read through Webb's file again, focusing this time on the details of his victim.

Reilly tried to imagine the horror for a 17-year-old girl, attacked, raped, beaten . . .

Shaking these distracting thoughts from her mind, she forced herself to read on. Amanda Harrington was a secondary school student and lived in a well-to-do area of South Dublin. She focused in on the family details. The girl's parents were listed as Sally and David Harrington. The mother worked as a teacher, the father was an architect and she had one older brother.

The obvious conclusion was that someone close to this girl had to be responsible for these murders. But who? Who was picking off one by one those they believed were collectively responsible for this miscarriage of justice? Was it the mother, father . . . close relative or boyfriend, even?

Reilly ran her hand through her hair, and tapped her pen on the edge of the table. She looked at the names again – they could probably eliminate the mother, as it would have been necessary for someone strong to control and manipulate the bodies into the scenarios the killer had set up. And although anything was possible, she doubted that a woman would have been able to do it.

What about the father or brother then? Architecture seemed like a mild-mannered profession, but God only knew the kind of things grief could drive a person to. Reilly made a short annotation beside David Harrington's name.

The brother was a possibility too, but he was only a few years older than Amanda, now in his early twenties, and again someone strong and very capable had been responsible for the level of expertise and planning that went into the murders. Then again, a college kid might well be very familiar with Dante's *Inferno*. It was worth checking out.

For now, Reilly supposed the simplest thing to do was to talk to the parents. There was a phone number in the file . . .

She dialled and immediately got an automated message: '*We're sorry, but the number you have dialled is no longer in service. Please check the number and try again.*'

Dead end. So what now? Reilly looked at the address again: the Harrington residence was in Sandymount, only a few miles from here. She could be there within fifteen minutes.

She was tired of waiting around, tired of sitting

in her office poring over all that evidence that was getting them nowhere . . .

She grabbed her handbag, pulled her coat off the back of the chair and headed for the door.

A few minutes later, she was driving past impressive Georgian houses, their bay windows bright with Christmas trees and fairy lights, her windscreen wipers slapping out a rhythm against the driving icy rain.

She found the Harrington house just off Sandymount Square, and parking her car, stepped out into the rain.

The bright lights of a Christmas tree filled the front window of the tidy house. Reilly scurried up to the front door, the rain cold on her face, and rang the bell. She listened as it echoed through the house, the ringing soon replaced by the sound of footsteps.

Reilly was dreading this conversation – asking grieving parents to recall the one thing they would have been trying their utmost to forget.

The door opened. A middle-aged woman looked at Reilly with interest. She had short highlighted hair, and wore jeans and an elegant cashmere sweater. 'Hello. Can I help you?'

Reilly briefly showed her ID. 'Hi. I'm Investigator Steel with the GFU. I'm looking for Mrs Harrington?'

The woman's face showed a look of surprise. 'I'm sorry. The Harringtons don't live here anymore.'

Reilly's was immediately disappointed. 'Oh, they've moved. Any idea of their new address?'

'Sydney actually.' The woman looked out at the biting rain. 'Do you want to come inside? It's pretty nasty out there.'

Reilly nodded, eager to get out of the rain. 'Much appreciated. Thank you.'

The woman led her in through the narrow hall and into a warm living room – a fire crackled in the hearth, and the Christmas tree sat prettily in the bay window. She offered Reilly her hand. 'I'm Sarah – Sarah Miller.'

'Reilly Steel, pleased to meet you.'

Sarah perched on a chair beside the fire, and indicated for Reilly to sit in one on the opposite side of the hearth. 'Please make yourself comfortable.'

Reilly shook the rain from her hair, slipped her coat off and draped it over the back of the chair. 'Thank you.' She sat, and looked across at Sarah. 'You knew the Harringtons then?'

'Yes, we lived nearby. Everyone in the village knew them . . .' Her face fell. 'But after what happened with their daughter . . .' She left the remaining words unspoken.

Reilly helped her out. 'The family decided to move?'

Sarah nodded. 'They couldn't get away quick enough and I don't blame them.' She looked up, met Reilly's probing gaze. 'This might be Dublin but Sandymount has always had a village feel to it, a community, if you like. And while that's wonderful most of the time, when something terrible happens, something like Amanda's death . . . well, it affects everyone. David and Sally would have been reminded of it each and every day, every time one of us said hello, or how are you doing . . .'

'So it was common knowledge that she took her own life?'

'Sadly, yes. Nobody knew why, of course, at least not at first . . . Such a terrible thing, and for someone so young.'

'Dr Jennings, Amanda's GP, did he practice locally?'

Sarah frowned. 'Not in this area, I don't think. I've never heard of him, although now that you say it, the name does sound familiar. Wait a second,' she said, as realization dawned. 'Do you mean the doctor that was in all the papers? The one who was . . .' Her face paled. 'But what does that have to do with Amanda?'

Side-stepping an answer, Reilly quickly changed the subject. 'And do you ever hear from the Harringtons now?'

Sarah stood up, and lifted a festive card off the mantelpiece. 'Just a Christmas card once a year.' She handed it to Reilly.

Reilly looked inside, though it seemed somehow impolite, like spying on someone. The card read: 'Merry Christmas – hope you're very happy in our house. Love, David, Sally and Luke.' She looked at the handwriting – it was elegant, but completely different from the writing on the package they'd received with the DVD.

Sarah smiled. 'They wrote that last year, too, as though they're going to come back some day, and despite the fact we bought the house from them.' She sighed.

'Do they ever visit?'

'No. It's been almost two years since they left, and I've never heard anything about them having the slightest wish to come back, even for a visit. Too many painful memories, I'd imagine.'

Too many painful memories, Reilly echoed.

A rape/suicide incident like this created painful memories for so many people, not just the family.

But who would have been so badly affected by such memories that they would feel compelled to take the law into their own hands – and in such a destructive and elaborate way?

Having thanked Sarah Miller for her time, Reilly drove slowly back through the showers to the GFU building. Visibility was poor, and not just from the rain – it was one of those dark winter days when it never truly seems to get light, when the sun never rises, never sets, just slopes along, low to the horizon, hidden behind a wall of thick gray cloud.

Once again, almost every aspect of this case was proving to be elusive. Even when they got a break, thought they'd made some progress – they were still going round in circles.

With Ricky Webb now free from prison (ironically the one place where he'd be safe from the killer) – the clock was ticking.

And Reilly guessed they were fast running out of time.

CHAPTER 35

Late that evening, little by little, Harcourt Street Station grew quieter, as the reunited investigative team struggled to find something, anything that might help them either identify the killer, or find his next victim.

'So Webb's just . . . disappeared?' Reilly perched on the edge of Chris's desk after her return from the Miller residence.

'Vanished,' he replied shortly.

Kennedy stood up and stretched. 'Look, sorry to break up the party but I've really got to head away. It's our anniversary and I promised Josie I'd take her out to dinner tonight,' he muttered, reaching for his coat. 'If anything happens—'

'Don't worry, you'll be the first to know,' Chris replied.

He'd calmed down somewhat after his outburst earlier, but given Reuben's assessment, Reilly was still worried that something was blurring his vision and obstructing his objectivity. She was in two minds as to whether to say something about it, but didn't want to run the risk, and figured Chris wouldn't appreciate such prying questions, especially at such a crucial point of the investigation.

In any case, the guy was a professional, and Reilly was confident that if Chris did happen to have any . . . preconceptions, he would be able to overcome them, and do whatever it took to get to the bottom of this case once and for all.

'Speaking of dinner,' she said, after Kennedy left, 'if we're planning on making this an all-nighter, we'd better load up on carbs. Anything good in the canteen?'

Chris checked his watch. 'They closed an hour ago so it'll have to be something from Crappy Sandwiches R Us. Fancy anything in particular from the vending machine?'

'When you make it sound so tempting how can I refuse? Get me a ploughman's.'

Reilly kept on reading, trying to view the entire investigation through fresh eyes: the GFU evidence reports her team had produced at each murder scene, the autopsy reports, the case files. Nothing. There was nothing at all that jumped out, nothing that revealed anything new.

She turned to the report on Amanda Harrington's death.

The same pattern was repeated: coroner's report, evidence, interviews. She looked again over the interviews . . . the grief-stricken mother, Sally, the stoic father, David.

Suddenly Reilly froze. There on the page was a simple footnote, added almost as an afterthought . . .

She looked up. Where the hell was Chris? She tried to engage her brain – where had he said he was going? They were hungry – the canteen was closed. The vending machines . . .

Reilly strode across the floor, and almost wiped out another officer as she flew through the double doors into the corridor. At the end of the hallway she could see Chris standing in front of the machine, counting out some change. He looked up as she approached.

'You're in one hell of a hurry. Did you change your mind?'

She looked confused. 'Change my . . .?'

Chris pointed to the sandwiches. 'You said for me to get you a ploughman's.'

Reilly waved his comments away. 'Forget the damn sandwich, Chris. I think I know who our killer is.'

He just stared, waiting for her to come out with it.

'Amanda's parents, Sally and David—'

'They're in Australia, you said it yourself.'

'Right. But David Harrington wasn't her biological father. He was her stepfather . . .'

Suddenly the hallway grew very quiet.

'Her real father still lives here in Dublin. But here's why I know for sure that he's our guy,' she added, as the details of Reuben's original profile came back to her. 'Remember what Reuben said about this guy casting himself in the role of Minos?'

Chris nodded.

'Rearrange the letters a little, for a more modern alternative.'

He seemed to think for a moment, then looked at Reilly, eyes widening. 'Her father's name is Simon?'

Reilly nodded. 'Simon Darcy. And get this: he works as a court artist.'

Although the central criminal court was closed for the weekend, Chris managed to press the onsite security guard hard enough to give him the emergency phone numbers. If Simon Darcy worked there as a court artist, then he would have been issued a permit to do so, and they needed the details from that permit.

It took several calls, Chris gradually working his way up the food chain, before he had finally got hold of the head of Human Resources. The man was not pleased at being disturbed at home at seven o'clock on a Sunday evening, but when Chris explained their urgency, he finally agreed to meet him at his office.

Chris had talked the security guard into letting him back in, and was waiting in the lobby when Francis Dowling hurried up the steps and into the building.

The security guard watched carefully as they both passed through the scanner, then he dropped back into his chair and resumed his study of the *Sunday World.*

'Thanks for coming in,' said Chris as they hurried down the corridor. Dowling was in his mid-forties, with gray flecks in his dark hair. He was casually dressed in dark trousers and a navy sweater.

'So you said on the phone that you think Simon Darcy is tied in to those horrible murders in some way?'

Chris nodded. 'He may be in danger,' he said cryptically, figuring this was the best way to get Dowling on side.

Dowling unlocked his office door, and motioned Chris in. 'Well, I don't know him personally, but all artists and photographers need a permit so of course he'll be in the system.' He dropped into his black leather chair, and flicked on the PC. 'It's a bit slow . . .'

Chris stood behind Dowling, impatiently looking over his shoulder.

The screen eventually came to life and the man looked up at Chris. 'I need to put in my password,' he said pointedly.

'Sure.' He looked away while Dowling did the necessary.

'OK, here we are.' Within seconds, Simon Darcy's court permit popped up and Chris turned back to the monitor. 'Let's see . . .' Dowling clicked through the pages. 'Well, there's his current address and phone number . . .'

Chris scribbled a note. Darcy lived in Ringsend,

not far from the city center. They could have a unit there within minutes.

But obviously, Darcy hadn't been holding his victims there. He thought again about the other evidence, the horse feed . . . the Kildare-based soil . . .

Chris looked back at the screen. 'Does he have any other addresses listed, one for next of kin . . . anything?'

Dowling moved the page up screen. 'Nope, nothing at all.'

Afterwards, outside the courthouse Chris met up with Kennedy, whom he guessed wasn't too disappointed about having his romantic dinner interrupted. Josie's opinion on it would be another matter.

'Anything?' his partner asked.

Chris nodded. 'I got an address.'

He thought about what he'd just learned from Simon Darcy's file and tried to measure it against not only the evidence, but Reuben Knight's profile.

'By all accounts the guy sounds like a real hermit,' he told Kennedy. 'I just called his contact at the *Clarion,* and he said that although he was a brilliant artist, and they run a lot of his sketches, he's never met Darcy, has no idea what he's like.'

'Well then, I suppose it's up to us to find out,' Kennedy replied, throwing down his cigarette and stubbing it out with his foot. 'Let's go and pay this guy a visit.'

CHAPTER 36

It was almost eight by the time the detectives pulled up in front of Simon Darcy's house. As they approached the house itself, Chris grew even more confident that this really was their guy.

'Look,' he said, pointing out a restaurant on the approach to the street of red-brick terraced houses in which their suspect lived.

Kennedy followed his gaze to the Malaysian restaurant and its brightly colored sign. 'I'm sure you are hungry, Chris, but maybe when we've finished—'

Chris rolled his eyes. 'No, you eejit, I'm thinking of that sauce that kept popping up in the trace evidence. Malaysian food is spicy, isn't it?'

'Ah, now I get you.' Kennedy looked sideways at him. 'Looks like this thing is really starting to come together now. Are we heading for the endgame, do you think?'

Chris was feeling precisely the same way. They were indeed close. Simon Darcy had to be the guy. He had motive, opportunity, and access to all the players. Not to mention, given his profession, a first-hand knowledge of how the justice system worked.

Through their actions, Coffey and Crowe had each had a bearing on Webb's case. Morgan had had the opportunity to do the right thing and give Webb the statutory sentence at trial, but because of the so-called 'missing evidence' he'd bottled it, and ordered a minimal jail term at best.

Then to add insult to injury, a government representative had influenced the parole board, ensuring that Webb had barely begun his sentence before he was once again a free man. This early parole must have been the trigger, or 'stressor' as Reuben Knight had described it, to set Darcy on his menacing revenge spree.

And then there was Jennings, the doctor who'd let Simon Darcy's poor damaged daughter die in his care. It was one hell of a list of people to punish, but Darcy had managed it.

And now, at the very top of the list, was the man who had caused all the heartache in the first place, Ricky Webb. The rapist – destroyer of lives.

What would Chris have done were he in Simon Darcy's shoes, and it was his daughter, his own flesh and blood, who had suffered at the hands of such an animal? Could he honestly say he would do any different?

Chris couldn't be certain, and this was all forcing him into a corner. As a man who had sworn to uphold the law, of course he couldn't condone Darcy's actions, but there was little doubt he could identify with them.

Well, there was no time to think about that now,

Chris told himself as he and Kennedy got out of the car, and rang the doorbell of the house listed as Simon Darcy's last known address.

They needed to ring the bell twice before they heard a shuffling behind the door and finally a man opened it.

Chris and Kennedy exchanged a surreptitious glance as a slight, middle-aged man wearing glasses appeared at the door. What the hell . . .?

'We're looking for Simon Darcy,' Chris said, finding his voice before Kennedy did. 'I believe he lives here.'

'You're looking at him,' the man said softly as he looked from one to the other. Chris stared at him.

This couldn't be their killer, it was impossible.

'What can I do for you?'

Kennedy took out his badge. 'I'm Detective Kennedy and this is Detective Delaney from Harcourt Street Station. Sir, are you the same Simon Darcy who is permitted to work in the Central Criminal Court as a sketch artist?'

'That's me,' the man replied. 'What is it? Have I done something wrong?'

He leaned forward through the open doorway and looked nervously up and down the road, as if worried about what the neighbors might think, and again Chris was flabbergasted. This man couldn't possibly be . . . *wasn't* the killer.

'Could we possibly come inside for a moment? We'd like to ask you a couple of questions.'

'Of course. I really don't know what this could be about but . . .'

Simon Darcy moved back to make some room for them in the narrow hallway. From there, he directed them into a small living room.

Glancing around, Chris immediately noticed the prevalence of religious iconography – there was a large Sacred Heart painting over the mantelpiece, a child of Prague on a shelf in the far corner, as well as a photograph of Pope John Paul II hanging on a nearby wall.

The religious stuff certainly fit with the profile, but . . .

'Mr Darcy, we understand that a member of your family, namely your daughter, Amanda, was the victim of an unfortunate incident some years ago,' Chris began.

'An unfortunate incident, Detective?' Simon Darcy said, his sad gray eyes boring into Chris's, and immediately he regretted his choice of words, keenly aware of how understated they sounded. 'I've never heard vicious rape and assault being described quite like that before, but if that's what you want to call it . . .'

'I'm sorry, you're right, of course . . .'

'Your daughter took her own life shortly afterwards,' Kennedy cut in, also somewhat indelicately, Chris noticed, but he knew that they couldn't assume anything. Darcy might look harmless, but he was the chief suspect in a murder investigation and they already knew that the perp was as cunning

369

as they came. Who knew what kind of ruse the guy was prepared to use in order to manipulate the law yet again?

'That's correct,' Darcy replied, his voice catching a little, and Chris was almost certain he saw him swallowing a lump in his throat. 'The nightmares, the panic and fear . . . it all became too much for Amanda to take.'

Chris immediately felt for him, but struggled not to project that. This guy was a suspect, possibly a murdering thug.

'The police identified the perpeprator, Richard Webb,' Kennedy said, reading from his notebook as if he were seeing the information for the first time. 'He was duly convicted and sentenced to three years in Mountjoy.'

'Yes. But my understanding is that he is now once again a free man,' Darcy admitted in a move that surprised them. 'I believe he was paroled this weekend?'

'How do you know that, Mr Darcy? Have you been keeping tabs on Webb?'

Darcy looked at them, his eyes filled with sadness. 'Detectives, there isn't a day goes by when I don't think of Richard Webb and the misery he caused my daughter, my family. But at least I have the comfort of knowing that he was punished for his crimes and has been rehabilitated.'

OK, now they were getting somewhere. 'You think eighteen months in prison is enough of a punishment for a guy like that?' Kennedy asked.

Darcy shrugged. 'I have no idea. But when recently I looked into the man's eyes, I—'

'Hold on,' Chris interjected. 'What do you mean, when you looked into his eyes? Have you seen Webb since his release?'

'Not since his release, no. But I went to see him in prison. I didn't tell him who I was, of course; I couldn't do that. But I needed to see him. I needed to see if I could capture his essence, decide for myself if he was well and truly repentant. And I believe he was – is – sorry for what he did to my little girl.'

Chris couldn't believe what he was hearing.

'Capture his essence? What the hell does that mean?' Kennedy asked.

Darcy shrugged. 'I'm an artist. To me, as to many artists, the eyes are windows to the soul. I arranged it with the authorities to draw Mr Webb as part of a collection I'm working on. I hope to exhibit it soon.'

Chris's mind was spinning. What Darcy was saying was incomprehensible. 'So you went to see Webb in prison, shortly before his release, just to paint him? Didn't you want to strangle this man, tear him limb from limb for what he did to your daughter?'

Darcy fixed his gaze on Chris. 'There were many times over the years that I thought about doing just what you describe. Yet, I would find no peace in doing so. If there is justice to be served, ultimately we will all be judged in the end. It's not my place to do the Lord's job for Him.'

'What about the devil's job then?' Kennedy asked.

'Drowning a guy in his own shit, hanging another from a tree with his guts pouring out, leaving another one out for the maggots to feed on?'

Simon Darcy looked genuinely shocked. 'Those horrible things that they're talking about in the newspapers? What in heaven's name has that got to do with . . .?' Then suddenly, it seemed to dawn on him. 'That's why you're here? You think, someone like me – ' he looked down at his thin, wasted frame – 'would be involved in something like that?' He snorted. 'Honestly, Detectives, I don't know whether to laugh or cry.'

'We're going to need access to your medical records in order to prove—'

'You're more than welcome to anything you want,' he interjected shortly, and with that, Simon Darcy lowered both arms, and wheeled himself out of the room.

CHAPTER 37

Chris was stumped. There was no way this guy in the wheelchair could be their killer. Even overlooking his disability, Simon Darcy was a slight, feeble-looking 60-odd-year-old man. There was no chance he could have carried out the heavy lifting required at the murder scenes.

Upon further questioning, Darcy informed them that he'd been quadriplegic since the late nineties, following a car accident. His disability was largely the catalyst for the breakup of his marriage to Amanda's mother.

While the man was talking, Chris noticed something. He'd actually been aware of it all the time he'd been here, but was initially so distracted by Simon Darcy's condition that his mind hadn't been able to process it.

Present in the house was an incredibly potent ammonia smell, the kind of smell that Reilly had tried to describe to them throughout the investigation as similar to skunk spray. Clearly there was something else going on here, something they weren't getting. Simon Darcy might not be directly involved in the killings, but the police were on the right track. However, the ammonia smell may well have been some side effect of Darcy's condition . . .

But Chris didn't believe in coincidences, and there were already way too many to ignore. Darcy's connection to Webb, the spicy cooking sauce, and now the smell . . .

'Do you live alone, Simon?' he asked suddenly.

'No, my son lives with me,' the older man replied easily. He sighed. 'Actually, I thought it might have been him you were looking for at first.'

The hairs on the back of Chris's neck stood up.

A son. Someone who would have also been deeply affected by the rape, and who quite possibly didn't share his father's noble ideas about justice and punishment.

He recalled the details from the Harrington case file. An older brother had indeed been listed under family, but because they'd discovered the Harringtons had subsequently emigrated . . .

Evidently the brother had decided to swap surf-boards and koalas for magpies and maggots. Chris's mind raced and his pulse quickened. He looked at Kennedy 'Where is your son now?'

'Out with friends, I believe. Whatever it is, can't it be dealt with during work hours?'

Kennedy looked baffled. 'Work hours?'

'Well, yes. I presume you wanted to ask him something about the morgue.'

Now Chris was confused. *The morgue?*

Simon shook his head. 'I'm sorry – my mistake

again. I just assumed you both knew Luke, and this was work-related. He works as a volunteer assistant at the city morgue. Goodness knows why. I can't imagine a more macabre position, but of course he's always been interested in the darker side of . . .' Then, at the same time that Chris made the connection, Simon did too. The older man stared at Chris, a world of pain in his eyes. 'Oh, no . . . no . . .' he cried out. 'The drawings . . . I had no idea.'

Chris was by now holding his breath. He let it out slowly. 'What drawings, Simon?' he asked carefully. 'What are you talking about?'

'You said something · before – about those appalling murders . . .' he said, addressing Kennedy now. 'About a man . . . hanging from a tree with his . . .' He shook his head, and Chris recalled that the more horrific details of Jennings' death had been purposely concealed from the media. 'I thought it was a rendering of Dante, such a vivid, expressive scene . . .'

'Simon,' Chris said, gently touching the man on the shoulder, 'show us the drawings.'

'Luke? The son's name is Luke? How deliciously perfect!' Reuben was agog with exhilaration when, following an update from Chris, Reilly phoned the profiler to pass on the details of their most recent find.

She frowned. 'How so?'

'Well, all along I had envisioned our killer as

375

Minos, when of course he was acting in the name of the devil himself! Lucifer,' he added quickly, when at Reilly's end there remained a baffled silence. 'A rare blunder on my part, but it happens occasionally, if truth be told,' he added with typical modesty. 'But given his familiarity with Dante, I'm guessing our Lucifer must have been keenly aware of not only the connotations of his namesake, but his responsibilities too. In the *Inferno*, Minos ordains the punishments, but it's the devil who carries them out.'

Luke . . . Lucifer . . .

The quiet college kid from the morgue, capable of so much destruction? It seemed incomprehensible. Yet at the same time it fit.

From his position at the morgue, Luke Darcy would have had access to the case files and the evidence reports, and was keeping himself abreast of the investigation every step of the way.

Then another thought struck her. Luke's made-up goth face the last time she'd seen him . . . and that unidentified white dust mark on Crowe's shoulder on the DVD . . .

Reilly knew that poor Karen Thompson would be devastated to learn that this amiable kid she'd entrusted with the city's dead had deceived her in such a way.

Judging by the drawings that Luke's poor devastated father had shown the detectives – a sketchpad of perfectly rendered illustrations of all five Dantesque murder scenes – it was clear that the younger Darcy was also quite the artist, which fit in perfectly with the pencil and rubber traces.

Not only that, but the proximity of the takeaway restaurant (and Simon's reluctant confirmation that his son was a regular customer) tallied with the cooking sauce, and Chris was adamant that in the Darcy house, he too had picked up that same so far unidentified ammonia-type smell.

Now all they needed to do was find out where Luke was, and if he was indeed holding Ricky Webb, the man he held ultimately responsible for his sister's death.

Reilly was certain that the key to this was the equine slant to the remaining evidence – the horse feed and the alkaline soil that Lucy had identified as being from the Kildare area.

Reuben was on his way to the GFU building to help with the search, while Chris and Kennedy planned to remain temporarily at the Darcy house until Luke returned from his supposed 'night out with friends'.

They were also keen to continue questioning Simon about his knowledge (or lack of it) of his son's recent pursuits, and to determine whether the older man could shed any light on the rural location in which Luke had been holding his victims. If they could identify this, they might just be able to save Ricky Webb.

'Check the Land Registry, see if either is registered as owning property other than this one,'

Chris suggested. 'Simon says he doesn't, but I'm not taking anything for granted.'

'I'm on it,' Reilly told him.

She'd just hung up the phone when she heard Gary's footsteps in the hallway outside. He hurried into her office, laptop in his hand.

'I just got your message. What do you need?'

Reilly was already tapping on her own keyboard. 'Property search,' she replied briskly. 'We need to know if Simon Darcy owns any property around the Kildare area.'

Gary slid his laptop from its case. 'Like a stables, or stud farm maybe?' He stretched his fingers and cracked his knuckles. 'This is my kind of search.'

Reilly looked over as his fingers flicked nimbly across the keyboard. Always good to have a techie on the team.

Some twenty minutes later, Reuben breezed into the office, full of excitement.

'Pray tell, my beloved, what news?'

Gary, temporarily distracted from his search, gave the profiler a curious glance, and despite the fraught circumstances Reilly couldn't resist a smile.

'We're trying to figure out where Darcy's keeping his victims,' she told him. 'Chances are it's where he's got Webb right now.'

'Ah, my favorite part of the story,' Reuben intoned in a singsong voice. 'Now that the true culprit has been unmasked, we must swoop in, find our villain and save the day. Only then will order be restored.'

'This isn't a TV show, Reuben,' Reilly scolded. 'Someone's life is at stake here.'

'Agreed, but I must admit I'm rather in agreement with the object of your attraction on this one. The life at stake could hardly be considered a treasured one.'

Reilly couldn't believe what she was hearing.

'Then why are we doing this, Reuben? Why the hell do we do this job at all? Why not just allow every sicko to get away with whatever random form of justice he fancies?'

'Calm down, I jest.'

'Do you, though?' she asked. 'Do you really care about what happens to Ricky Webb? Or have you already made up your mind that he's not worth saving?'

If they – the authorities, the ones who were supposed to uphold order and justice – could be prejudiced, then surely they were no better than viligantes themselves, deciding at will who merited protection or who didn't?

'My dearest Reilly, that is precisely the reason I'm here. To assist and illuminate you on your quest to save our man,' Reuben replied in his typical mocking tone, though for once there was a modicum of seriousness in there too. 'And truth be told, I have an idea—'

'I think I've got something.' They both turned to look at Gary, who was still tapping away on his computer. 'It's a bit of a long shot, but . . .'

'What is it?' she demanded.

He looked at her. 'I know you said to search for property ownership under the Darcy name, but then I had a thought. The son, Luke, he and his sister lived with their mother and stepdad at the time of the attack, yes? Then he emigrated to Australia with them after the sister died—'

'But subsequently returned to ye oul sod,' Reuben finished.

'Yes. And went to live with his real father, Simon, who lives in a small terraced house in Ringsend.'

'I'm not following.'

'So who's to say the stepfather doesn't still own property here?' Gary continued, excitement in his tone. 'The Harringtons are reasonably well off, and while they were able to sell their Dublin house before they emigrated—'

'They might still be trying to offload another place down the country,' Reilly finished, sitting down and scooting her chair closer to Gary's.

'Yep. There is indeed a property still registered to one David Harrington formerly of Sandymount, Dublin – in Clane, County Kildare. A quick MyHome search confirms it's currently on the market . . .' He spun his laptop round so Reilly could see the screen, and grinned triumphantly. 'And here's what it looks like.'

Her breath caught. It was a two-acre farmstead, a house and an old stone barn located on the property. For sale and abandoned, yet Luke Darcy would have easy access to the place, probably had his own set of keys, and with the property market in the doldrums, could likely go about his business completely undisturbed.

'Gary, you're an absolute genius!' Reilly exclaimed, and in her excitement she reached forward and kissed him on the lips.

The lab tech's face colored with surprise, and he smiled.

'Hmm . . .' Reuben raised an eyebrow as he surveyed the exchange. 'Clearly, I'm in entirely the wrong field.'

CHAPTER 38

Ricky Webb slowly opened his eyes. Where the hell was he? He tried to move, and found that he was bound hand and foot, strapped to a chair with thick bands of duct tape.

He looked around – he was in an old shed or barn or some sort. There was straw on the dirty concrete floor and a single bare light bulb hanging overhead casting deep shadows to the far corners of the room.

Ricky turned his head – he could hear some movement behind him.

'Hey! Anybody there?'

Footsteps approached from behind his back, a shadow passed across and a tall figure stood before him. Ricky looked up. The man was slim, with glasses and dyed jet-black hair, his skin scarily white, as if he were wearing make-up or something. 'Why the fuck have you got me tied up here?' Ricky raged. 'Let me go, arsehole. I'll fucking get you for this!'

Luke considered him carefully. 'That's hardly an incentive to let you go, is it?'

Ricky seemed to think about this for a moment.

'All right – let me go, and I'll just walk away, won't say nothing, won't tell anyone.' He looked up, pleading. 'Deal?'

'No deal.' Luke pulled up a chair and sat down facing Ricky. 'I brought you here for a reason. Can you guess what that might be?'

Ricky shrugged. 'You fancied me? You could have just asked me for a date.' He couldn't keep his cockiness from his voice.

'You really are a despicable little worm, aren't you? A pampered posh git trying to sound like a hard man.'

The obvious menace in the cold tones of his voice chilled Ricky. He said nothing, and waited for him to continue.

'You spent eighteen months inside for raping a teenage girl. You think spending a paltry few months in prison constitutes justice?'

Ricky looked back at him, belligerent. 'What the hell is this? Do you think you're some kind of caped vigilante, is that it? Ha, you need to put your underwear on over your tights to do that.' He laughed nastily. 'Anyway, what's it to you if I got my leg over with some tramp?'

Luke's dark gaze bored into Ricky while he struggled to contain his fury. 'That . . . *girl*,' he said, emphasizing the correction, 'was my sister.'

Ricky couldn't maintain eye contact as the full impact of his situation suddenly struck him. 'Look, I'm sorry, right?' he blustered. 'I didn't mean to do anything, you know, we were just messing around and things got a bit out of hand.'

Luke stood up so suddenly that his chair flew across the floor. 'An accident? An accident?' He suddenly flicked out an arm, smashed the back of his hand across Ricky's right cheek. 'The police said you violated her at least three times!' His hand slammed against the other side of Ricky's face. 'You beat her, left her on the side of the road – and you say that was a fucking accident?' He smashed his fist into Ricky's face again and pulled it back – his knuckles were cut and bleeding.

Ricky slumped against the chair and felt around his mouth with his tongue – two teeth were gone. He could feel them rolling round in his cheeks.

'I didn't mean to. Like I said, things just got out of hand. She threatened me . . . clawed at me – I just lost it, man, you know how it is.'

He spat out a gobbet of blood and broken teeth, and looked up at Luke, who stood over him, breathing hard.

'No I don't.' Suddenly Luke turned and marched behind Ricky, out of his sight. Ricky strained at his bindings; desperate to keep an eye on what was going on. Bad as it was getting a beating, at least he could see him.

'Where are you?' he pleaded. 'What are you doing?'

There was no reply.

He squirmed, strained in his chair. 'We can work something out, right? I said I was sorry, didn't I?'

He could hear Luke moving around.

'I'm different now – I've been inside, done my time – I'm rehabilitated – that's what the parole board said.' He turned his head from side to side, desperate to see what the other man was doing.

'Rehabilitated? Different?' Luke's voice was venomous. 'You forget that last night I caught you about to commit the same act. You'd been out only a few hours.'

'What? No way!' Ricky turned his head as far as it would go and could just see some movement in his peripheral vision. 'That girl wanted it, was gagging for it!'

'Liar.'

Something hard caught Ricky across the back of the head and sent him sprawling across the floor, still strapped to the chair. He landed hard, his world spinning. He felt a wave of nausea, closed his eyes, and passed into black.

'Wake up!'

Ricky spluttered, and blinked. A wave of cold water soaked him. He opened his eyes, to see the weird-looking guy standing over him, a plastic bucket in his hand.

'This is no time to sleep. You've got work to do.' Luke bent over and, with strong hands, hauled Ricky and the chair back upright.

Ricky shook the water from his eyes, and blinked hard against the glare. There was a spotlight trained on him, a video camera on a tripod set up facing him. He looked up, confused. 'What's this?'

Luke wiped his face with a rough cloth. 'Your last chance.'

'Chance?' He grasped at the faint tinge of hope. 'What do I have to do?'

Luke stepped over to the camera. A small red light blinked as he turned it on. 'This is your last chance for a confession.'

Ricky could see his face, half hidden in the shadows behind the camera. 'What . . . what am I supposed to say? Just tell me – I'll do it.'

Luke smiled. 'Of course you will. You are going to confess to your crimes – all of them.'

Ricky screwed up his eyes against the glare of the light. 'All of them?'

'My sister wasn't the only one, nor the first, was she?'

Ricky's body shook. He wouldn't meet Luke's gaze. 'I don't know what—'

'Be a man and tell the truth for once in your sorry life. Your daddy isn't here to bail you out now. Tell me about them – all of them.'

Ricky was thinking over his options. 'And if I do . . . if I do exactly what you say . . . will you let me go free?'

Luke gazed back at him, his dark eyes unblinking. 'Maybe . . .'

CHAPTER 39

It was safe to say that Inspector O'Brien was even less pleased to be disturbed at home than the court's HR manager had been. His sour face when he saw Chris and Kennedy on his doorstep was worth a thousand words.

'This better be important,' he growled as he ushered them into the kitchen. 'We're entertaining – my wife will murder me.'

He flicked on the kitchen light, and headed straight for a corner cupboard and pulled out a bottle of whiskey. The detectives waited impatiently as O'Brien poured himself a generous measure into a cut-glass tumbler. He took a sip.

'So what's so important that you have to come and disturb me at home at ten o'clock at night?'

'We're pretty sure we know who the perp is,' Chris announced, gritting his teeth as, out of nowhere, another wave of pain struck.

'Pretty sure?' O'Brien raised an eyebrow. 'If you're here at this time I hope to God you have a solid reason for your suspicions.'

Kennedy jumped in. 'The murders are all linked

387

by one incident, sir, a rape a few years ago of a girl called Amanda Harrington.'

O'Brien gave them a sharp glance; the name obviously meant something to him and Chris wondered if Reilly had been right about Crowe's comment in the video about this particular case going higher up the food chain. He couldn't process something like that just now, not when his faith in the system he himself was a part of had already been shaken to the core.

Their boss contemplated his drink and Chris was thinking that he wouldn't mind one of those himself. The tremors were particularly bad at the moment, possibly because it was such a long bloody day.

'Nasty affair – Roger Webb's son was involved, as I recall?'

Involved? Well, that was one way of putting it. Seemed like their boss was another one of the deceased developer's cronies.

'At first we believed that the girl's biological father was the one responsible for the murders,' Kennedy told him quickly, when Chris remained silent. 'Her parents moved to Australia the year after the trial, but her real father, Simon Darcy, lives in Dublin – he's a court artist, works down at the Central Criminal Court.'

O'Brien looked thoughtful. 'An artist? The guy fits the profile Knight gave, then, and he's certainly got motive if this is indeed about the Harrington case.'

'It's not the father – he's disabled. But we're pretty sure it's his son, Luke Darcy, Amanda's brother.' Chris explained about the sketchpad of drawings Simon had reluctantly shown them.

When they'd got the call from Reilly about the farmhouse location, they'd left Simon in the custody of a couple of local officers, under instructions that he be brought in for further questioning. From there they'd gone straight to O'Brien.

The older man looked incredulous. 'Well, what are you doing here then? Bring the son in, question him.'

The detectives exchanged a look. 'He's currently off the radar.'

'Then find him.' O'Brien glanced at his watch.

'We think Ricky Webb is his next victim,' Chris said.

'Webb. He's inside, isn't he?'

'He was released yesterday. Now seems he's disappeared – no one knows where he is.'

O'Brien lifted his glass, took another sip of whiskey. 'Well, he's been inside. He's probably lying drunk in a ditch somewhere, or shacked up with some woman.'

'Actually, sir, we believe Luke Darcy has seized Webb, and is currently holding him at a farm in Kildare,' Kennedy said quickly. 'It's why we're here. We need you to authorize the response unit. And a search warrant.'

'A tactical weapons team? You're that sure?'

Chris met Kennedy's eye. They both trusted

Reilly's judgement, knew that she wouldn't have given the location unless she was absolutely sure. 'Yes, sir.'

A woman in her early sixties with a nervous, thin face poked her head out of the dining room. 'Are you coming, Donal? I'm nearly ready to serve dessert.'

O'Brien nodded to his wife. 'I'll be back in a minute.'

He looked at the two detectives. 'You'd bloody better be sure. These guys cost a feckin' fortune, so for your sakes, you'd better hope this doesn't turn out to be a fool's errand.'

Having located the Harrington farm, Reilly then called Lucy to her office and asked her to describe in greater detail the farmsteads she'd visited on her recent renegade trip to Kildare.

'A woman in the pub pretty much gave me the heads-up about where to go,' she told Reilly. 'The places I checked out all fit the profile: isolated farmhouses with stables or a barn onsite, totally unoccupied . . . apart from the one with the dogs, of course.'

'Dogs?' Reilly's ears pricked up at this. Why would dogs be present on an unoccupied farm? Either they would have left the property at the same time as their owners, or they were being kept there for a reason. As guard dogs perhaps?

'Actually,' Reuben put in, 'this is what I had come to tell you.'

'Tell me what?'

'Once again it all comes back to *Inferno*. In the Seventh Circle, there are a selection of hellish torments meted out to sodomites and rapists – a rain of fire, rivers of boiling blood . . . And while our man is inventive, I'm not entirely sure these are torments anyone could reconstruct. But another such punishment,' he added with a pause, his tone heavy with meaning, 'is being is torn apart by dogs.'

Reilly met his gaze, understanding immediately. 'So if Luke has got Ricky Webb,' she finished, 'he's going to throw him to the dogs.'

Kennedy turned on the blue strobes and siren and maneuvered impatiently through the traffic at speed. He glanced over at Chris.

'What's up with you? You've barely said a word since we left O'Brien's. Having second thoughts about all this?'

Chris gripped the door handle tightly, as his body was once again racked by convulsing pain. He tried to keep his voice even. 'Of course not. Reilly will have done her homework. This is the endgame, I'm certain of it.'

They cleared the suburbs and the road opened up before them. The engine growled as Kennedy pushed the hammer down.

'Although, to be honest with you, I'm still not sure why we're rushing . . .' Chris said to his partner quietly.

Kennedy shook his head. 'I know what you're thinking but don't even go there.' He changed down, tore past two slow-moving lorries. 'Our job is to catch criminals, and prevent crimes. We have the opportunity to do that today.' He glanced over at Chris, frowning. 'What are you saying, mate? That you want me to slow down, that you'd rather we get there after Darcy has done a number on Webb?'

Chris gazed out the window at the dark fields dashing by. 'The guy's a convicted rapist, not exactly a great loss . . .'

Kennedy didn't reply. He slowed to thirty as they entered a village near Kildare. The bright lights of a pub loomed up ahead. 'OK, maybe we'll stop here then,' he suggested archly. 'We could have a quick drink, talk about the weather for a while . . .'

Chris gazed at the pub. Through the window he could see people talking, drinking, relaxing. Safe. Secure. And who kept them safe?

People like him and Kennedy, that's who. Or at least, they tried to.

Kennedy drove slowly through the village, past the bright lights of the pub Lucy had visited before. 'We'll be there inside five minutes.' He glanced across at Chris. 'You ready for this – or not?'

Chris nodded automatically, thinking he might be ready if he had any idea what 'this' was likely to be.

CHAPTER 40

Luke kneeled down behind Ricky, and with a quick flick of his knife sliced through the bands of duct tape that secured his wrists.

Ricky started to move his arms and tried to relax them, but before he could get any feeling back in them, Luke seized first one, then the other, and clamped a pair of handcuffs on him.

Ricky twisted in the seat and looked back at him. 'You're going to release me, right? I did what you said.' He glanced back toward the video camera. 'You got it all, everything . . .'

Luke stood up, and walked round to stand in front of him. 'I agree you were very co-operative. But I can't let you go right away – I need to check on some of the information in your confession, make sure you were telling the truth.'

He kneeled down again and cut the bands that secured Ricky's feet. He was about to stand back up when Ricky kicked out hard and sent him sprawling.

Luke looked up in surprise. Ricky got to his feet and quickly delivered another vicious kick, this time to the other man's ribs. Luke fell backwards,

393

landed hard on the concrete floor, and tried to roll away, but Ricky knew this was his one and only chance. He stumbled forward toward Luke, and kept lashing out with his feet, delivering one wild kick after another.

For a moment it looked like he had done enough. Luke had been caught unawares, was unable to fight back, unable to ward off the kicks. His glasses were knocked off, flew across the floor and disappeared in the dirty straw.

But Luke had waited too long to let everything slip away so easily. Crawling across the floor he finally managed to dodge one of Ricky's kicks. Then he reached out and grabbed at his leg, pulling hard.

Without his arms free to balance him, Ricky toppled over, landed on his back, his arms pinned beneath him. Luke half jumped, half crawled across the floor, and threw his body on top of Ricky's, landing punches down on his defenseless victim.

Blow after shattering blow rained down, Luke's flailing fists finding their target again and again, pulping Ricky's face, splattering blood across the floor, until he could no longer muster another.

Finally he rolled off him, and lay panting on the floor beside him. He couldn't see clearly without his glasses, but it was obvious that Ricky wasn't going to be giving him any more problems for a while.

Luke pushed up onto his hands and knees. His ribs ached from the kicks he had absorbed, his lip was busted and bloody, while his hands and arms smarted from the reckless, relentless blows he had delivered.

Half-blind, blood and saliva running from his mouth, he crawled around on his hands and knees, desperately feeling among the mud and straw of the cold floor for his glasses. Suddenly his hand hit something cold, hard and metallic. He closed his fingers around his missing glasses, gave a gasp of relief and slipped them on.

One lens was cracked, but Luke could still see well enough. He sat up and looked around.

He climbed to his feet, his ribs aching with every movement, and looked down on his captive. Ricky lay on the floor a couple of yards away. His face was a bloody pulp, his nose clearly broken, one eye already half closed, blood flowing freely from his nose and mouth.

For a moment Luke thought that he'd killed him, but as he watched, Ricky took an almighty heaving gulp of breath, coughed violently and tried to open his eyes.

Luke stood a safe distance back from him. 'I could kill you here and now.'

Ricky looked up at him through his bloodshot eye. 'Go ahead.'

'Not yet. I've got something special planned.'

He leaned over Ricky, grabbed him beneath the armpits, and hauled him to his feet. Ricky was still dazed from his beating, was barely able to stand, even with Luke supporting him.

'Where are we going?' he mumbled.

'To get you cleaned up.'

Ricky looked confused, and tried to twist round and look at Luke. 'Cleaned up? Why?'

'I've decided to let you go,' he told him, his voice calm, soothing.

Ricky blinked his one good eye. 'Let me go . . .'

'I have your confession. The police will lock you up for a lifetime once I give them that.' He led Ricky toward a door at the end of the barn.

'But you'll definitely let me go?' It was a crumb, a life raft, something to cling on to in the waters of despair.

'Yes.' They had reached the door. 'Let you go, give you a head start before I go to the police with the tape.' Luke reached for the door handle. Before he could open it, an eruption of savage barking sounded from behind the door.

Ricky flinched against him. 'What the fuck is that?'

'My security.' Then Luke glanced back toward the main doors of the barn. 'Oh. I think we might have visitors . . .'

'Visitors?' Ricky was still dazed, confused by the sudden change of events.

'I think the police are here. Let's get you cleaned up, then I'll stall them while you escape.'

Kennedy rolled the car slowly into the driveway with the headlights off. He cut the engine, and looked over at Chris. 'Looks like someone's home . . .'

They peered out through the rain-splattered

windscreen. There was a plain white van parked right outside the barn, and a faint glow of light from inside the building.

Getting out, they closed the car doors as quietly as possible, then crept across the muddy yard, Kennedy's torch showing up the maze of puddles. They were halfway across the yard when a fresh bout of pain struck Chris and he stumbled, and splashed into a deep puddle, twisting his ankle.

'Crap!'

No sooner was the word out of his mouth than the dogs responded, striking up a howling cacophony like a savage, ever-vigilant siren.

Kennedy glared at him. 'So much for stealth.'

'Shit, sorry.'

Kennedy went on ahead, making straight for the main doors to the barn. The light was creeping out from around the edges of the double doors, illuminating the driving rain that pelted down upon them.

Chris followed, panting, his drenched hair plastered to his head. He didn't need this, not now, of all times.

Reaching the wooden doors, he paused and wiped his face, then put his eye to a crack in the door. Kennedy was pressed close – Chris could feel the heat of his body – his head above his, also peering through the crack.

The barn was dimly lit, but he could see the chair lying on the floor, the video on the tripod, a small table and chair in the corner – an artist's sketchpad and a set of pencils on the table.

Chris sniffed the air outside the door, realizing he was yet again aware of the strong ammonia smell that had been present in the Darcy household. It was especially strong here, by the door.

Reilly was spot-on. This was definitely the place.

Then out of the corner of his eye, something caught his attention, something moving in the darkness across the yard.

'Did you see that?' he whispered to Kennedy.

'What?'

'A movement. In the bushes over there.'

'What kind of movement?'

'I don't know, but we'd better check it out.' He was hoping against hope that Kennedy would offer to take a look, because at that very moment, the pain was so bad that Chris didn't trust his own legs to hold him up.

'I'll go. You stay here and keep an eye out,' his partner offered. 'Where did you see it?'

Chris indicated the thick bushes surrounding the perimeter, and Kennedy duly crept over, his footsteps slow and cautious. Then after a couple of seconds, he turned back and looked at Chris. 'You eejit,' he hissed, his voice a high whisper. 'It's just a bloody fox.'

A fox? he repeated silently, when suddenly it came to him. Of course, fox spray . . . that was the source of the ammonia smell, he realized instantly. Chris knew from experience that foxes were notorious for marking their territory; they used to have terrible problems with them at his

398

parents' place in Enniskerry. The scent would get dragged into the house from walking in the garden, and the smell was so pungent it was nauseating.

The animals were particularly territorial when their feeding grounds were disturbed. Such as a farm that was usually abandoned but had been recently reoccupied . . .

Evidently, Luke Darcy had been walking fox spray he'd picked up here into the various murder scenes, and Reilly's delicate nose had picked up on traces of it in smaller, more enclosed areas like the church tower and factory freezer.

Kennedy moved back to the door and nodded inside. 'Looks like this is definitely the place,' he said.

Chris nodded. 'It's all there – but does he have Webb?'

The dogs continued to bark, roaring and snapping out their rage.

Kennedy pulled his face away from the crack, and turned back. 'From the sound of those dogs, he's probably in there right now. Could already be dead.'

Chris shook his head. 'If he were dead, the dogs would be too busy eating to make that much noise.'

'God, that's disgusting . . .'

'It's true.'

'You want to go in there?'

Chris nodded.

'What about the dogs?'

'Dogs I can deal with.'

Kennedy seemed to know the decision had

already been made. He put his hand on the rusty handle. 'I'll follow your lead – the usual, OK?'

Chris winced, trying to ride out yet another burning spasm. 'No problem . . .'

Ricky flinched as Luke shoved him into the room. The dogs were huge, three enormous Rottweilers, chained up in a horse stall on the far side of the room, snarling, snapping and jerking at their chains. It looked as though they could pull them free of the wall at any moment.

Racked with fear, Ricky felt his bowels loosen. 'Jesus Christ . . .'

Luke gave him a hard shove, and he fell to his knees in the stall, just a couple of feet from the snarling dogs. Seeing him so close and covered in blood simply inflamed their fury.

'Say hello to my boys.' Luke snapped the door of the stall closed, then walked calmly into the stall adjacent to the dogs. He peered over the short wall at Ricky – the rapist's eyes were fastened on the dogs, primal fear gripping his face.

'In Dante's *Inferno*,' Luke informed him, 'rapists are torn apart by dogs – that's what I call justice. Savagery to match a savage crime.'

Ricky looked up at him, and began to blubber. 'Please, man! Please! Anything but this . . .'

Luke reached over the low wall dividing the stalls. 'May the devil have mercy on you, because I have none.'

CHAPTER 41

While Reuben decided to follow the team to the farmhouse location, Reilly chose to remain at the station and wait for news. She'd done her job in finding the place, so really there was little else for her to do.

Except perhaps try to uncover the answer to one single outstanding question.

Adams, wasn't it? Melanie Adams. Hoping she'd remembered correctly, she turned back to the police computer and typed the name into the system.

And there it was.

A medical report, transcript of victim statement, and follow-up supplemental statement from victim's partner.

Reilly's heart sank, and she began to read the details of exactly what had happened to Chris's ex-girlfriend seven years before.

The pub was busy with the usual Friday night crush, but in one corner of the room there was a special celebration going on. A group of young men and women stood with their glasses in the air.

Peter, a handsome 31-year-old with short blond hair,

was giving a toast. 'Here's to Chris and Melanie,' he proposed.

A dozen or so glasses clinked together. 'To Chris and Melanie!'

Chris smiled. His dark hair was buzzed short, his features lean and hardened, but his face still wore an air of innocence. 'Here's to you, Mel.'

Melanie was beaming.

Peter clinked his glass against Chris's. 'You lucky dog, I can't believe she said yes.'

Chris nodded, and looked over at Melanie. She was chatting with some of her friends, her dark silky hair catching the light. 'I can hardly believe it myself,' he admitted.

Melanie gave a shy smile, reached across the table and squeezed Chris's hand. He slid over beside his new fiancée. 'You doing all right?'

She nodded, the big smile still fixed firmly on her face. 'I still can't believe we're getting married. It was just so unexpected . . .'

Chris gave her a quick kiss. 'Believe it.'

The sudden sound of his mobile phone broke the moment. He pulled it from his pocket, and looked at the screen – his face showed surprise. 'It's my dad. I'd better take it outside so I can hear him. Back in a minute.'

He stepped away from the crowd, and brought the phone to his ear.

'Dad, what's up?' It was clearly not good news as his father rarely phoned his mobile; in fact, Chris was amazed his old man even knew the number.

'It's your mother,' his father said, his voice trembling, and Chris's stomach sank. 'She's had a little accident – fell off a stepladder while trying to change a light bulb. God only knows what she was doing up there in the first place – that kind of thing is my department but—'

'Is she OK? How bad was the fall?'

'They reckon she's broken her arm – she's in Beaumont Hospital – I'm with her now – but they want to keep her in overnight for observation. She banged her head too, so they think she might have a concussion.'

'I'm coming over.' Saying goodbye, Chris slipped his phone back in his pocket, and walked back over to the table.

Melanie looked up, concerned. 'What's up, hon?'

'It's my mum,' he informed her, explaining about the accident.

'You need to go see her,' she said immediately.

Chris nodded. 'Dad's with her now, but he's got to leave in a few minutes – he's working nights . . .'

He turned to his mates, who were all listening with concern. 'I'm afraid I'm going to have to cut out early.'

'No problem, mate – say hi to your mam.'

'Yeah – hope she's OK.'

Chris turned to Melanie. 'I can drop you home now if you want?'

She shook her head. 'No, don't worry about me – that'll take you too far away from the hospital.' Melanie lived on the opposite side of the city to

Beaumont Hospital. 'I might have one more, and then take the DART back with Fiona later,' she insisted, referring to her best friend, who lived in the same locality. 'You go on – and give your mum my love.'

Chris looked uncertain.

'Seriously, go. We've done it a hundred times before. I'd go with you, only not being family, they probably wouldn't let me in.'

'Not being family – yet,' Chris reminded her with a soft smile. But she was right. The Dublin hospitals were especially strict on non-family visitors outside normal visiting hours.

'Are you sure you'll be OK?'

'Of course. Don't worry about me. Anyway,' she joked coquettishly, 'who's gonna mess with the fiancée of a cop?'

Melanie stepped out of Shankill DART station, and wrapped her jacket around her. It was mid-February, and temperatures had been barely above freezing in the past few days. She looked left and right, and stepped out briskly toward home. Unfortunately Fiona had neglected to mention that she was staying the night at Steve, her boyfriend's, place in the city center, which meant that Melanie had had to take the DART home by herself.

The streets were quiet – it was just after eleven – and she soon left the bright lights of the station behind her.

As she walked along she thought about Chris,

wondering how he was getting on at the hospital. She turned onto the main road, her heels clicking in the still night air.

Halfway down she turned and glanced behind her – she'd thought for a moment that she had heard footsteps, but all she saw was the dark street, the parked cars gleaming beneath the streetlights.

At the end of the street she slowed a little. Take the long way round, three blocks down, or the shortcut down the alleyway? She paused, pulled the collar of her denim jacket up around her neck. She really should have worn a much heavier coat tonight.

She peered down the alleyway – it had been the subject of much mythologizing and scary stories when she was a kid. Bogymen lurked down there, the ghost of old Mr Jacobs, who had broken his neck when he fell from his apple tree and whose spirit haunted the alleyway . . . Melanie had walked down there hundreds of times during the day, but at night it looked different, more menacing.

She thought of what Chris always told her: 'Walk with confidence, look around you, meet people's gaze full on and they won't mess with you.'

She was tired from the excitement of the celebrations, her feet were killing her and she was feeling the cold – she just wanted to be home. Quick as a flash, Melanie turned and headed into the darkness.

She was only about fifty yards along the narrow pathway when she heard footsteps behind her. There was no doubt about it this time, someone was back there. Following her, or just walking home from the station?

She picked up her pace a little, and listened to the footsteps – they definitely increased speed too.

Her breath quickening, she passed under the big oak tree, out into the open section of the path – the tree loomed large on her left-hand side, the open park behind it, an inky pool of blackness under the dark night sky.

Melanie glanced back, feeling very afraid now – a shadowy shape was definitely moving quickly behind her, no more than ten yards away. Was she imagining things? It could just as easily be someone else coming home after a night out. Still, despite her attempts at rationale, some deep primal instinct was warning her that danger was imminent. She thought about running, but knew that in her high heels, and on this broken pathway, she would almost certainly stumble and fall.

A shiver of icy fear raced down her back. Why had she come this way? Why hadn't she accepted Chris's offer of a lift home? The footsteps were close behind her, strong, steady.

Don't run, Mel, stay calm, she told herself. In all fairness, it was probably nothing, probably just someone else who was feeling the cold and in a hurry to get home . . .

The assault was so sudden that Melanie didn't have time to scream. Her attacker closed on her quickly, fast and silent – one hand grabbed her tight around the waist while the other clamped itself over her mouth.

They tumbled to the ground together, strong hands holding her firm, making sure Melanie landed first, with his weight on top of her, driving the air from her lungs.

Before she could react she was down on her back on the cold ground. She looked up into the darkness – she couldn't see the face clearly, but could smell the tobacco on his breath.

With his free hand he brought a knife up in front of her face. It glinted in the faint light of the distant houses. Melanie thought about how close she was, how close to people who could help her . . .

The rough face was closer, though; she could feel his hot breath on her cheek. 'You make one sound, one squeak, I'll slice you. You got it?'

She nodded, struggling to breathe with the rough hand over her mouth.

Slowly, one finger at a time, he lifted his hand from her face. 'That's a good girl.' He was breathing hard. 'We're gonna have fun . . .'

Melanie could see his eyes glistening in the dark. She stayed silent, hardly daring to breathe.

'You know what I want?' It was a rhetorical question – he was already pawing at her, pulling her jacket open, his breathing growing rapid in his excitement. 'You do what I ask – everything, exactly the way I want – and I'll let you go free? Got me?'

She nodded, and squeezed her eyes shut as he ripped open her clothes.

CHAPTER 42

Kennedy pushed open the door of the barn, Chris on his heels. They had no difficulty knowing which way to go – the sound of the barking dogs came clear through the door on the far side of the room.

He stopped, one hand on the door handle. 'You sure you want to do this before the big guns get here?'

Chris nodded. 'I don't think we can afford to wait.'

'OK.'

Kennedy pushed at the far door, and a grim tableau revealed itself – a bloody Ricky Webb on his knees in the horse stall, the three savage dogs straining every sinew to reach him with their slavering jaws. Luke Darcy in the next stall, his hand hovering over the catches that held them.

As the door opened Luke paused, momentarily surprised.

'Oh thank God . . .' Ricky Webb blubbered. 'Help me . . . . please!'

Chris went to take a step forward, then stopped suddenly.

408

Kennedy showed no such hesitation, and pushed past Chris into the room. 'Stop,' he ordered Darcy. 'You don't have to do this, we can ensure that justice is served.'

Luke paused, looked at the two of them. 'You think that sending someone like him to jail makes any difference? He hasn't changed at all.' He gave Webb a look of absolute disgust. 'Do you know where I found him? Do you?'

Chris edged closer – maybe if he could get a little closer . . .

'With another girl,' Luke went on. 'He'd been out of prison for only a few hours, and I caught him, about to rape another poor defenseless girl . . .'

At these words, Chris froze.

'It wasn't like that, I swear!' Webb cried out.

'Whatever he's done, it's still not our place to dispense justice,' Kennedy pleaded, glancing toward Chris. They were trained for this; had been in similar situations a few times before, and Chris knew by Kennedy's tone that he was hoping to distract Darcy by talking to him, while Chris himself tried to take him down.

Luke looked up, and met Kennedy's gaze. 'No,' he said, his voice becoming frantic. 'The authorities had their chance and you failed. Now it's my turn.'

'No, stop him please! Help me!' Webb wailed.

Casting his eyes about the gloom, Chris found more details springing up at him. There was a large easel in one corner of the room, a gargantuan heavy art board affixed to it.

It bore a life-like image of the present scene, reinforcing the severity of the punishment as Luke (or indeed Dante) had imagined it, the twisted and screaming figure of the rapist depicted as suffering his torment through the viciousness of the three dogs.

As he stared at the realistic rendering, Chris thought about Melanie, about all that she'd gone through, all *they'd* gone through.

'You don't have to do this, Darcy . . .' Kennedy stared back at Chris as if to ask why the hell wasn't he doing something.

But Chris couldn't move. Still taking in the gross power of the painting, a rough and vitriolic anger reared its head, and flooded forth into his being as if from some primal well.

'Chris . . .'

'Jesus, man . . . help me!' Webb cried.

Luke shook his head, a look of inestimable sadness on his face. 'You're wrong,' he told Kennedy. 'I do.'

As he said it, his hand popped the clasps that held the dogs' chains. The Rottweilers burst forward, their powerful muscles rippling beneath their glistening black coats.

'Chris!' Kennedy roared, as Ricky Webb screamed out in terror. 'Do something, for fuck's sake!'

But Chris stood rooted to the spot, unable to do anything else but watch.

The fury of the assault was astonishing – the three dogs tore into Webb, their powerful jaws snapping and tearing. He shrieked in anguish, once, twice, before one of the dogs locked its massive jaws on his thigh, shook and ripped, tearing at his flesh. It was as if they'd been starved for months.

'Chris, what the fuck . . .?' Kennedy hurried round the side of the stall, grabbed Luke and threw him to the floor. The young man didn't even resist; the menacing smile never left his face.

The blood splattered the dogs, sprayed up against the wooden sides of the barn, and left a streak across Luke Darcy's face. The young man barely noticed. As he watched the carnage, he had an expression of calm contentment. Finally, after so much planning, so much torment, he had his moment, and it was worth it.

Chris stood there, paralyzed, completely immobile. Kennedy stared at him, mystified at his partner's inaction. 'What the fuck is wrong with you?'

'You get it, don't you?' Luke called out, and with considerable effort, Chris slowly turned to look at him. The loose-fitting white cotton of the younger man's clothes was splattered with flecks of blood, the two colors intermingled in a ghoulish marbling that gave added weight to his chilling words. 'You can feel it, yes? You understand that I'm right. This is the only true justice.'

Kennedy grimaced in confusion. 'What the hell . . . Chris . . .?'

'I—'

Suddenly a single shot rang out, sending the entire room speechless apart from Webb, still screaming as he lay on the ground, his body torn to pieces by the hungry pack.

It was the last sound Chris heard before he slumped to the floor.

CHAPTER 43

Reilly stood by Chris's hospital bed, her thoughts going a hundred miles a minute as he lay there immobile. A nurse stood at the head of the bed, the white of her uniform stark against the crimson syringe she'd used to extract his blood.

'How long has he been out?' she asked Kennedy, when the nurse, having finished tending to Chris, had left the room.

'It's a couple of hours since we left Kildare.' He ran a hand through his hair, exasperated. 'Jesus, Reilly, I don't know what the hell happened back there.'

According to him, Chris had been edgy and distracted on the way to the farmhouse, but seemed to regain focus by the time they were ready to enter the building for the takedown.

'He completely froze, Reilly,' Kennedy continued. 'Darcy was just about to release the dogs . . . I was trying to talk him out of it, trying to distract him so that Chris could get to Webb. But Chris just stood there, doing nothing. It was almost as if . . . almost as if he didn't care if the dogs got to the guy. Then all of a sudden he just collapsed in a heap.' He shook his head. 'Thank fuck the cavalry arrived when they did.'

He went on to explain how, fortunately for Webb, the response team had arrived just in time, their gunshot frightening the vicious Rottweilers into a retreat.

Webb was now laid up in another hospital, still alive but in a bad way from his injuries.

Luke Darcy was under arrest for a catalogue of charges: the murders of Coffey, Crowe, Jennings, Fitzpatrick and Morgan, and the attempted murder of Ricky Webb.

Reilly struggled to figure out what had happened based on Kennedy's outline of events. Had Chris been rendered immobile, torn by a moral dilemma about rescuing the rapist because of Melanie's experience?

The thought was deeply unsettling. Chris Delaney was one of the good guys, she'd always been certain about that, and whatever his misgivings about Webb (projected or otherwise) she just couldn't imagine that he would stand back and condemn the man to such a horrible fate.

Then again, didn't Reilly know better than most the terrible things people were capable of – irrespective of how well you knew them, or how much they were loved . . .

Kennedy seemed to be struggling with a similar notion. 'In all my time working with the guy I've never seen that side to him. But thinking about it now, all throughout the case he was acting weird. You saw the way he was with Reuben. It's my job to be cranky – Chris is usually good cop.' He looked sideways at Reilly. 'Did he say anything to you? Was there something going on with him that I don't know about?'

She swallowed hard, not sure what to say. She couldn't very well tell Kennedy about her discovery concerning Melanie, when it was pretty obvious that Chris had never confided in his partner about it. 'Well, he never actually mentioned anything but reading between the lines . . .' she took a deep breath, '. . . I do know he was having some personal issues lately.'

'Personal issues?' Kennedy frowned. 'What kind of issues? He isn't seeing anyone as far as I— Oh . . .' His voice trailed off and he looked at her questioningly. Reilly was quick to assure him that Chris's issues had nothing whatsoever to do with her.

'His ex-girlfriend got married this week,' she said. 'I get the impression it was something he was still dealing with.'

'His ex?' Kennedy made a face. 'What ex? Only one I've ever heard about is some crackpot he dumped years ago.'

'Well, maybe there's a little more to that story than meets the eye – who knows?' Reilly replied diplomatically. 'In any case, I doubt it has anything to do with what happened earlier,' she finished quickly, just as Reuben – fresh from a questioning session with Luke Darcy – came into the room.

His eyes widened. 'What's this? I would have thought that by now our Prince Charming would have been awoken by a kiss from the Fairy Princess,' he said in his usual mocking tone, but Reilly could hear genuine surprise in his voice that Chris was still out.

'Shut it, Knight,' Kennedy spat. 'That's our mate you're talking about.'

'Indeed. I'm rather sorry I missed all the drama earlier,' Reuben continued, referring to his arrival at the farmhouse just after Darcy had been apprehended. He looked at Reilly. 'However, seems like I was right about our good detective's personal stake in this unhappy story. Why else would he have faltered?'

'Look, I've had just about enough of your bullshit,' Kennedy began, rounding on Reuben. 'Spouting shite might be the name of the game for you, but Chris Delaney is a good cop and a great man . . .'

'Hmm . . . if he's such a good cop then why didn't he save the day?' Reuben countered. He cast a surreptitious glance toward Reilly. 'Of course, some of us understand better than most the capability for darkness inside us all, don't we?' he continued, and she looked away, unnerved.

She turned her attention again to Chris lying unconscious on the bed. 'You said he just collapsed?' she asked Kennedy, briskly changing the subject.

'Hit the ground so fast, I thought he'd been shot at first, but our guys only fired a warning shot to scare off the dogs. Paramedics said it was some sort of blackout.'

'And the doctors can't say what caused it?' Reilly asked, thinking about Chris's problems from before, and the crippling pain he used to endure. What if this was a recurrence of it? Whatever 'it' was. The blood tests she'd run last year on his behalf were inconclusive, and when in the meantime he'd confessed that the symptoms had stopped, and he was feeling great . . . Reilly realized now that she needed to mention this to the medical staff, at least let them know that there was a precursor. Granted, by doing so, she ran the risk of breaking Chris's confidence, but what was she supposed to do when he was lying unconscious in a hospital bed, and everyone was baffled as to what was wrong with him?

Kennedy shook his head. 'Well, one good thing about today at least is that the investigation is over. The less we have to look at your ugly mug, Knight, the better.'

Reuben smiled. 'Worry not, Detective Dinosaur, now that our unsub is no longer unidentified, I shall be out of your hair soonest – tomorrow, actually.'

'Can't come fast enough for me,' Kennedy replied, giving the profiler a dark look. 'I'm going outside for a fag. Catch you later, Reilly.'

'Sure. I'm going to stay on for a while, see if I can find anyone who'll tell me what's going on with Chris.'

Kennedy nodded, and without another word to Reuben, he turned on his heel and walked out of the room.

'Another conundrum for the inimitable Ms Steel to solve?' Reuben teased. 'I'm impressed. I appreciate your talents are extensive, but even I wasn't aware they extended to medicine.'

Reilly was startled. Unbeknownst to himself Reuben had just given her an idea . . .

Her mind flashed to her kitbag, tucked safely under her seat in the GFU van parked outside, and inside, the syringe not dissimilar from the one the nurse had just used.

The nurse had finished her rounds, Kennedy was gone and no doubt Reuben would be leaving soon. All it would take was one tiny blood sample . . .

Could she risk trying to figure out this particular puzzle all by herself? Or more to the point, should she?

Torn by indecision, she looked again at the prone figure on the bed. With everything she and Chris had been through together, and how much they'd shared . . .

For Reilly Steel, it was a question that only had one answer.

CHAPTER 44

Chris was terrified. Throughout his career he'd faced down syringe-brandishing junkies and gun-wielding scumbags and would happily do so again rather than tackle what was to come.

As he stepped into the elevator at the GFU building and pushed the button for the floor to Reilly's office, all manner of horrific possibilities were running through his mind.

A week before, after the Darcy takedown, Chris had woken up in St Vincent's ER to see the concerned face of Kennedy beside him.

'What the hell happened, mate?' his partner asked, his face uncommonly solemn. 'Something's been going on with you lately, and I think we both know you completely bottled it back there.' He took a deep breath. 'The question is – why? I covered for you this time with O'Brien, but if there's going to be a next time . . .'

'Pete, I'm sorry; I'm not sure myself what happened. I was feeling faint and . . . I must have blacked out or something.' While Chris's brain still felt fuzzy, he was alert enough to know that back at the farmhouse, he had been rendered completely immobile – not because he was torn by any moral dilemma regarding the rescue of Ricky Webb but because his pain-racked limbs had quite literally failed him. 'I've been having a few niggles here and there lately, but I'm sure this place will sort me out in no time,' he reassured Kennedy and, much to his relief, he seemed content to leave it at that, but something in the other man's eyes told Chris he wasn't convinced.

However, it turned out the medics at the hospital were stumped as to the root cause of Chris's blackout, and he was subjected to a battery of scans and tests, until eventually the worst of the pain subsided, and he was sent home, none the wiser. The enforced medical leave meant he'd done little else this past week but fret about his condition and how it might impact not only his job, but his life. The problem was he wasn't sure how next to tackle the issue, not while he remained in the dark about what was happening to him. And if the hospital couldn't figure out what was wrong with him, then who the hell could?

Chris was beginning to descend into despair when first thing this morning, out of the blue, Reilly had called him from the GFU lab and asked him to come in and see her.

'I'm pretty sure I've figured what's wrong with you,' was all she said, refusing to reveal anything further until he agreed to visit the lab in person.

Now, as he knocked lightly at the door to her

office, he wondered what on earth he was about to face.

'Hey there, come on in,' Reilly said, her typically calm demeanor once again betraying nothing.

'You said you think you know what's wrong?' Chris urged, curter than he'd intended before adding lightly. 'Go on then, put me out of my misery.'

'Well . . .' She stood up and came around the front of her desk. 'I was thinking about the last time you suffered badly with this thing – remember throughout the whole Jess . . . episode?' While her tone was even, Chris could still hear it waver when she mentioned her sister's name.

He nodded.

'Well, it always seemed strange to me, and not entirely coincidental, that the whole thing seemed to stop right after you got shot. Remember all that blood you lost?'

'Yeah, but what's this got to do with anything?' he asked, unable to restrain his impatience.

'Those tests we took before . . . I looked through the results, specifically the transferrin saturation test Julius did, and compared them with a more recent sample.'

She met his questioning gaze head on. 'Don't ask, just trust me, OK?'

He exhaled heavily, not sure what was coming.

Reilly continued. 'Last year your transferrin was just above sixty percent. Now it's eighty-five.'

He blinked, thoroughly confused. 'Reilly, as

Kennedy might say, just give me the meat-and-spuds version . . .'

'OK, high transferrin is often indicative of a blood condition that can only be identified via a genetic scan. It's possibly why the hospital didn't pick up on it. You'd need to be aware of the condition to identify the anomaly, and many medical staff aren't.'

Chris felt a knot form in his stomach. Genetic scan . . . blood condition . . . what in God's name . . .? His heart thumped heavily in his chest.

'Have you ever heard of hemochromatosis?' she asked then.

'Hemo . . . what?'

'Hemochromatosis. Like I said, it's a genetic condition, which basically means that your body is absorbing too much iron, and prone to storing it in the blood. It might be hard to pinpoint, but is actually a pretty common condition – especially amongst people of Celtic origin.'

'Too *much* iron?' If anything, he was thinking he was deficient.

'Yes, the opposite of anemia.'

Chris frowned, unsure what to think. 'I take it that's not good?'

'It depends. If it goes untreated for too long then the iron can build up in your organs – and that's very bad. It's why you were in so much pain last year, and over the last few weeks. The excess builds up over time, and affects your muscles and limbs.'

'So how do you treat the damn thing?' he asked,

not at all certain he wanted to hear the response. '*Is* there any treatment?'

She moved back around the desk to her computer. 'I saved this for you earlier.' She turned the screen so Chris could see for himself.

'Treatments,' he read, scanning the page quickly as his heart rate gradually began evening out. He struggled with the next term. 'Therapeutic phlebotomy . . . what the heck is that?'

Reilly looked at him. 'Vampirism – of sorts.'

'What?'

'You'll need to have blood exsanguinated on a regular basis,' she explained. 'It offloads some of the iron in your system so as to stabilize the condition. It's why you were fine for so long after the shooting.'

Of course. He'd lost so much blood . . . Suddenly things started to fall into place.

'Chris, this might be treatable but isn't something you can just ignore – people have died from it. And,' she added meaningfully, 'you need to let O'Brien know. Kennedy too.'

He shook his head, suddenly terrified. 'No way, I can't do that. What if—'

'What if you freeze again at another crucial moment?' she argued. 'We can't have that happening, not when there are lives at stake.' She gave him a defiant look. 'I'm sorry, but if you don't tell them then I will.'

'OK, OK, I know what you're saying, but I just found out about this. At least give me a little time to see a doctor, find out how bad it is.'

'Fine.' Reilly's tone was brisk. 'But do it soon. It's gone untreated for so long now there may well be some form of organ damage or something even more serious. Either way, things won't be plain sailing.'

OK, Chris thought exhaling. Maybe he did have a problem, but at least it seemed treatable.

'Take this stuff home with you, and read up on it for the moment. You'll need to keep a close eye on your diet.' Reilly keyed in a command, and her printer came to life, spewing out several sheets. She eyed him knowingly. 'And lay off on the drinking too.'

Chris looked away, ashamed. So she had noticed. He should have known better than to think the reason for his absence on the day of Melanie's wedding would have gone unnoticed, especially by Reilly.

He couldn't help it; that day the tremors were particularly bad, and anyway, all he'd wanted to do was get shit-faced, to help shut out the physical pain, drive away the memories and, in all honesty, the raw hurt that someone else and not him, had finally managed to rescue Melanie from her demons.

Chris wasn't proud of it, but at the time the drink had been a balm to him in more ways than one.

He scanned briefly through the material she had given him. While he was relieved that the question mark hanging over his condition had finally been answered, there seemed to be an awful lot of reading for something supposedly so straightforward.

Maybe it was a much bigger deal than he'd thought?

As to whether it would hold him back in the job remained to be seen, but Chris could only hope for the best.

After all, a little joint pain never killed anyone, did it?

'Well, thank you for getting to the bottom of it,' he told Reilly. 'I don't know what to say . . .'

She looked up and flashed him a smile that made his stomach do a somersault.

'Hey, you know me,' she winked. 'Always looking for a puzzle to solve.'